THROUGH MY EYES
(A FOREIGN VIEW OF THE 2008 US ELECTIONS)

THROUGH MY EYES
(A FOREIGN VIEW OF THE 2008 US ELECTIONS)

By

OMOLOLU ELEGBE

London
2009

iUniverse, Inc.
New York   Bloomington

THROUGH MY EYES
A FOREIGN VIEW OF THE 2008 US PRESIDENTIAL ELECTIONS

iUniverse books may be ordered through booksellers or by contacting:

iUniverse
1663 Liberty Drive
Bloomington, IN 47403
www.iuniverse.com
1-800-Authors (1-800-288-4677)

ISBN: 978-1-4401-3341-1 (pbk)
ISBN: 978-1-4401-3342-8 (ebk)

Printed in the United States of America

iUniverse rev. date: 3/20/2009

TO

My lovely and loving wife, without whose unyielding
support this book would never have been possible.
You are the love of my life and my best friend.

My darling daughter. I cannot wait to hear your
opinion when you are old enough to understand the
contents of this book.

Table of Contents

FOREWORD

Any research endeavor on politics and its impact on the socio-economic well being of the people carries with it the unenviable potential of being an awful drudgery, especially for those whose interest is less keen in political activities than the political gladiators themselves and their hangers-on. The drift of the conclusion of such academic exercise is almost always predictable. The researcher, after having taken his readers on a voyage on why and how elections are won and lost, not forgetting to lace the work with anecdotes on the heroic deeds of super-human beings who impose themselves on the rest of the people and why it is they who must continue to rule, rounds off with the worn out cliché on the need for all and sundry to join hands to "move the country forward".

These writers, often commissioned to deliberately distort historical facts, weave all manner of stories into a ridiculous fiction, deceiving the unsuspecting and the naïve of the authenticity of their spin. They come in different shades. They are either biographers or academic politicians of the worst type. They are seen as omniscient experts, whose opinions are almost as infallible as God. These peddlers of mendacity do great disservice to the dwindling proclivity towards reading. They contribute to the growing but regrettable culture of ill-literacy.

One is, thus, bound to pay glowing tributes to the efforts of the author of this book Omololu Elegbe not only for the sublimity of style, but also, and more significantly, for a detailed, well-researched and painstaking analyses of events and situations, putting in context every assertion of fact. The tantalizing effect of the simplicity of style is such that a reader may likely get stuck reading from the first page till the end. The transcripts of speeches at the end of the book are an invaluable research material on the subject. Near perfect is the rendition that one easily forgets that the writer is not an American. The accounts of what transpired during the last election in America is presented in such a manner that makes the reader to leave with the impression that he or she is now seised of the intricacies of American politics and the manipulation of the system by a group bent on protecting its parochial interest against the general aspiration of the rest of the people.

Democracy, as practiced in the US, is a model worthy of emulation by both developed and developing countries of the world. This book affords the reader the opportunity of drawing inferences from the variants of this political concept as they are operated in the world today. It also exposes the severe limitations of the American brand of democratic governance.

The just-concluded American presidential election was phenomenal in every respect. The emergence of Barack Obama, not only as the candidate for the Democratic Party, but also as the first Black President, is historic. Nobody genuinely thought that he could go far in the primaries, let alone clinch the slot as the candidate of his party. If anyone had prophesied this novelty he would have been laughed to scorn. To have predicted that, right **before our eyes**, a man of recent black African ancestry would become the most powerful person in the world should have, ordinarily, warranted justifiable disparaging comments on the person's state of mental health. To pretend, under whatever guise, that the history made at the elections was foreseeable is patently dishonest. Most people had written him off at the outset of electioneering campaign. He was considered as an unknown personality craving popularity for future contest. Now that history has been made and the erstwhile unthinkable has been achieved, it is instructive that everyone takes stock and determines the aspect of the phenomenal occurrence that will be of benefit to him or her.

The Obama phenomenon promises to be a constant reminder to the despondent that all is not lost. It rekindles hope in the hopeless. It recognizes that power is useless without responsibility and proclaims the virtues inherent in humility even against an adversary dwarfed by the ubiquity of one's potentials in every respect. The American story should be an abiding lesson to any nation or an aspiring one. Nation becomes and not decreed into existence.

I enthusiastically recommend this book to political scientists, Historians, researchers, academics, lawyers, students of international relations and others who may take interest in American history, especially as it relates to the last election. It would not be out of place to ask those who can read among the politicians in third world countries to spare some time to know about how the game of politics is played in other climes.

On the whole, I consider writing the foreword to this excellent work a rare privilege. I am confident of its instant acceptance from the reading public.

OLUWAROTIMI O. AKEREDOLU ESQ. SAN.
PRESIDENT,
NIGERIAN BAR ASSOCIATION.

INTRODUCTION

Why did I decide to write this book? What does a Nigerian national have to do with the US Presidential elections? The whole world followed the elections, but why write a book about it? Why not write about, say, the Nigerian Presidential elections? Why not even talk about politics in the UK, where I am resident? Why the US and why this year?

The truth is that, I've been asking myself these questions and I'm still not sure which answers are the right ones.

What I do know though, is that the 2008 US Presidential elections affected me in a way I never thought I could be affected by politics, either in the US or in any other part of the world.

My interest in politics started when I was really young, probably about eleven or twelve years old. Whenever my Dad got back from work, I would ask him for newspapers and read about current affairs in Nigeria and around the world. I was always particularly interested in news from and about America, but I'm not entirely sure why. It probably had a lot to do with the fact that I was a movie buff and 99% of the movies I watched were American. It could also have been the fact that in school, my teachers always talked about America as the world's greatest and most powerful country and always had passion in their voices that was absent when talking about anything else. Even history lessons were often times dominated by American history. It could also have been because whenever I watched the Olympics, America seemed to dominate almost every sport. Or it could have been the fact that most of the music videos and songs I heard in parties or heard older ones singing were mostly American.

Which ever one of these it was, I grew up with dreams of America. To me, America was a myth because it was so far away, but yet so close because of everything I had read, heard and watched.

When Saddam Hussein decided to invade Kuwait in 1990 and the possibility of a US led attack on Iraq was mooted, I could not get enough of the news. I would get back from school and do my homework in front of the TV, not waiting for cartoons or Sesame Street which usually started around 4pm, but waiting for news of both the diplomatic and military options. When my Dad got back from work, I would get the day's newspapers from him, stay in my room and read with my dictionary by my side. There was so much I did not understand about the conflict and I tried to find answers. I asked my teachers in school, but they did not tell me anything I had not read in the newspapers or heard on TV, so I stopped asking them. I asked the older ones around me, but their explanations might as well have been in Chinese because I did not understand any of it. I then decided that I would listen and watch the news more and try to understand it on my own. And at a point, I actually started to understand the issues or at least I thought I did. I would listen to my uncles and older cousins arguing about whether or not a US led attack on Iraq would be the first shots fired in World War 3. One of my aunts who was convinced that the war would be the beginning of WW3, rented the movie, "The Man Who Saw Tomorrow", to justify her conviction!

I listened intently and tried to ask questions, but no one really paid attention to me. In retrospect, I guess an 11year old asking questions about war, invasion and international politics would have been hard to take serious.

The start of the war in January 1991, I think was the beginning of an obsession with International Politics and International Law that I still have today. Even at that age, I was fascinated with International relations. I wondered why Iraq would invade Kuwait, knowing America would always intervene if any country is attacked by another (This was the thinking of an 11year old boy). I tried to understand why Iraq was attacking Israel with scud missiles, when Israel had done nothing to Iraq. After the war, I tried to understand why George H Bush lost the next Presidential election very badly to an unknown Arkansas Governor, after leading the country to victory in a war that ended in record time.

It was not until years later, when my I started my degree in Law that a lot of these issues became very clear to me. With this new clarity, came the realization that a lot of the things I thought I understood were not really that clear cut. I had read dozens of history books, but it was not until this period that I really began to understand things I had read years ago. I discovered that the world is a lot more complicated than I thought it was. I discovered that America is a very complicated country, with a very complicated history. I discovered that America has a leadership role in the world like no other country in world history. I discovered that the responsibility that goes with this leadership role, makes America either the greatest force for good in the world or the greatest complication in the world. Finally, I discovered that winning a war is not enough to guarantee winning an election, especially when the economy is in a downward spiral.

The more I understood these issues, the more fascinated I became with US politics, International Law and International relations, because I believe all three are interwoven. Consequently, I have been an avid student of all three, especially the election aspect of US politics, particularly the Senatorial and Presidential elections. I dreamt of going to Law school in America and practicing Law in America, but the cost meant that was more fantasy than dream.

So, following John Kerry's nomination as the Democratic candidate for President in 2004, I could not wait for the conventions for both Parties to start. To be perfectly honest, the only thing I was looking forward to was John Kerry's acceptance speech. I was hardly interested in what anyone else had to say, because the conventions I had watched usually had boring speeches until the nominee took the stage. I liked watching their families join them on stage after the speeches amidst all the cheering and confetti.

But by the time the 2004 Democratic Convention

was over, I had not only changed my perception that all speeches were boring; I had allowed myself to start fantasizing of the day when a serious African-American candidate would run for President of the United States. Barack Obama's 17minute speech at the Convention had led to that fantasy. It was not just the oratory, but a combination of the oratory, the delivery and the response. The response from the audience so amazed me that I actually made myself believe that this man could one day run for President. I did not think he could win if he did run, but I felt he could do well enough to maybe be considered for Vice President (Even this I thought was a long shot).

I knew Shirley Chisholm, Jesse Jackson and Al Sharpton had all run for President in the past, but I don't think any of them had a serious chance of winning the Party's nomination, not to talk of the Presidency. I always had this belief that a black person, a woman and a Muslim could never be US President. I just did not see any scenario in which anyone of these three groups could be President of the United States, at least not for a good few decades. It's funny because I believed this so strongly and at the same time, believed very strongly that America is one of the world's most tolerant countries.

It was the strength of this belief that was responsible for my thinking that despite Barack Obama's obvious charisma, the fantasy of his running for President would always remain just that.

When he did announce his intention to run in February 2007, I was surprised because first of all I thought, America is not ready for a black President. Secondly, I thought he had only spent two years in the

Senate and was just 45 years old, why didn't he just wait? If he waited another eight or even twelve years or so, America might have changed significantly enough to seriously consider having a black President.

But in the last 22 months, every one of my preconceived notions about America's readiness for a black President has been knocked down one by one. In place of my skepticism and cynicism, is the realization that America is ready and indeed has moved on. I saw that America is color blind to excellence. Americans were looking for a President who could lead the country out of the current situation and they did not care about race or gender. It suddenly became clear to me that when I asked the question, "Is America ready for a black President?" I was asking the wrong question. The question I should have asked was, "Is there a black candidate who is ready to be President?"

Ready in terms of showing that he is not the black Presidential candidate, but the American Presidential candidate who happens to be black;

Ready in terms of showing that he is running because he believes he can better the lives of all Americans and not just African-Americans;

Ready in terms of moving forward from the racial issues of the past, without ignoring the racial discrimination of the present;

In short, he needs to show that he is running for President because he feels that he is the best person for the job and not because he feels it is high time America had an African-American President.

During the last 22 months, Barack Obama showed

all these factors and so much more. He inspired a whole generation of not just Americans, but people all over the world. As I would point out later in this book, the most touching tribute I heard to Obama was when Caroline Kennedy, daughter of John Kennedy, said, "I have never had a President who inspired me the way that people tell me that my father inspired them. But for the first time in my life, I believe I have found that President; not just for me, but for a new generation of Americans".

As much as I had followed and enjoyed US politics, never before had I wished I had a chance not just to vote, but also to do something to make sure that a candidate is elected. Obama represented the kind of President I only read about from history books or saw in movies. His speeches, though sometimes rhetorical, sounded like stuff I had read from Abraham Lincoln or JFK. I could even understand the rhetorical aspect because I believe the rhetoric is what initially grabs a person's attention, before substantive details come.

As conversant as I was with US politics, especially US elections, I had never followed an election from the primaries with the same level of intensity as the 2008 elections. I usually waited until the nominees had been picked (although, I still remember Howard Dean's bizarre screams during the 2004 primaries).

This time though, with a candidate I believed was good enough but would probably not win it in Barack Obama and two candidates I had always liked and respected in Hillary Clinton and John McCain, I decided I would follow this election from start to finish. I made this decision mostly because I wanted to follow Obama's campaign and see how far it would go.

This is the story of that decision. This is the story of my thoughts, my fears, my tears, my hopes, my anger and my joy. This is the story of that thin line between the ecstasy of victory and the agony of defeat.

This is the story of the 2008 US Presidential Elections, through my eyes.

THE SOAP OPERA

July 27 2004 and the Democratic Convention was in full swing. Usually, when I watch US party conventions, I wait for the speeches from the nominee and running mate and don't bother with what anyone else has to say. This was going to be no different, or so I thought. I had rented "The Godfather Trilogy" and had watched the first part earlier in the day. For some reason, I wasn't able to sleep that night and decided to watch the second part. As I switched on the TV, I heard a news anchor talking about "the much anticipated keynote address by US Senate candidate from Illinois, Barack Obama" and I thought, "How does he expect to win the Senate race with a name like that?" Me and my cousin, who was also awake, made fun of the name and decided we would see what he looks like and then watch the movie. When he walked onto the stage, we thought, "He's actually good looking." We decided to listen to the speech for a few minutes before starting the movie.

For the next seventeen minutes, my cousin and I did not or maybe I should say could not say a word. After the speech, we looked at each other and it was like one was waiting for the other to find the right words to describe what we had just witnessed.

I said, "Wow! That was possibly the most effective political speech I've ever heard. It would be interesting if he ever ran for President."

My cousin said he was thinking along the same lines and for the next hour we launched into a discussion cum debate as to why America may or may never have a black President. I thought Obama's name, especially his Arabic middle name, all but guaranteed he could never become US President if he ever ran. The speech was being shown again and just as we were talking about his name, he was saying, "The hope of a skinny kid with a funny name who believed that America has a place for him too".

There was a particular line in that speech that I have never forgotten and I still replay it over and over again in my head; "There is not a liberal America or a conservative America, there is The United States of America; There is not a black America or a white America or a Latino America or an Asian America, there is The United States of America!"

To hear a politician have the audacity to utter those words was a breath of fresh air from the suffocation of divisiveness and partisanship that has so plagued American politics, especially since George W Bush became President. When he uttered those words, Hillary Clinton, Chelsea Clinton, Jesse Jackson, and everyone in the VIP section rose to their feet, started cheering and whispering into each other's ears. I could only imagine what they were saying. Possibly, "Who is this guy and why haven't we heard about him until now?" (That's just my idea). I found out later that Emile Jones, the President of the Illinois State Senate said after the speech, "I felt embarrassed that tears dropped from my eyes, but when

I looked around me, everyone had tears in their eyes. I was so proud of him!"

After our debate, my cousin went to bed and I got on the internet to try to find out about Barack Obama, since I liked to see myself as a follower of US politics, but I did not have a clue who this guy was. I found out he was from Chicago, Illinois and had been a State Senator since 1997. I also found out that he was now running for the US Senate. I read a bit of his history and was quite fascinated by the fact that he was the first black president of the Harvard Law Review. After that speech, it seemed like the whole of the US had fallen in love with him. His speech became the main talking point of the 2004 Democratic convention. I'm not sure John Kerry's acceptance speech got as much post event analysis. One thing was obvious to anyone who watched or heard Obama that night; a star had been born. Even before he announced his intention to run for President, if you typed in 2004 Democratic Convention into Google, 8 of the first 10 hits were about his speech. That was why when the elections were held in November 2004, it came as no surprise to me or anyone else who was watching that he won with 70% of the vote. Landslide was an understatement!

After that, I did not hear that much about him again, mostly because I had lost interest and was just waiting for the candidates for the 2008 Presidential elections to line up.

I've been reading Time magazine for about fifteen years now and always look forward to the annual Top 100 Influential People in the World edition. I'm hardly ever surprised by any name on the list, but nothing prepared me for the shock I got when I opened the 2005 edition.

Under the group, "Leaders and Revolutionaries", Barack Obama's name was on that list! I could not believe it! I read the write-up on him and was amazed to discover that groups all over the country had been inviting him to speak and almost every time he obliged, he was asked the same question, "When are you going to run for President?" I was even all the more surprised at the fact that a lot of these groups went beyond party lines. But I willed myself not to get too excited and convinced myself that the people asking him this question still had residual feelings from his electrifying speech at the Democratic Convention in 2004.

In October of the following year, I got another shock, this one, more intense than the year before. I got the October 23 2006 issue of Time magazine and stared at the cover for what I thought was a long time before I finally opened the magazine. The front cover had a picture of Barack Obama, with the caption, "Why Barack Obama could be the next US President".

I now started to really ask myself, "Is it possible? Would he actually run for President and if he did, could he actually win?"

If I was eagerly anticipating the start of the 2008 election season before, now I was almost willing time to move quickly just to see if Obama would run. Even my fantasy could not have been that optimistic. When I watched his speech in 2004 and thought it might be interesting if he ran for President, I was thinking along the lines of 2012 or 2016, not 2008! Now I could not wait for the candidates to start announcing their intent to run.

One by one, the candidates stepped forward. The one that obviously garnered the most press coverage and public attention was Hillary Clinton. The former First Lady had long been rumored to favor a White House bid, and her formal announcement in January 2007 came as no surprise.

A new game then started in Washington, "Will Barack Obama run for President?" Talk show hosts, analysts, strategists and anyone who looked good enough or sounded smart enough to be on TV spent the later part of 2006 trying to predict if Obama would run. He was invited to talk show after talk show and asked the same question, "Will you run for President in 2008?" Oprah Winfrey asked him on her show, "Will you announce on our show?" He did not. The now late Tim Russert asked him on the news program, Meet the Press, "Will you run for President in 2008?" He never said he would and never said he would not either. Instead he said he's "considering it". Even merely saying that became headline news. Analysts and pundits tried to define and dissect what the word, "consider" actually means! Some have said he did this whole, "will he, won't he" dance just to boost interest in his book, "The Audacity of Hope". This wasn't the first time something like this had happened in American politics. In 1995, the press was pre-occupied with the same dance with Colin Powell when he released his book, "My American Journey". Colin Powell eventually decided not to run, but by the time he made that decision public, his book had become a bestseller. So when analysts began to look at similarities between the two while the song and dance was going on, I wasn't really surprised.

On 10th February 2007, in front of the old capitol building in Springfield, Illinois, where fellow Illinois native, Abraham Lincoln gave his "House Divided" speech, Barack Obama, flanked by his wife and daughters and cheered on by a crowd of about 17000 people, finally announced his candidacy for President.

The Democrats now had an all star cast consisting of, Hillary Clinton (Former First Lady and Junior US Senator from New York), Barack Obama (Junior US Senator from Illinois), John Edwards (Former US Senator from North Carolina and John Kerry's running mate in the 2004 Presidential Elections), Joe Biden (Senior US Senator from Delaware and Chairman of Senate Foreign Relations Committee), Chris Dodd (Senior US Senator from Connecticut and Chairman of the Senate Banking Committee), Bill Richardson (Governor of New Mexico, former US ambassador to The UN and former Energy Secretary), Dennis Kucinich (US congressman from Ohio), Mike Gravel (Former US senator from Alaska) and Tom Vilsack (former Ohio Governor, who dropped out before the start of the primaries).

At this point, to be honest, I actually did not think Barack Obama had a chance. I, like most of the analysts and polls, believed Hillary Clinton would secure the nomination. I had always believed a woman could never be elected US President, but if it was going to happen now, it would be Hillary Clinton. I heard an analyst on TV say, "I just cannot see any scenario in which Hillary

Clinton will not be the nominee". Another news anchor was even more colorful, when he said, "The Democrats are not going to have a convention, they're going to have a coronation. The coronation of Hillary Clinton."

While I would not have put it so dramatically, I honestly thought he had a point. Hillary Clinton had everything going for her. She was a powerful US Senator, a former First Lady and a very powerful one at that, her husband wasn't just a former President, he was Bill Clinton! Together, they were the most powerful force in the Democratic Party and possibly in the country.

In Obama's case, I just did not see how a freshman Senator could successfully win the Democratic Party nomination after 2years in the Senate. When you add the fact that I just did not see how a black man could be elected President, you begin to get an idea of the way I was thinking. However, this line of thinking received a massive shock after I began to watch the debates.

The first debate I watched was the CNN/Youtube debate in South Carolina in July 2007. I was so impressed by Senator Obama's carriage of himself and the obvious respect he had from his rivals, that for the first time, I actually began to think, "It IS possible". During that debate, he was the youngest candidate, but sounded smarter than everyone else on that stage. There was just something about the way he portrayed himself that seemed to transcend his race. I looked at the polls and saw that Hillary Clinton was way ahead in public perception. Fundraising, however was a different issue. Granted, Hillary was ahead, but the speed with which Obama was catching up was beginning to cause a stir. Suddenly, Clinton's status as the "inevitable nominee in waiting", as she had been widely described, seemed to be in jeopardy. Obama was drawing huge crowds everywhere he went and unsurprisingly, news of jitters from the Clinton campaign began to filter through. She asked her campaign manager, Mark Penn if she should be worried about "this guy raising serious money and drawing huge crowds everywhere". Mark Penn's reply, "Don't worry about Obama, he's a flash in the pan, he'll fizzle out eventually". I would give anything to have seen Mark Penn's face on 3rd of June 2008, when Obama effectively wrapped up the nomination.

Back to the debate, Obama was asked this question, "Would you meet with the leaders of Iran, North Korea, Syria and Cuba, without pre-conditions, within the first year of your Presidency?" Nothing (and I mean that literally) prepared me for Obama's response. He said, "Yes, I would, because this notion that if we don't talk to countries we don't like, we're punishing them, is ridiculous. America should be willing to talk, not just to our friends but also to our enemies" I looked at my fiancée and said, "Did you hear what he just said?!?" This is exactly what America needs after 8years of unilateralism and "for us or against us" approach to foreign policy. I could not believe that a politician, a Presidential candidate at that, could have the audacity to say what he just said. Statements like that were seen as political suicide.

President Bush's confrontational approach to foreign policy effectively turned diplomacy into an afterthought, rather than the primary focus of foreign policy. War seemed to be the first, rather than the last resort. Don't get me wrong, when necessary, war should be an option. But I think the problem with the Bush approach is in not being able to walk that fine line between what is necessary and what is not. Tony Blair once said, "Sometimes, the only chance for peace is the readiness for war." While I accept this as true, should diplomacy, TOUGH DIPLOMACY, not be pursued first? I'm not a military man, but I'm educated well enough to know that war should be a last resort, unless in very dire and very specific circumstances.

Nations, like human beings, have and will always have disagreements, but I have always believed that disagreements do not necessarily have to escalate into conflicts. While the issues with these particular countries go beyond mere disagreements (they're far more serious than that), isn't a refusal to sit down and talk with them not a strengthening factor to what these issues are?

Take Iran as an example. This is a proud country with a proud leader, who supposedly does not understand why the world has a problem with his country's nuclear ambitions. He says it's for peaceful purposes but I'm sure he knows no one believes that. The Bush Administration's policy has been isolation, sanctions and threats of military action. This is a proud leader and a proud country. Does anyone really believe these are the kinds of actions that will convince the Iranians to abandon their nuclear program? Even if Ahmedinajad was worried about these threats, he obviously would put up a strong face and say, "We are a sovereign nation, you cannot tell us what to do." As ridiculous as I think some of his comments are, he would have had a point, had he said that. A nuclear armed Iran is not in anyone's interests, period. President Bush's Iran policy has given Ahmedinajad the excuse to tell his people that the whole world is against them and so they need to protect themselves. This leads to increased support from Iranians. And there is nothing that emboldens a country's leader as much as having the support of his people. Genuine support, that is. This isolationist policy is what has led to an acceleration of Iran's nuclear program.

Some people have argued that if the USA has nuclear weapons, why is it trying to stop everyone else from having it? Let's be serious about this: can you imagine a world where every country has nuclear weapons? Can you imagine a world where terrorists get their hands on nuclear weapons? Can you imagine a world where there is a coup in a country that happens to be a nuclear power? The truth is that the world is too unstable for that kind of scenario. Countries with civil wars, with coups, even civil unrests can destroy the planet if they had nuclear weapons.

It would be lovely of we lived in a nuclear-free world, but the sad reality is that we don't. There needs to be a balance of power in the world. My belief is that the world's most powerful countries use it as a deterrent and would only consider using it under the most extraordinary conditions. At least I hope so. With Iran, how on earth does President Ahmedinajad expect Israel and the rest of the world to sit back and allow him to develop nuclear power when he keeps talking about "wiping Israel off the face of the earth?"

What President Bush should have concentrated on, was getting the Iranians to the table to talk, instead of giving speeches about Iran being part of an axis of evil. If they insist that their nuclear ambitions are peaceful and for energy purposes, offer to help with alternative energy sources that do not involve nuclear power. Make this case, not in a pacifist manner, but clear enough for Iran to know that nobody on earth will sleep peacefully if Iran continues to pursue its nuclear goal. Teddy Roosevelt said, "Talk softly, but carry a big stick." In other words, talk first, but make sure the person you're talking to understands that you're talking because you want to avoid the last alternative. John Kennedy probably said it best when he said, "We must never negotiate out of fear, but we must never fear to negotiate."

Of course the backlash from Obama's response came instantly, first from his fellow Democratic rivals and later from the Republicans and even some Independents. His response was described as, "naïve and dangerous." These attacks began to get quite a bit of traction, because they fed into the biggest criticism by Obama's rivals; inexperience. They said, "How can a US President say he will meet with someone like Ahmedinajad without pre-conditions?" That is just dangerous and it is clear that Barack Obama is not ready to be President." Obama's advisers tried to explain that he meant lower level meetings and not Presidential meetings. People were ready to accept this until Obama himself repeated what he said and added, "The Bush policy of isolation of these so called rogue states is clearly not working. Why don't we try something else?" He went further to say that as President, he would reserve the right to meet with anyone at anytime and at a place of his choosing if he thinks it will keep Americans and the rest of the world safe. I said at the time, "Obama is absolutely right, but is America ready to hear that kind of brutal truth?" It turns out, they were! On blog sites I visited after these comments, people began to respond saying, "Why not try diplomacy?" "The Bush way has not worked, it's not made our country safer, so why not try Obama's way?" "We're tired of Bush's war rants, let's give diplomacy a chance", "Senator Obama is right, what is wrong with talking to our enemies if we're trying to achieve peace?", "JFK did it and it worked, Ronald Reagan did it and it worked, why don't we try it again?"

I'm not American, but seeing those comments brought a pride in America I never thought I could have for another country. For the first time, I actually began to see that Americans were sick and tired of the direction the country had been heading, especially in the last 8years. You might ask, "Why should it concern you so much that America is headed in a wrong direction?" The answer to that question is very simple; "When America sneezes, the rest of the world catches a cold!"

The rest of the year saw all the candidates jockeying for air time in TV ads and TV interviews. They were getting ready for the first primary battle in Iowa.

Polls initially showed Hillary Clinton ahead and Barack Obama in second place, but the more time Obama spent on the ground campaigning, the higher his poll numbers got. When he eventually caught and overtook Hillary Clinton, the whole world really began to pay attention.

Election night, January 2008 and I could not wait for the results to come in. When Barack Obama was declared the winner, I was almost in tears. When I listened to his victory speech, I actually had goose pimples! His speech started with, "They said this day would never come!" I hated to admit it, but I was one of that "they" and for a very long time too. This probably sounds dramatic, but let me explain. From everything I had seen and heard leading up to Iowa, it was clear that Obama's race was not an issue for a surprisingly huge number of voters. But even my most optimistic predictions would not have expected him to win Iowa, a State with a 96% white population! When you consider this fact, you start to get an idea of where the goose pimples came from.

I heard an African-American Professor remark that Obama's Iowa victory was like a jolt of electricity had run through the African-American community, because, "if he could win in a State like Iowa, with a mostly white population, this is no longer playtime".

I could understand where they were coming from. When Obama announced his candidacy, African-Americans must have been thinking along the lines of, "We'll vote for him, but we all know he's not going to win anyway. We'll vote for him, but white people will not and he'll become another statistic of the number of African-Americans who have run for President".

Iowa changed that line of reasoning because if he could win in a State where African-Americans only make up 4% of the population, then the possibility of him securing the Democratic Party's nomination did not seem that farfetched!

His Iowa victory proved that Obama had won the State strictly on merit and race was the last thing on voters' minds. I hoped and prayed that voters in all the other States would cast their votes based on who spoke to their concerns and not who looked a certain way.

The "inevitable nominee in waiting", Hillary Clinton did not even finish second in Iowa, she finished third, behind John Edwards! (Although she still had more delegates than he did). Senators Biden and Dodd dropped out of the race after very disappointing showings. The delegate count had started and by the end of the Iowa caucuses, it looked like this;

Obama – 16
Edwards – 14
Clinton – 15

One interesting thing that came on the back of the Iowa victory was a debate that was now in full swing: Change versus Experience. Exit polls in Iowa showed that a large number of young voters cast their votes for Obama and most of them cited a need for change from the way Washington operates and Obama's message of change as their main reason for voting for him. Since the change versus experience debate raged until the end of the election season and even became more heated, I will delve into that a bit more later.

So it was official, Barack Obama was now the frontrunner, not Hillary Clinton. It would now be interesting to see if Obama's new role would propel him on a tidal wave of delegate counts in the upcoming states or if he would crack under the pressure, as has been known to happen in Presidential level politics.

Some doubters however believed that Obama was just a flash in the pan. They believed he was the man of the moment, at the moment, but would eventually run out of steam. But as one analyst put it, "I saw firsthand the professional manner in which the Obama campaign was run in Iowa and I knew he was not going anywhere anytime soon".

The next State was New Hampshire and the polls reflected Obama's new role as frontrunner. I was getting pretty excited and kept thinking, "Wow! He actually has come this far!"

The media went "Obama-crazy" and there were headlines all over the world on his win in Iowa, his expected win in New Hampshire and the possibility that he might be the Democratic nominee and possibly, President of The United States. I remember watching an evening news story, touting "Barack Obama's extraordinary ties to The UK"! I was surprised when I saw this and was really curious to find out what these extraordinary ties were, since I did not know of any. It turns out it was about a trip Obama made to The UK a few years ago and went with some friends and family to a local bar! The bartender was interviewed and asked what he thought of the fact that he had once served the man who could possibly be the next US President! I could not believe what I was hearing! That THIS was Obama's "extraordinary ties to The UK???" I liked Obama from the moment I heard his speech in 2004 and enjoy watching stuff about him, but that news program bordered on ridiculous!

Even the Republicans could not resist. Republican Presidential candidate, Mitt Romney said, "Obama is a Senator killer, he's taken care of Senator Clinton, he's taken care of Senator Edwards, if John McCain is our nominee, he'll take care of him too. I'm the only one who knows how to deal with Obama." I can only imagine by that, he meant since he was not a Senator, he could deal with the "Senator killer". Sounds nice, but when you think about it, you remember that John McCain was the only serious Republican candidate, who was running as a seating Senator. So, anyone of the others could actually deal with Obama, based on Mitt Romney's logic. Anyway, we'll get to the Republicans in a bit.

I don't think anyone (myself included) even conceived of the idea that he might not win New Hampshire. The polls had been wrong before, so why were we all so sure that they would be right now?

A day before the primary, I saw something that I wasn't sure whether to be amused by or if it was touching. While campaigning in New Hampshire, Hillary Clinton had a sort of round table question and answer meeting with some female voters. One of the women asked her this question: "How do you do it? How do you keep upbeat and so wonderful?" Hillary responded, "You know, this is very personal for me. It's not just political, it's not just public. I see what's happening and we have to reverse it. Some people think elections are a game, lots of who's up and who's down, but it's about our country, it's about our kids' futures, it's really about all of us together".

You might ask, "What is the big deal about that?" The big deal is that when she answered the question, she was visibly fighting back tears. Her voice was shaky and at one point, I actually thought she was going to break down. Don't get me wrong, there's absolutely nothing wrong with being emotional. But the reason I wasn't sure whether to be amused or touched was because it was Hillary Clinton. I did not know if this emotional moment was for show or if she actually felt that way at that moment. I was with my fiancée and my cousins the first time I saw the video clip of that moment. My fiancée and one of my cousins thought it was genuine, another one of my cousins thought it was fake and I just wasn't sure what to make of it.

Election night, January 8 2008 and I was already reading up on the demographics for the next State because I believed New Hampshire had been won even before election night. So imagine my shock when the results came in and I saw that Hillary Clinton won! I could not believe it! Even the pundits on TV were initially lost for words (That doesn't happen very often),but when they did find their voices, they started talking about the Clinton family's history of comebacks and the validity of polls, since according to the polls, Obama should be the one giving a victory speech, not Hillary Clinton. To be perfectly honest, I had always questioned the idea of polls. I had always tried to understand how the opinions of about 1000 people out of a population of roughly 300million could be representative of the country's opinion. I desperately wanted to believe the polls were right, since they had been right in Iowa. I wondered if the "Bradley effect" had taken place in New Hampshire. The Bradley effect was coined from a situation in the 1982 California Governorship election, between African-American candidate, Tom Bradley and white candidate, George Deukmejian. Opinion polls leading up to the elections showed Bradley with a sizeable lead, but on Election Day, Bradley surprisingly lost the elections. Exit polls taken showed that a large number of white undecided voters ended up voting for Deukmejian. Also, a significant number of white people who had stated in opinion polls that they would vote for Bradley, ended up voting for

Deukmejian instead. If this was what had happened in this case, I was worried that it could happen again in the subsequent States and eventually derail Obama's chances at being the Democratic Party's nominee. I also hoped that if he did win the nomination, the Bradley effect would not be responsible for costing him the Presidential elections in November. However, I knew the pundits only question the validity of polls when they turn out to be wrong and was quite sure that by the next race, everyone would be hungrily mopping up the polls again. Anyways, New Hampshire was over and it was obvious that the race had been turned on its head again. Hillary Clinton was still very much in the race and Barack Obama had to put the champagne bottle back in the bucket. I found out something interesting though. The woman who asked Hillary Clinton the question that led to that emotional moment, voted for Obama!

Governor Bill Richardson dropped out after the New Hampshire primary, while Congressman Dennis Kucinich dropped out on January 23rd. Mike Gravel would eventually quit the party to join the Libertarian Party.

Now, the next State should have been Nevada, but trouble on the horizon meant there would be a bit of drama first. Florida and Michigan, in defiance to Democratic Party rules had decided to schedule their primaries at an earlier date than the DNC scheduled dates. Michigan decided to hold theirs on January 15, while Florida decided to hold theirs on January 29. The DNC had warned that if both states went ahead with these plans, they would be stripped of all delegates and their primaries would not be reflected in the final delegate count. In keeping with this agreement, the candidates did not campaign in either state and Clinton's name was the only major candidate on the ballot in Michigan. She eventually won both states. Since the Florida and Michigan primaries became such a major issue later in the campaign, I will get back to it. Back to Nevada, Hillary Clinton won the state as expected on January 19, without incident.

The stage was now set for what would prove to be a major test for the candidates, South Carolina. The State was a major test for a variety of reasons;

1. South Carolina has a large African-American population and it would be interesting to see how potentially the most successful African-American Presidential candidate would fare among this key constituency, some of whom had accused him of not being black enough;

2. Hillary Clinton had tremendous support within the African-American community and I could not wait to see if this loyalty would remain in place when faced with the first serious African-American contender;

3. John Edwards was born in South Carolina and his father worked in South Carolina for most of his life, so he also had a huge following in the state;

4. South Carolina has a large number of people serving in the US military, at a time when an unpopular war was being fought in Iraq and the

candidates' positions on this issue could swing
the state's contest one way or the other.

The polls however put Barack Obama in the lead,
with Hillary Clinton second and John Edwards third. I
was careful this time, not to read a lot into this, after New
Hampshire.

The next debate was going to be held in South
Carolina, just days before the State's crucial primary. This
debate had garnered quite a bit of interest and I started
wondering if it wasn't being overhyped and may even end
up not living up to it.

The debate started and I listened intently to what the
candidates were saying. It was obvious that Clinton and
Obama were trying to establish themselves as the favorites.
John Edwards was holding his own, but it was obvious
that most of the attention was on the two frontrunners.
Any pre-conceived ideas I may have had that the debate
would end up being like watching paint dry, was shut
down less than an hour into the debate.

One of the debate moderators, Suzanne Malveaux,
had brought up an assertion made in the campaign
by Hillary Clinton against Barack Obama about fiscal
responsibility. The gist of the assertion was that Obama
had highlighted a series of programs he would enact
as President, but had not explained how he intends to
pay for about $50B worth of these programs. Obama's
response was that this was not true. He then went on
to raise instances where Hillary and Bill Clinton had
distorted his positions and even called his opposition
to the war in Iraq, "a fairy tale" (Bill Clinton actually
said that) and pointed out that voters are looking for
something different and not the typical Washington

political games. Hillary's response was a clarification of the criticisms, including her and her husband's issue with Obama's Iraq war opposition and Obama's purported fondness for the Republican economic ideas. Obama's reply was like a whiplash! It almost sounded like a younger brother scolding an older sister for being silly! I will try to remember his exact words. He said something along the lines of, "What I said is that Ronald Reagan was a transformative political figure because he was able to get Democrats to vote against their economic interests to form a majority to push through their agenda, an agenda that I objected to. Because while I was working on those streets watching those folks see their jobs shift overseas, you were a corporate lawyer sitting on the board at Wal-Mart!"

The audience went crazy! I could hardly believe my ears. Before I could recover from the shock, he went on. "So I want to be clear. What I said had nothing to do with their policies. I spent a lifetime fighting against Ronald Reagan's policies. But what I did say is that we have to be thinking in the same transformative way about our Democratic agenda. We've got to appeal to Independents and Republicans in order to build a working majority to move an agenda forward. That is what I said"

At that point, Hillary Clinton tried to step in to object to what he was saying, but he cut her off and went on, "Hillary, you went on for two minutes, so let me finish. The irony of this is that you provided much more fulsome praise of Ronald Reagan in a book by Tom Brokaw that's being published right now, as did Bill Clinton in the past. So these are the kinds of political games that we are accustomed to."

By this time, I was on my feet screaming the house down. My fiancée woke up and asked what was going on. I kissed her and said, "I'm sorry babe, nothing's wrong, go back to bed. I'll try not to shout anymore."

Just as I said that, I saw that they were still at it! Clinton was trying to explain that some comments should not be attributed to her. This was how that dialogue went:

Clinton: I just want to be clear about this. In an editorial board with the Reno newspaper, you said two different things, because I have read the transcripts. You talked about Ronald Reagan being a transformative political leader. I did not mention his name

Obama: Your husband did

Clinton: Well, he's not here, I am

Obama: Well, I can't tell who I'm running against sometimes.

Oh my God!! I literally had never seen anything like this before. I had seen debates with a lot of back and forth and I had seen debates with some really heated exchanges, but not from two Presidential candidates who were this high profile. The rest of the evening went on with a few more exchanges, most of them between Clinton and Obama, but nothing resembling those few minutes. John Edwards had to keep reminding everyone that the debate was between three people and not two. He largely stayed out of the attacks, probably trying to do a John Kerry. By that, I'm referring to the 2004 Democratic Presidential campaign, during which frontrunners Howard Dean and Richard Gerphardt's constant attacks on each other turned voters off. John Kerry stayed above the fray and ended as the unlikely nominee.

My second favorite moment of that debate was when Obama was asked if he thought Bill Clinton was the first black President, as observed by Nobel Prize winning author, Toni Morrison. After praising Bill Clinton for his affinity with the African-American community, he went on to say, "I would have to investigate more of Bill's dancing abilities and some of this other stuff, before I can accurately judge if he was in fact a brother". The audience loved that and applauded loudly. Even Hillary Clinton could not help herself, she burst out laughing hysterically and said, "I'm sure that can be arranged", which drew an even bigger applause from the audience. I was loving every minute of it! I was almost sad that the debate had to come to an end. When my fiancée woke up the next morning and asked me how the debate went, I said, "That was the most interesting politics related thing I've ever seen on TV, never mind debate. It had absolutely everything, from civility to nasty exchanges, to sarcastic comments, to humor. It was just fantastic. She said, "Glad to know you enjoyed it. Now, what do you want for breakfast?"

On the day of the State's primary, Bill Clinton started a storm with comments that were viewed by many as being racially tinged. All the polls suggested that Obama was heading for a big win in South Carolina. When Bill Clinton was asked about this, he said, "Well, Jesse Jackson also won South Carolina".

This was seen as diminishing Obama's accomplishments, since Jesse Jackson's win was largely as a result of African-American voters and very little else, if any. So, to take away from a guy who won in a State with a 96% white population and had done quite well among white voters in every State was seen as a low blow. It was made even worse by the fact that these statements came from a man who had such enormous respect within the African-American community. Of course, Bill Clinton stated that was not what he meant, but the fact that this was another in a series of scathing criticisms of Obama by the former President did not sit well with a lot of people. Some even began to question if Bill Clinton was an asset or a liability to his wife's campaign.

Personally, I thought Bill Clinton's point was that a black Presidential candidate will always win in South Carolina or any State with a sizeable African-American presence. Whether or not this was a racially motivated comment, only he will know, but let's face it, he did have a point. It's pretty hard to see how an African-American candidate would not do well in a South Carolina. When you then consider the fact that Barack Obama was the first African-American candidate, who seemed like he had a pretty good shot at being President, you understand that for a lot of African-Americans, even if they did not agree with his policies, there was a "feel good" factor in voting for him. If they voted overwhelmingly for Jesse Jackson, who I do not think ever had a serious chance of being President, I think it only makes sense that they would also overwhelmingly vote for Obama who is a lot more popular than Jesse Jackson was. Further, since African-Americans are not the only voting bloc in South Carolina, if Obama could win majority of their votes and do as well with the white voters as he had done in other States, it was hard to see how he would not win South Carolina. The fact is that regardless of the Clintons' popularity with African-Americans, if and when an African-American runs for President, that loyalty will always be tested. Bill Clinton's comment was ill-timed and frankly, it was not the smartest thing to say, but I don't think he meant it in the way that it was portrayed.

When the State's primary results were announced, Barack Obama won convincingly with 55% of the vote and 25 delegates. Hillary Clinton came second with 27% and 12 delegates, while John Edwards finished third with 18% and 8 delegates. Exit polls showed that an overwhelming majority of African Americans had voted for Obama.

This win had shown that Obama could do well with both whites and blacks. He had won in Iowa, which had a 96% white population and in South Carolina, a State that had a large African-American population. The "Obama is not black enough" mantra did not seem to be an issue for African-American voters in South Carolina.

After the South Carolina primary, John Edwards dropped out of the race. Both Hillary Clinton and Barack Obama actively sort his endorsement, but he decided not to endorse anyone just yet.

Barack Obama did receive two high profile endorsements though. The first came on January 27 from Caroline Kennedy, daughter of former President, John Kennedy. She wrote a piece in The New York Times, explaining why she had decided to endorse Obama. The most touching part of that piece was the last sentence; "I have never had a president who inspired me the way people tell me that my father inspired them. But for the first time, I believe I have found the man who could be that President — not just for me, but for a new generation of Americans." It was touching and quite amazing for the daughter of an American icon to make that kind of comparison. I had heard the comparisons, I had heard the similarities, but I wrote it off as dramatic Obama fans, who would say just about anything to explain why he would the best President for America. But to hear Caroline Kennedy describe him in those words was something very powerful indeed. The following day brought an even bigger endorsement from one of the "Big Three", Ted Kennedy. The "Big Three" are the three most powerful and respected people in the Democratic Party. They are Bill Clinton, Al Gore and Ted Kennedy. I think we already know who Bill Clinton endorsed, while Al Gore had not endorsed any candidate yet.

Ted Kennedy's endorsement of Barack Obama was seen as a coup for Obama, as both candidates had actively sought it, because of the sense of legitimacy (for want of a better word) that such an endorsement would give the campaign of whoever got it. He was joined by his son, Patrick Kennedy and niece, Caroline Kennedy. They all made the same comparisons with the iconic former President. These endorsements, coupled with Obama's surge in the national polls meant the upcoming "Super Tuesday" contests would be very interesting and would definitely be a long night for both candidates.

At this point, I have to ask a question; why is so much emphasis and importance placed on endorsements? I can understand that a candidate wants the support of major players in the game, but why call a press conference to announce who you are supporting? There is the obvious argument that a public figure will always be asked who he or she is supporting, but my point or maybe I should say my question is how much of a difference does an endorsement ultimately make when it all comes down to the voters on election day? Will voters cast their votes for someone they initially did not plan to vote for because a respected public figure did, or will an endorsement help sway undecided voters on election day? In the more extreme scenarios, would an endorsement from someone a voter dislikes make that voter change his/her mind, just because he or she has never agreed with the endorser's views? These were the question I had always asked, without ever getting a completely satisfactory answer. I found out later in the year though, that the reason I never got a completely satisfactory answer was because there wasn't one.

Endorsements can work for or against a candidate. In my opinion, the endorsement of Obama by the Kennedys was supposed to make three things happen:

1. It was supposed to show that the comparison that people were making about Obama and JFK were echoed by the former President's family as well;

2. It was supposed to show that Obama was a serious contender and if one of the most respected politicians in the country was putting his support behind someone described by critics as inexperienced, that might make others take another look at him;

3. It was supposed to win him the Massachusetts primary, which was coming up in a few days;

Did these three things happen? I would say the first two did to a certain extent. The last, you will see soon if it did.

The first debate since the Democrats had only two candidates left was held on January 31 in California. The venue was the Kodak centre, where the Grammy awards are held and the venue was packed full with celebrities. Apart from the obvious draw of seeing these two superstar candidates, there were those who were expecting another drama filled debate like the South Carolina debate. I have to admit, I was one of those people.

When Obama started the debate with this statement, "Hillary Clinton and I were friends before the campaign and we will be friends after the campaign", I knew there would be no fireworks. Needless to say, the debate was dangerously close to boring because they both seemed to be trying too hard to be gracious.

Everyone's attention now turned to "Super Tuesday", the day when 23 States held their primaries. This particular day was February 5, 2008. It is interesting to note that just a few months ago, most analysts, including some of Hillary Clinton's advisers, believed that she would have the Democratic nomination wrapped up by Super Tuesday. This was obviously far from it. In the delegate race to 2117, the table stood like this:

Obama – 63
Clinton – 48
Edwards – 26

Questions were now being asked as to whether the race could be wrapped up by the end of Super Tuesday, either by Obama or Clinton. It most certainly did not look that way, but this race had produced quite a few surprises already, so no one was making any predictions. From what I was seeing though, one thing was clear to me; Super Tuesday would not be the end of this race, either for Clinton or Obama.

Slowly, the results started to trickle in. By the end of the night, Obama won 13 States (Alabama, Alaska, Colorado, Connecticut, Delaware, Georgia, Idaho, Illinois, Kansas, Minnesota, Missouri, North Dakota and Utah) and finished with a total of 847 delegates, while Clinton won 10 states (American Samoa, Arizona, Arkansas, California, Massachusetts, New Jersey, New Mexico, New York, Oklahoma and Tennessee) and finished with a 834 delegates. The total delegate count now stood at:

Obama – 910
Clinton – 882

As you saw from the list of States won by the candidates, Clinton won in Massachusetts and not Obama, as analysts believed, due to the Kennedy endorsements. Another reason for an expected Obama win in Massachusetts was the fact that former Presidential candidate, John Kerry, who had endorsed Obama in January, was a Massachusetts Senator. Even more of a reason was the fact that Obama's close friend and co-chair of his campaign, Deval Patrick, was the Governor of Massachusetts! As a result, it is noteworthy that Hillary Clinton did not just win the State, she actually won big! She won with 56% to Obama's 41% and gained 55 delegates, while Obama gained 38 delegates. So, I ask again, why is so much emphasis and importance placed on endorsements? As we go on and different endorsements come in for both candidates and also in the general election season, I will attempt to answer this question again.

The fact that Clinton had won the big States like California and New York led some observers to question Obama's ability to win these States in the general elections. This turned out to be the first in a number of quite ridiculous statements made by analysts, Clinton supporters and sadly, Hillary Clinton herself. California and New York are two of the most Democratic leaning States in the country. One might say, the "bluest States" in the country. I don't think either State would suddenly vote Republican in the general elections for the first time in decades, just because Barack Obama is the nominee. But I suspect the people making these silly statements already knew that!

The day after Super Tuesday, Hillary Clinton announced that she had loaned her campaign $5million. Although this news came as a shock, it settled rumors that had been going around for a while about Clinton's campaign finances. The rumors that powerful donors were worried about the way the race was going, since they expected Clinton to have won it by now and the rumors that Clinton had not planned for post Super Tuesday, as she expected the race to be over by then. Even though her supporters responded by raising $6million within the 36 hours after her announcement, she was dealt a further blow by the Obama campaign, when it announced they had raised $7.5million within the same period.

Obama was raising mind bending amounts of money and setting fundraising records every month. In January, he raised $36million, a record amount for a Presidential candidate in a single month. In February, he blew that record apart, raising $55million. When you consider the fact that for so long, Hillary Clinton was the frontrunner, both in polls and fundraising, this was a remarkable feat. I wondered how and why Clinton could be in such a position, while a relative newcomer was shattering fundraising records every month. Clinton had the support of some of the most powerful people in the country, while the powers that be were still sizing Obama up.

I decided to do some research to get a better understanding of why Obama was the one at a financial advantage. What I found was not only stunning, it was also very touching.

First of all, I found out that Barack Obama had made use of the internet in a way never before used by any politician for fundraising. I found that hundreds of thousands of people had donated as little as $5 to his campaign. Since the maximum allowed by law was $2300, some people set up direct debits online to donate different amounts per month, as long as the total individual donation did not exceed the maximum allowed by law. I found that mind boggling! I liked Obama, I would definitely vote for him if I was American, but for people to believe in his candidacy so much that they were willing to make those sort of financial commitments at a time when the economy was in trouble was touching. I saw a news program with a single mom who earns $22000 a year. She had 3 kids and every month, after paying the bills, there is little or nothing left over until the next pay day. She said, "I can sit back and wait for a miracle to happen or I can make sure I do what I can to see that the next President is someone who understands what I and millions in this country are going through, so that my children can have a better future". Her contribution; $20 a month! When you multiply people like her by the little amounts they gave and add the ones who could afford to donate even more, Obama's fundraising prowess starts to make a lot more sense. Also, the Obama campaign registered millions of new voters, who most likely ended up contributing to his campaign. Obama explained this in a very simple sentence; "A movement for change does not start from the top down, it starts from the bottom up"

In Hillary Clinton's case, she used the more traditional fundraising platforms, which would usually attract the more affluent contributors. She did have contributions from less affluent voters, but nothing on the scale of the Obama campaign. If the rumor that she had not planned for post Super Tuesday was true, then it was really no surprise that her campaign was experiencing the kinds of financial problems I was now hearing about. Even though she raised millions, she spent the bulk of it on the earlier primaries in the hope of delivering an early knockout to her rivals. She (let's face it, like most of us) did not anticipate the Obamamania that had swept across the country. One thing was starting to become clear; Hillary Clinton did not have a plan B if she did not win the nomination by Super Tuesday. And since Super Tuesday was over and not only had she not won, she was behind (even if only slightly) Obama in the delegate count. They still had 28 primaries and caucuses all the way through to June. I started to wonder how Hillary Clinton would survive in the race with inadequate planning beyond February 5, if the race went all the way to June or even the convention in August. One thing I did know though, was this: Never count out a Clinton!

February is supposed to be shortest month of the year, but February 2008 was a very long month for me, because I was moving houses at the time and had also just changed jobs. Due to the move, my cable TV was not fixed until the last week of the month. My internet was also not sorted until that same time, as the new place did not have a phone line, so we had to wait for a couple of weeks to get one fixed. We were finally given a date for the cable install for February 20. I checked the calendar and saw that was the day after the last primary in February and I thought, "Just great! Is someone or something trying to prevent me from watching the drama of the February primaries unfold?" I felt so frustrated because I felt like I was disconnected from what was going on. Since I could not use the internet at work for anything other than work, I went to internet cafes after work to see what was going on, but could only spend so much time in there before my fiancée came to drag me out of there. The British TV channels only covered the results of the primaries and the coverage obviously was not as in depth as CNN or ABC or MSNBC or the entertaining FOX News.

Due to the time difference, I had to wait till early morning each day to find out who won which primary. So every morning, I would wake up before 7am and switch on the TV to catch the 7am news, since it was always one of the lead stories.

On February 9, what I heard was: "Barack Obama has won all 4 primaries that were held earlier today. He won in Louisiana, Nebraska, US Virgin Islands and Washington caucuses. He finished the day with 104 delegates, to Hillary Clinton's 57.

The next day, it was: Barack Obama has won the Maine caucuses, finishing with 15 delegates, while Hillary Clinton finished with 9.

The day after that, it was, Barack Obama has won the primaries in DC, Maryland, Virginia, and the primary for Democrats abroad. He finished the day with126.5 delegates, while Hillary Clinton finished with 68.5 delegates." I wondered for a second if the anchor was mistaken. Did she really say 112.5 and 62.5? Where did the ".5" come from? When I got into the internet café the next day, the first thing I did was to check what exactly .5 delegates meant. I found that in that particular primary, pledged delegates have only half a vote and not a full vote to the convention. Didn't make a lot of sense to me, but that's what it was and that's how it's always been. I had an American colleague at work and decided to ask him if he knew what this meant. He said the same thing, that it's a rule he's never understood, but it's always been that way, so he's given up on trying to understand why they don't just get a full vote.

On February 19, it was: Barack Obama has won the Hawaii caucuses and Wisconsin primaries, finishing with a total of 66 delegates, while Hillary Clinton finished with 38 delegates.

The next day, my cable was fixed and I felt a breath

of fresh air! It wasn't until an analyst on TV mentioned something that it occurred to me. And when it did, the realization hit me like a thunderbolt! Obama had won 11 different State primaries in 11 days! He had won every single primary since Super Tuesday and some of them in states where Hillary Clinton was heavily favored to win. I sat back and said, "Is this really happening?" It felt like one of those moments when you hope something will happen, but deep down you have doubts about whether it will, but when it does happen, you start to ask yourself if it's really happening. How was this guy doing it? By this time, my fear of the Bradley effect had all but disappeared, but there was always still that nagging feeling that "Obama is one of the most intelligent and charismatic politicians I have ever seen, but will his race ultimately become an issue?" I knew it had not really been an issue to date, but I also knew that November was a very long time away and a lot of things could happen before then. The strange thing was that these thoughts would push themselves to the top of my thinking only when Obama seemed to be doing well. I decided I would keep watching and banish those thoughts to the outer parts of my mind and just focus on what I felt and saw as history in the making, because if I allowed those thoughts to gain traction, I would lose interest in the race.

The delegate count now stood at:

Obama – 1192
Clinton – 1035

In all, February was not a very good month for the Clinton campaign. Highly respected Clinton adviser,

Patti Solis Doyle, who had been with Hillary Clinton since 1992, left the campaign. Whether she was fired or she resigned, no one will ever know, but the point is that the Clinton campaign was starting to implode. Clinton surrogates could not understand why or how they found themselves in this position, when according to established wisdom, she should by this time have started her search for a running mate. I heard some analysts (talking heads, as they're called), saying they just did not see how Clinton could overturn the delegate lead in the upcoming States, unless she won by substantial margins. If the trends of the race since Iowa were being followed, I also did not see how she would win some of the upcoming States by substantial margins.

The next set of primaries was to be held on March 4. March turned out to be the most eventful month of the campaign, as attacks and controversies dominated the news. Hillary Clinton was heavily favored to win the big States of Texas and Ohio. The Clinton campaign's calculation was that if she was able to win both States and win as big as the polls suggested, then she might just be able to knock Obama off in terms of delegate count. However, they were also aware that if the victory margins were not large enough, or if she even lost one of these two States, the race was as good as over. The other two States to hold their primaries on March 4 were Rhode Island and Vermont. The polls in Texas and Ohio showed Clinton with a huge lead, as much as 20 points. Obama spent a lot more time campaigning in Texas than Ohio. I guess the reason was because he saw Texas as easier to overcome Clinton's lead or at least reduce it. Ohio was a little more complicated, because of the large number of the so called "working class white voters". This voting bloc had been the most loyal Clinton base throughout the primaries and had a less than enthusiastic reception to Obama. Ohio also had a large number of older voters (over 60); this age group had overwhelmingly preferred Clinton to Obama in the previous primaries. These facts, coupled with the vocal support of Ohio's Governor, Ted Strickland, made Ohio almost impossible to lose for Clinton.

In Texas, a large Latino presence was also seen as a good thing for Clinton, who was very popular within that community. But something started to happen.

The more time Obama spent campaigning in Texas, the higher his poll numbers got. By the end of February, he was running evenly with Clinton in Texas! I was amazed at this and something I had thought about earlier started to occur to me.

Before the primaries started, everyone in the country knew who Hillary Clinton was. Barack Obama was unknown outside his home State of Illinois until his speech in 2004 and his subsequent election as a US Senator and even then, the people that knew about him were the ones who followed politics. Most people interviewed stated that they liked Hillary Clinton and they also felt like they knew her. They stated that they liked Obama even more, but didn't really feel like they knew him and they would rather vote for someone they know, rather than for someone they like. The bottom line is that a lot of people voted for Hillary Clinton more out of name-recognition than a disagreement with Obama's ideas or policies. This is not to take anything away from Clinton, but when you ask someone a question about Hillary and they talk about her accomplishments and what a wonderful person she is and what brilliant plans she has for the country. If you ask those same people about Obama, they usually say something like, "I like him, he seems like a nice guy and he's got a lovely family, but I don't really know much else about him". Using this scenario, I probably would vote for Clinton instead of Obama. Plus, I don't think people really paid that much attention to Obama until he won Iowa. But I found out that in any State Obama campaigned in, the more time he spent on the ground, the more people listened to him, the more they felt comfortable voting for him. The situation in Texas was a perfect example. By the time Obama had campaigned in the State for a few days, Hillary Clinton's lead was at first reduced and then, they were tied. Some polls even put him ahead. His rallies in Texas made headlines, because of the sizes of the crowds. At one particular rally, the crowd happily cheered and applauded when Obama blew his nose! I had never seen anything like it! Crowds like these were more commonplace at music concerts and sports events, not political events and certainly not from a hitherto unknown politician.

A few days before the March 4 primaries, a "controversy" erupted. I have put that word in quotes because I believe it was a generated controversy, one meant to derail Obama's campaign. He was accused of plagiarism. I was initially worried when I heard this accusation, because plagiarism charges had effectively ended Joe Biden's first campaign for President in 1988. When I found the facts out though, I relaxed because I knew it was just another political game. During a campaign event in Milwaukee,

Obama gave a speech, which had similarities to a speech by Massachusetts Governor, Deval Patrick.

Obama's words were, **"Don't tell me words don't matter! 'I have a dream.' Just words. 'We hold these truths to be self-evident, that all men are created equal". Just words. 'We have nothing to fear but fear itself.' Just words, just speeches"**.

Deval Patrick's words during a 2006 campaign event, while running for Governor were, **"We hold these truths to be self-evident, that all men are created equal'-just words. Just words. 'We have nothing to fear but fear itself'-just words. 'Ask not what your country can do for you, ask what you can do for your country'-just words. 'I have a dream'-just words"**.

Sounds similar, right? Right. But the real question is, What does the word plagiarism mean? It means, "the use of or close imitation of an author's work as one's own without permission of the original owner".

Deval Patrick was a co-chair of Obama's campaign. He and Obama were close friends. He said himself that he and Obama talk regularly about strategies and he suggested those lines to Obama, as it was in line with Obama's theme during that campaign event. How that qualifies as plagiarism is certainly beyond me. Obama used a line from a speech of his campaign co-chairman, not only with his permission, but Governor Patrick actually suggested he use it and is accused of plagiarism. I believed I had now seen it all in this campaign! Obama's supporters and even some Hillary Clinton supporters condemned the accusation and it eventually died as suddenly as it had erupted, at least until Clinton brought it up during the next debate.

The last debate before the March 4 primaries was the Texas debate on February 21. Just like in California, the Texas debate was surprisingly civil, considering the fact that the campaign trail had witnessed fireworks from both candidates. There were arguments and there were exchanges, but nothing really heated, apart from one moment late in the debate. Obama was asked about the plagiarism accusation. He and Clinton responded to this question. The dialogue went like this:

Obama: "I've been campaigning now for the last two years. Deval is a national co-chairman of my campaign and suggested an argument that I share, that words are important and the notion that I plagiarized from somebody who was one of my national co-chairs, who gave me the line and suggested that I use it, I think is just silly. And, this is where we start getting into silly season in politics and I think people start getting discouraged about it. What we shouldn't be spending time doing is tearing each other down, we should be spending time lifting the country up."

Clinton: Well, I think that if your candidacy is going to be about words, they should be your own words. That, I think is a simple proposition and you know, lifting whole passages from someone else's speech isn't change you can believe in, it's change you can xerox"

Clinton's response drew huge boos from the crowds. A woman interviewed by CNN after the debate said of that moment, "It's silly, unnecessary statements like that from Hillary that makes me question her character".

Two days after the debate, I was driving home, I think from London. My fiancée called me and asked, "What did Obama do wrong?" I asked, "What do you mean?" She said, "I just saw Hillary Clinton on TV, holding some papers and shouting, Shame on you Barack Obama".

I didn't have a clue what was going on and my mind started racing. I wondered what had happened. Had Obama done something wrong? Had something he did or said in the past come to light? Had he said something silly? I was about 45mins away from home that day, but I got home in 30mins and switched to CNN, but they were talking about something else. I switched to FOX, but they were also talking about something else, so I got on the internet.

Since there was no headline news on Obama or Clinton, I relaxed a bit. My relaxation turned into amazement, then amusement and finally, to hysterical laughter, when I found out what Hillary Clinton was so upset about. Apparently, the Obama campaign had released some fliers in the last few weeks, comparing and contrasting his and Senator Clinton's health care plans and their positions on the North American Free Trade Agreement (NAFTA). She felt the fliers distorted her views on these issues and decided to voice her anger, with the Ohio Governor, Ted Strickland, nodding gravely behind her. I thought, "Hillary Clinton is such an actress! I'm sure she knew about these fliers before today, why is it a few days to the Ohio primaries and when Obama seems to be closing the gap in Ohio that her anger at the "distortions" became evident?" Obama's response was one of surprise at the sudden outburst, since these fliers had been around for weeks. He also stated that there was nothing untrue about Clinton's positions in the fliers. I found it very curious that Clinton was "upset" about her positions supposedly being distorted, since she had constantly done that with Obama's positions and with John Edwards's positions as well, when he was still in the race. I'm not saying Obama did not or could not have distorted her positions. But the fact of the matter is that in putting forward your political positions and contrasting it with your opponents', omissions, distortions (knowingly or otherwise), will always exist. No one in this election cycle used that rule more than Hillary Clinton, so if indeed her positions were distorted, she should be the last person to be upset or even complain about it.

The personal attacks were stepped up, both by the candidates and their surrogates. Hillary Clinton unleashed what Obama called, "the kitchen sink attacks", referring to the almost daily attacks on him. Bill Clinton joined in and I wondered if these attacks would pay off eventually. Even the media was not spared. They were accused of being in love with Obama and not giving him as much scrutiny as Hillary Clinton. I remember a cartoon I saw which I actually found quite funny. In the cartoon, Obama was relaxing, while the media was fanning him, and tending to his needs. Obama responded with attacks of his own, leading some analysts to question his promise to run a campaign free of negativity and attacks, never mind the fact that most of his attacks were in response to attacks on him.

Just before the March 4 primaries, Hillary Clinton came up with two master strokes. One backfired spectacularly. The other however, was a spectacular hit!

The first was an astonishing comment she made to

reporters. She said, "I think I have a lifetime of experience that I will bring to the White House. I know that Senator McCain has a lifetime of experience that he will bring to the White House and Senator Obama has a speech that he gave in 2002".

Shock was an understatement for what I felt! How could she go this far?!? It was bad enough that two Democrats were mercilessly attacking each other in a bid to secure the party's nomination, while the Republicans had all but wrapped up their contest. It was bad enough that the Republicans seemed a lot more organized and decisive than the Democrats, but why give them more ammunition for the general elections? To go as far as endorsing the Republican Party's presumptive nominee over a fellow Democrat was just plain wrong! It's one of those unwritten rules that you just follow. Did it not occur to her that if Obama won the nomination, the Republicans would use that statement against him?

This statement led analysts, party elders and even some Clinton supporters to question Hillary's commitment to the party. They saw her comment as a sign that she would rather destroy the party's chances of winning the general elections in November than give up the nomination. Some saw something even more sinister going on. They felt she knew she did not have a chance of winning the nomination, so she wanted to spoil Obama's chances of winning the general elections so badly, that she would be the presumptive nominee in 2012. A lot of Democrats began calling for her to withdraw from the race. As the March 4 primaries drew closer, these calls for Hillary Clinton to withdraw got even louder.

The second masterstroke was a TV ad that definitely

changed the momentum of the race. I hated to admit it, but the ad was brilliant!

The ad shows a little girl asleep at 3am. The red phone in the White House situation room rings. The voice in the ad says, "It's 3am and your children are safe and asleep, but there's a phone in the White House and it's ringing. Something is happening in the world. Your vote will decide who answers that call. Whether it's someone who already knows the world's leaders, knows the military; someone tested and ready to lead in a dangerous world. It's 3am and your children are safe and asleep; who do you want answering the phone?"

The ad was an instant hit! It was replayed over and over again on news channels and on Youtube.

It was no doubt aimed at voters who still questioned if Obama had enough experience to deal with international crises. It was also another point for the pro-experience voters in the Change versus Experience debate. Whichever way you looked at it, the ad was brilliant and more importantly, it was a success. So successful in fact, that the general election candidates released their own versions of the ad later in the year. Even though I thought the ad was brilliant, I also believed that what was more important, was what the person who picked up the phone said and not who actually picked up the phone.

The day before the primaries, Hillary Clinton appeared on my favorite talk show, "The Daily Show with Jon Stewart". That day's show turned out to be my favorite election season episode. I loved that particular episode because of something Jon Stewart said to Clinton; "Tomorrow is perhaps one of the most important days of your life and you've chosen to spend the night before talking to me. As a host, I'm delighted; as a citizen, I'm frightened". Clinton's reply, "It is pretty pathetic!"

"Conservative" radio talk show host, Rush Limbaugh then decided to mix it up a little bit. Since the Texas primaries allowed anyone to vote (not just Democrats), he advised his listeners to vote for Hillary Clinton, so that the Democratic race could be prolonged. Whether or not this was responsible for the primary results is anyone's guess.

March 4 finally came and I was itching to see what would happen. Four States were being contested, with a total of 415 delegates up for grabs. All eyes were on Ohio and Texas, as they had a combine delegate total of 334. The polls suggested that Hillary Clinton would win Ohio. Texas was a bit more difficult to predict because the polls there were very tight.

The results came in, and unsurprisingly, Hillary Clinton won big in Ohio, with 53% of the votes, to Obama's 45%. The delegate count was closer though, with Clinton gaining 74 delegates, while Obama got 67. She also won Rhode Island as expected and gained 13 delegates, while Obama gained 8. Obama won Vermont, gaining 9 delegates, while Clinton gained 6.

Hillary Clinton won the Texas primary with 51% of the votes and 65 delegates, while Obama finished with 47% of the votes and 61 delegates. As Texas also had a caucus as well as a primary, the Texas drama was not over yet. When the caucus results eventually came in, Obama won it with 56% of the votes and 38 delegates, while Clinton finished with 44% and 29 delegates. This meant that Obama ended up with more delegates in Texas than Clinton. He got a total of 99, while Clinton got a total of

94. These results meant that the race was far from over. This was made an even worse situation for the Democrats because John McCain had wrapped up the Republican nomination on the same day.

There were two more contests in March, Wyoming on March 8 and Mississippi on March 11. Obama won both States convincingly. The delegate count now looked like this:

Obama – 1402
Clinton – 1240

A few days after the March 11 primaries, the most serious controversy of the primaries and possibly of the year erupted. It was a controversy that would make a lot of voters, some of them Obama supporters, question Senator Obama's judgment, relationships and even his character. It was a controversy that would make an Obama supporter say, "I'm disappointed. I thought Senator Obama was different, but it's obvious he's just another angry black man".

THE REVEREND WRIGHT CONTROVERSY

This controversy was about sermons given by Obama's former Pastor, Reverend Jeremiah Wright. Some of the sermons were about 7years old, but that did not make any difference, not in the internet and Youtube age.

Among other outrageous remarks, Reverend Wright said, "They want us to sing God Bless America. No, no, no, not God Bless America, God damn America – that's in the Bible – God damn America for killing innocent people. God damn America for treating our citizens as less than human. God damn America as long as she tries to act like she is God and she is supreme!"

In another sermon, he said, "I am sick of negroes who just don't get it. Hillary was not a black boy raised in a single parent home; Barack was. Barack knows what it means to be a black man living in a country and in a culture that is controlled by rich white people. Hillary can never know that. Hillary has never been called a nigger. Hillary has never had a people defined as a non person. Hillary has never had to work twice as hard to be accepted by the rich white folks who run everything"

In another sermon, he said, "Yes, 9-11-01 happened to us, but so did slavery happen to us! Yes, the World Trade Center happened to us, but so did white supremacy happen to us. Yes, the Pentagon happened to us, and so did the Tuskegee experiment happen to us; Yes, Shanksville Pennsylvania happened to us, and so did the Sharpeville massacre happen to us!"

I was literally in shock when I heard these comments. Clips of these sermons were played over and over again on TV stations and on the internet. I hoped that the media had taken these comment out of context, as they usually do. I figured that these excerpts must have come from sermons and maybe when I listen to the entire sermon, it would be easier to understand why he said these things or what exactly he was talking about. I went online and searched for his sermons, but a lot of the stuff I saw and read was quite disturbing, and frankly, I don't believe a Pastor, any Pastor, has any business saying the kinds of things Reverend Wright was saying.

My attention now turned to Obama. How was he going to handle this? Analysts tried to predict if this was going to hurt his chances. Some said it may not, because the comments came from his former Pastor and not from him. But I knew that it was impossible and probably even naive to think that these comments would not hurt Obama's chances. It was obvious that a lot of voters were still sizing Obama up. Some had never voted for a black man before in any capacity. Others were still waiting to see if he was as different as his supporters have claimed. That was why these comments could not have come at a worse time for Obama. Even though the comments were not made by him, I knew his closeness to Jeremiah Wright would obviously be a problem. Reverend Wright was the one who introduced Obama to Christ, he was the one who married him and Michelle in 1992 and he was the one who baptized his two children. They had an almost father and son relationship for twenty years. How was it possible that these comments would not make people take another look at Obama and say, "Are we sure about this guy? If he was so close to this guy for 20years, how do we know he does not share these same radical views? How could Obama have sat down in this man's church for 20years?"

The title of Obama's second book, "The Audacity of Hope", was taken from a sermon of the same title preached by Reverend Wright. I thought it was just impossible that this close personal relationship with Reverend Wright would not hurt his chances of securing the nomination. Even if he did secure the nomination, I knew the Republicans would attack him with it again during the general election campaign. Even though the presumptive Republican nominee, John McCain said he does not believe those views should be attributed to Obama, I knew that other Republicans would turn it into an issue if Obama did become the Democratic nominee.

Reverend Wright's comments ignited a debate across the country. Some said, "Why should Obama have to be held responsible for comments made by his Pastor?" Some said, "Reverend Wright's comments show Obama not only attended a racist and radical church for 20years, but was also very close to the Pastor; how do we know he does not share at least some of these views?" Some said, "If he disagreed with his Pastor's views, why did he remain in the church?" Some asked, "Was Obama present in church when these sermons and others like them were being preached?"

In the context of his immediate political future, the really damaging thing about these debates was that a lot of them were raging in States that had not yet held their primaries.

Whichever way you looked at it, it did not look good for Obama. My personal view was this: You should not be held responsible for comments made by your Pastor. I want to try to put the entire thing in context though.

African-American preachers are generally fiery, because majority of them grew up in a post-slavery but segregated America. A lot of them faced the dogs, the batons, the hoses, which were reminiscent of the civil rights struggle in America. The plight of African-Americans in America has obviously changed since then, but the residual feelings of discontent, coupled with the fact that African-Americans are among the poorest people in the country has led to some of the often inflammatory rhetoric heard in African-American churches. Don't get me wrong, I'm not excusing Reverend Wright's comments; I think it's shameful, ignorant and just downright wrong for a Pastor to use his pulpit as a stage to make his political views heard. If Reverend Wright wanted to be a part time political activist, that's fine, but to stand in front of thousands of people and say some of the things he said is something no religious leader should indulge in.

As I pointed out earlier, residual feelings of discontent and social inequality from the segregation era have now been mixed with the more recent feelings of social injustice and isolation. This combination has produced preachers who believe that for African-Americans to stand up and take control of their lives and their destinies, they need to be fired up, hence the fiery and sometimes inflammatory rhetoric. Whether or not this preaching style is helpful, not just to African-Americans, but to Americans as a whole, depends on how far the preacher goes with his rhetoric. In my opinion, Reverend Wright did not just go too far. He crossed a line he should never even have been close to. There is no question that African-Americans have had the short end of the stick for a very long time and still do. Consequently, anything that can help restore some of the parity is always helpful, but to go as far as saying some of the stuff Reverend Wright said is just inexcusable.

I could understand why a lot of white Americans were upset. Race relations have always been a sensitive issue in America, and I suspect that majority of white Americans want to move forward from what Obama called, "the tragic aspects of our past". To have a Pastor make statements like that definitely did not help.

I could understand why a lot of African-Americans were upset. I suspect that a majority want to move forward from tense race relations brought about by years of slavery, followed by years of segregation, followed by years of social inequality, injustice and isolation. Reverend Wright's comments most definitely did not help.

His comments gave a louder voice to the hitherto barely audible views of those who felt race relations in America could never improve because white people would always feel and act superior, while black people would always be bitter about their treatment, both in the past and present. It was this view that prompted an Obama supporter to call Obama, "just another angry black man". It was also this view that angered a number of people earlier on in the race when Michelle Obama said, "For the first time in my adult life, I am really proud of my country, not just because Barack is doing well, but I think people are hungry for change". On the one hand, I could understand why some people took issue with this statement. White people in America have become so used to hearing African-Americans make disparaging comments about the country, that even though Barack and Michelle Obama seemed different, there must have still been those that felt it was only a matter of time before they showed their true colors. I did not think Michelle meant what she said in the way that it was portrayed. I think the meaning of her comment should have been obvious. At no time in decades, had Americans been so involved in politics until now. The 2008 elections had made people who were usually cynical or just plain uninterested in politics, not only pay attention, but also start to participate in unprecedented ways. I think this was what Michelle Obama was proud of, but people that had been watching and waiting for either her or her husband to make a comment that could have racial connotations finally had something to pounce on.

Back to Reverend Wright, I suspect in his comments about September 11, his point was that other tragic events had taken place against African-Americans and other black people besides the terror attacks of that day, so what is the big deal?

The big deal is that almost three thousand people died on that day!

The big deal is that each one of those people was the most important person in the world to someone!

The big deal is that some families all over the world

will never be the same again after losing a loved one on that day!

The big deal is that loved ones of some of the people on the plane that crashed in Pennsylvania heard them tearfully saying goodbye while their plane was being hijacked!

The big deal is that New York City lost almost its entire Fire Department when the first tower collapsed!

The big deal is that the loss of one life is a tragedy, much less almost three thousand!

Besides, I think the terrorists decided to attack America as a country and not a particular group of Americans. This makes Reverend Wright's comments sound all the more ignorant.

Further, Reverend Wright trying to imply that slavery and segregation make September 11 pale in comparison is an insult to the memories of those who died on that tragic day. Slavery and segregation are dark periods in not just American history, but also world history, as is apartheid. But the fact of the matter is that these things happened and the whole world desperately wants and needs to move forward from that period, but people like Reverend Wright believe it is not yet time to do so. His comments sounded more like something that would come from a religious fanatic, rather than a Pastor. I remember reading somewhere that a fanatic is someone who cannot change his mind and will not change the subject. Unfortunately, everything I read and heard of Reverend Wright made me see him in that light. I use the word unfortunately, because I somehow believe that he is a better person than that.

The most scathing criticism of Obama's relationship with Reverend Wright, unsurprisingly came from FOX News, Sean Hannity especially. According to Hannity, Obama was guilty by association. The irony of this coming from Hannity is that not long ago, he stated that the views of a neo-nazi friend of his, Hal Turner, should not be attributed to him, since guilt by association is wrong. He initially denied knowing Turner, but when Turner himself confirmed that he and Hannity were good friends and was disappointed that Hannity denied knowing him, he reversed and said he did know him, but did not share his views.

While trying to understand what exactly was going on with this whole Reverend Wright issue, I went on different web sites, listening to and reading his sermons and watching interviews he had given. I saw one he had given Sean Hannity, when his church was being accused of being a separatist movement because he preached about black consciousness. One of Sean Hannity's last comments during that interview was, "You should be talking about American consciousness and not black consciousness, because that is racist". If you just read that on the surface, it seems like a fair enough comment to make, but when you delve into the reality of being black in America, you will see that Hannity's comment was made by an ignorant person. It's what Robert Ludlum called, "The arrogance of ignorance".

Reverend Wright is a preacher in an African-American community. Is it unreasonable to expect that his sermons would be tailored to fit a mostly African-American congregation? Black consciousness, as I understand it, teaches black people to be proud of who they are and stop feeling inferior or seeing themselves as being victims of what they see as "white America". According to Hannity, if a white preacher was preaching the same in a church and was talking about white consciousness, he would be called a racist. Very true, but I think the point Hannity is missing or is ignoring is that after years of slavery, segregation and social inequality, it is not difficult for a black person to think that there is something inferior about him/her. This is why African-Americans need to be taught that there is nothing inferior about them and they can achieve anything they set their minds to, if they work hard. Some have said that African-Americans need to work twice as hard to be considered as good as their white counterparts or even half as good. My answer to that is this: Since you know that, then work twice or three times as hard! I know that sounds simplistic, but I believe it really is that simple, at least to an extent. Besides, racism and racially motivated discrimination are concepts that will never go away. They can be significantly reduced, but I don't think they are ever going to go away, either in the US or anywhere else. The most prominent African-Americans learned this and that was why they were able to get to the levels they did. People like Colin Powell and Condolezza Rice are very good examples, because they're two of the most respected people in America and just happen to be black.

Neither of them was born with a silver spoon, but rose to the top of their professions and beyond. In Condolezza Rice's case, apart from the fact that she is black, she is also a woman, so she had both the barriers of race and gender to contend with. They are both members of a party many regard as being intolerant to minorities, but are among the most respected people within the party. The sad thing is that either because they are as successful as they are or because they are Republicans, a number of African-Americans, including Jeremiah Wright, see them a sellouts! He actually described them as such in one of his sermons!

Why is it wrong for black person to be that successful? Why is Colin Powell a sellout for being National Security Adviser to President Ronald Reagan, a Four Star General, Chairman of the Joint Chiefs of Staff and Secretary of State to George W Bush? Why is Condolezza Rice a sellout for being an accomplished scholar, a Senior Presidential Adviser to George H. Bush, National Security Adviser and later Secretary of State to George W. Bush? While I admit that not every African-American can be a Colin Powell or a Condolezza Rice or a Barack Obama, that should not be limiting factor to success.

Reverend Wright preaching in his church that these people are sellouts is an example of the unnecessary and inflammatory statements that plant, water and harvest hatred in the hearts and minds of his congregation. A preacher needs to understand that he has a huge responsibility to his congregation because of the influence he has on their lives. I think when a preacher makes statements that can potentially incite hatred, bitterness and anger, he is either taking his responsibility and influence lightly or getting carried away by them.

The other side of working twice as hard as whites is that generally speaking, African-Americans need to stand out to be considered for positions that an average white person would probably get. In this, I believe the Government needs to take equal opportunities monitoring

Omololu Elegbe

more seriously. There are obviously anti-discriminatory laws in the US, but the fact of the matter is that if it is not monitored properly, the laws might as well not exist. My point is that, it is one thing to work twice as hard, but a completely different thing to work twice or even three times as hard and still not be considered good enough because anti-discriminatory laws are not being properly enforced. The white Americans who are not so smart or so focused are not automatically considered no good. So why does an African American who is not so smart or not so focused considered no good? The playing field needs to be level, so that the best person for a job, any job, gets it and not just the one who looks a certain way. My favorite comedian, Chris Rock, once said, "A black man has to fly to get to what a white man can just walk to".

The playing field also needs to be level on other fronts. An example is in a report I read when the mortgage crisis hit. I found out that some banks were charging African-Americans and other minorities, higher interest rates than white Americans for mortgages of the same amount and with similar incomes. There is no excuse I can think of for this kind of blatant discrimination, other than being racially motivated.

I read another report that showed that African-Americans are more likely to be given a much harder sentence than white Americans charged with exactly the same crime and having similar histories. Again, the excuse for this kind of blatant discrimination eludes me, other than being racially motivated.

The fact is that racism and discrimination of some sort exists and is always going to exist, not just in the US, but in every country. Even in Africa, discrimination exists, but in the form of tribalism. In the same way, blacks and other minorities have to work twice as hard to be considered good enough, in certain instances, citizens of a different tribe from the ruling cadre of a country have to work twice as hard. I find tribalism more distasteful and it annoys me more than racism because now, the discrimination is against a fellow citizen, with the same skin color and probably even against people who grew up together.

Back to Reverend Wright, I don't think there is anything wrong with a Pastor telling his mostly black congregation to raise their heads up with pride and work hard to achieve their dreams. Almost every church with a predominantly African-American congregation preaches it, but I think Reverend Wright's church was singled out because Barack Obama happened to be a member of that congregation. Where I think Reverend Wright got it wrong though, was that while preaching about black consciousness, he sought to portray white people as the enemy. It doesn't make any sense to tell black people to stop seeing themselves as inferior and then tell them that "the white man is the enemy". So, on the one hand, while doing something noble by trying to pull his congregants out of the doldrums of poverty and inferiority complex, he effectively nullifies that act by making statements that exacerbate an already tense situation. The result of this is that these racial tensions remain or even worsen and the inferiority complex is multiplied because as long as African-Americans continue to see white people as the enemy, they can never come out of that inferior mindset.

I remember when I was studying for my Law degree,

I watched a movie with some of my friends. It was a true life story, titled, "The Hurricane" and starred Denzel Washington as Rubin Carter, the African-American boxer who was sentenced to three consecutive life sentences in 1966 for murders he did not commit. He ended up spending 19 years in prison before he was eventually released. According to the Federal Court Judge who released him in 1985, the prosecution was, "based on racism rather than reason and concealment rather than disclosure". After the movie, two of my friends were in tears. One of them said, "Which black person would watch this and not hate white people?" I looked at him and said, "I understand where you're coming from, but have you considered the fact that the people that gave up everything in their lives to help get him get released are white?"

It's very easy to blame white people for all the racial issues, but the truth is that this is just wrong.

Even in Nigeria, and I suspect other African countries where interaction with white people is not a daily occurrence, whites are still blamed for a variety of issues.

When Nigerians apply for visas and don't get them, white racism is blamed. When foreign airlines decide to charge almost double for flights to and from Nigeria, when other countries that are further than Nigeria pay much lower fares, white racism is blamed. When immigration officials in Britain clamp down on illegal workers and deport illegal aliens, white racism is blamed. When police search young black men in Britain for knives or guns, white racism is blamed.

In all these cases, racism might be present in specific

areas or aspects, but it is not the main reason. The fact is that we as black people bring these things on ourselves.

When Nigerians apply for UK visas, consular workers are suspicious and skeptical because of the sheer number of people that come into the country and disappear into the system. Even when they are caught and sent back home, they find all sorts of innovative ways to get back in. When we do things like this, why are we surprised that they scrutinize our applications and sometimes refuse them at the slightest suspicion of impropriety? White racism is not to blame here.

Foreign airlines can afford to charge Nigerians ridiculous amounts of money to fly to and from Britain, when Nigeria is only six hours away and then charge people in other countries half of that for a ten, twelve or even eighteen hour journey. The reason they can afford to do that is because Nigeria is one of a small number of countries without a National carrier that flies abroad. I could come up with a dozen reasons for this, but that is an argument for another day. The fact of the matter is that when a country as big and as rich as Nigeria does not have a National carrier, why the complaint about how much other airlines charge? White racism is not to blame here.

In Britain, immigration officials make random raids on places of employment or homes and arrest illegal aliens. 90% of the time, these workers are either black or of Asian descent. In some cases, they are sent back home and sometimes they claim asylum. I used to practice Immigration Law and I've heard a lot of stories as to why some people are claiming asylum. During almost every immigration raid, illegal aliens are caught. I guess what has not occurred to the people screaming racism at this is that, if majority of the time, these raids turned out to be fruitless, there would be reduced raids and eventually maybe even none at all. So when almost every raid yields results, why are we surprised that they continue? White racism is not to blame here.

In Britain, a very dangerous knife and gun culture is rapidly developing. Reports of knife and gun related deaths have increased in such a sharp and dramatic way. One of the sad parts of this is that in most cases, it involves black people. When a large majority of knife and gun related crime involves black people, why are we surprised that the police stop and search more black people than white people? White racism is not to blame here.

We need to start accepting responsibility for our actions and stop blaming white racism for problems we have caused for ourselves.

Back to the US, how exactly did Colin Powell, Condolezza Rice, Deval Patrick, Barack Obama, Oprah Winfrey, Bob Johnson and all the other successful African-Americans, get to the point in their lives where they are now? I believe the first thing was that they grew up with a mentality that said, "I'm going to make it in spite of what anyone says about the levels black people are allowed to reach; I live in a country where color or gender is not a barrier to success."

Did these people not ever experience racism? I'm 99.9% sure that they did. I remember Colin Powell talking about how he went to a hamburger joint decades ago and they refused to serve him because he was black. In spite of this and a lot of other racial issues they must have faced, I suspect what made them different was that, they chose to focus on their goals and aspirations and not the racism they had faced in their lives. Most African-Americans unfortunately, choose to focus on the racism they have faced or face, rather than their goals and aspirations. I believe the end result of both lines of thinking is evident for all to see.

What I think African-Americans need is a change of mentality. The mentality that:

- African-Americans live in a white world;
- An African-American cannot go beyond a certain level because of their color;
- White people are the enemy;
- African-Americans can only excel in music and sports;
- An accomplished, rich African-American is a sell out;
- A serious African-American student is acting white;
- An African-American cannot get a good job;
- College/University is not for African-Americans;
- An African-American born into poverty will live, grow and die in poverty;

Barack Obama said in a documentary that when he was a teenager, he was lucky to have lived in Hawaii, since there was no large African-American population there. I suspect what he meant was that his mother and grandparents' lessons that he could be anything he set his mind to, could not be negatively influenced by people with one of the mentalities mentioned above. If this had happened, he probably would have stopped trying because, what is the point of trying, when you cannot go beyond a certain level? It was this mentality that gave Obama the guts to run for President of the Harvard Law Review at a time when Harvard was a racially and politically divided institution and no black person had ever headed the review. It was this mentality that gave him the guts to go into politics the way he did and decide to run for President. It is this mentality, I believe African-Americans need. There have been some arguments that it was easy for Obama to have a different mentality because he was the son of an immigrant and not the son of slaves and he was also raised by his white grandparents. While the fact that his father came to America as a student and not as a slave and the fact that his white grandparents raised him may have helped with his mentality, I don't believe it would have made that much of a difference if he did not hold on to that mentality. I'm quite certain he must have had experiences that would have challenged or even made that mentality seem like the fantasies of a naïve black man, but his conscious effort to concentrate on his goals and aspirations has obviously paid off.

So, was Obama wrong to have stayed in Reverend Wright's church? I don't think anyone has the right to make judgments on the rights or wrongs of Obama's continued stay in the church because that is, or at least should be a personal decision. But I suspect the Reverend Wright he knew was a far better man than the one introduced to the world by Youtube. If I had a Pastor, who used incendiary rhetoric and I happened to have a close personal relationship with him, would I leave the church? To be honest, as long as I don't share those views, I don't think I would leave. But it's much easier to judge when you have a spectator's view, so until it happens to me, I guess a more realistic answer would be, I don't know.

A few days later, I heard on the news that Obama was going to deliver a major speech on race relations and talk about the Jeremiah Wright issue. I wondered initially if this was a good idea, but the more I thought about it, the more it sounded like the best thing to do. He had decided to confront the problem head-on, instead of allowing it to chase him all over the campaign trail.

On March 18, I listened to the speech. It was a 37minute speech, titled "A More Perfect Union". When it was over, I went on my knees and said a prayer, "God, please let this man be President".

It was one of the most powerful speeches I had ever heard and I don't mean from a politician, I mean from anyone. There was no shouting, no drama, no acting. Just an eloquent delivery of a bold speech about race relations in America. He denounced Reverend Wright's comments, but put them in the broader context of race relations in America. He talked about his own life, including racially tinged comments made by his white grandmother. He talked about why he could not denounce Reverend Wright as a person, even though he denounced his comments. He talked about the fact that white Americans need to understand that the bitterness African-Americans feel from the discrimination they have suffered over many decades is not going to simply disappear. He talked about the fact that African-Americans need to understand that America has changed and even though discrimination and racial tensions still exist, there has been progress. Maybe not progress to the kind of extent some would have wanted, but personally, I think the progress America has made should be viewed from where the country has come from, rather than where the country is. This progress is part of what Obama called, the quest for a more perfect union. The union that is the United States of America is not perfect. It never has been and it never will be, because there is never a perfect state. But the genius of America is that it continually strives to get to that perfection.

America has changed. Whether anyone, black or white, accepts that or not does not change the fact that it is true. Fifty or even forty years ago, the idea of a black man running for President seemed like a pipe dream. Thirty six years ago, that dream became a reality, even though nobody ever thought it would get very far. Today, a black man is running for President and for the first time, he actually is considered a favorite to win if he secures his party's nomination. America has changed. It is not perfect, but is has changed and will continue to change. Barack Obama's candidacy underlined the change America has gone through and I knew that no matter the outcome of the election, it was another hurdle scaled, another barrier broken, even though that was not what he set out to do when he announced his candidacy.

By the time Obama was through, the applause was deafening and I knew then, that what the audience had just heard, was possibly the greatest speech on race by a public figure, since Martin Luther King's "I have a dream" speech. I read later in a magazine that when Obama emailed the first draft of that speech to his campaign manager, his manger read it and replied saying, "This is why you should be President". (The full transcript of the speech is at the end of this book).

When it was time for the analysts and pundits to slice and dice the speech, I could not wait to hear what their views would be. I was actually waiting for the criticisms, but the astounding thing was that there was very little, if any. There was, of course from Sean Hannity and friends at FOX News. Apart from that, praise for the speech was almost unanimous. It was regarded as brilliant, well thought out and some even said this might finally put to rest the Reverend Wright issue. Even Condolezza Rice had nothing but praise for the speech. While I did not think we had heard the last of the Wright issue, I knew the response to the speech meant some of the damage done had at least been repaired. Some voters however were still unhappy that he only denounced the comments and not Reverend Wright himself.

Regardless of who was happy or unhappy about the Reverend Wright controversy and how it was handled, one thing I knew without a shadow of a doubt was this: If the clips of Reverend Wright's sermons had been released before the primaries started, Obama would most likely be out of the race by now. If it had been released at a time when Obama was just honing his political message, he would almost universally have been seen as, "just another angry black man".

Also, that he had gone as far as he did by the time those clips were made public, gave his supporters the chance to see it as a ploy to detract, either by the Clinton campaign or by the Republicans, since it was looking more and more likely that Obama would be the nominee.

THE SOAP OPERA CONTINUES

One surprising thing while the Reverend Wright debate was going on was that Hillary Clinton stayed out of the fray, at least initially. Her own controversy would make her start or at least attempt to talk about Reverend Wright. The Republicans must have been pinching themselves at their good fortune at the disarray the Democrats seemed to be in.

Her own controversy was about statements she had made regarding a trip to Bosnia in 1996, when she was First Lady. According to Hillary Clinton, she remembered landing in a hail of gunfire. She and the others who were with her, had to duck for cover from snipers and run to their cars. She also said that a welcoming ceremony at the airport had to be cancelled. She repeated this story on at least 3 occasions. The only problem with the story was that, it never happened!

She did go to Bosnia in 1996, but that's about the only thing that was true from Hillary's account. She was asked about it again at a press conference, when a reporter pointed out that the comedian Simbad, who was with her on the trip had said the only dangerous part of the trip was in trying to decide where to eat! She replied by first saying that Simbad is a comedian, (from that I assume she meant Simbad was joking). She then repeated her sniper story! She went as far as saying the US Secret Service did not want President Clinton to go, because Bosnia at the time was considered too dangerous, so the decision was made that the first lady and first daughter should go instead.

The true version of events was that she went to Bosnia, AFTER most of the fighting was over and Bosnia was relatively safe. When her plane landed at the airport, she strolled casually out of the plane with her daughter, Chelsea and the rest of the entourage to a welcoming ceremony AT THE AIRPORT. A little girl gave Hillary a flower and got a kiss and a hug from the First Lady. Doesn't sound like such a dangerous place, if there was so much time to do all that. Besides, what kind of husband or father would decide not to go to a region because of the danger involved and instead send his wife and only child? One of the military officers who accompanied the First Lady on the trip said he felt insulted when he heard Hillary's account of events, because it implied that they had put the President's wife in danger. The really sad, yet hilarious part of the whole drama was that when rumors first started flying around that Hillary's account was exaggerated, she actually tried to defend it. When the lie was finally exposed in its entirety, what do you think Hillary Clinton's defense was? She said she misspoke! As I was trying to rationalize that, she went on to say that she was sleep deprived and gotten her dates and locations mixed up. If my understanding of English is as good as I think it is, getting dates and locations mixed up means her account of events happened, but not in Bosnia and possibly not in 1996. So I did some research again and checked to see if the sniper story had happened anywhere else. I found nothing. I started to ask myself, why on earth she would say something like that, knowing fully well that it can be fact checked? Did it not occur to her that there were reporters and other people on that trip, who would no doubt wonder what she was talking about? I had a conversation about this with a friend of mine, who felt Hillary probably said it because she did not expect anyone to check on the truthfulness of the story. I said, "But that's what makes this so crazy! I'm not a political operative or a politician, but in the age of 24hour news cycles and the internet, I think it's naïve for anyone to make claims like that and not expect the truth to come out!" Also, if those events did take place, I'm sure it would have been headline news at the time!

I thought about Hillary Clinton's 3am phone call advert; if she was elected President, and international crises gave her sleepless nights, would she also misspeak at a time when the world needs a clear thinking American President?

To deflect attention from her Bosnia sniper story, Hillary Clinton decided to talk instead about Reverend Wright. She said, "You can't choose your family, but you choose your Pastor". And, "I think based on everything we have seen and heard, he would not have been my Pastor". Fortunately, everyone, even her supporters saw through her comments and no one took them seriously.

Polls taken just after Reverend Wright's comments showed that Obama's support had waned, but he had not taken as big a hit as was expected.

The next primaries would not be until the last week

in April, so this month and a half gap meant either candidate could either pull ahead or crash and burn.

By this time, it was clear to me that no matter what happened in the upcoming primaries, the delegate lead built up by Obama was too much for Hillary Clinton to overcome. It was obvious that they would split the remaining contests and the delegate difference would be more or less the same as it was. With the Democratic Party rules, a candidate had to reach the magic number of 2117 delegates, but I knew there was no way either candidate was going to reach that number, so I wondered what would happen in that case. I had heard of "floor fights" at conventions and hoped to God that it would not get to that, because I believed that the most powerful people in the party were still behind Hillary Clinton.

Since I started following US politics, this had never happened, so I wanted to know if there were any rules in place to deal with a scenario that looked more and more likely to happen.

I had heard vaguely about super-delegates, who were made up of the elected and former elected officials in the Democratic Party. Some were even called super-super-delegates, who had the power to appoint another super-delegate! All this was a bit too complicated for me, so I decided to do a bit more research.

I found that if no candidate gets to the target number of delegates by the last primary, the super-delegates would decide who the nominee should be. This seemed like an unfair rule because I did not see any reason why a bunch of "important people" should be the ones to decide a major party's nominee in a Democratic country like the US. What happens if majority of ordinary people vote for one candidate, but that candidate does not get to the magic number and then the super-delegates decide to go with the other person? What would have been the point of having any primaries at all? How could this be part of the democratic process in the world's most admirable democracy? It almost seemed like the leadership of the Democratic Party was saying to voters, "You had your chance, you blew it, so now, we the wise old men and women will decide for you".

It reminded me of a situation in Nigeria during the Presidential election season in 2007. The ruling party, Peoples Democratic Party (PDP), had a number of heavyweight candidates and I could not wait to see which of them would get the party's nomination. The sitting President, Olusegun Obasanjo had already endorsed Umaru Yar' Adua, but he did not seem like the one who would get the nomination, because he was relatively unknown outside his home State of Katsina, where he was Governor. President Obasanjo held closed door meetings with each of the candidates, and after each meeting, the candidate would come out and declare he was withdrawing from the race and endorsing Governor Yar' Adua, the President's candidate!

As if the Speaker of US House of Representatives, Nancy Pelosi heard me, she made a statement advising super-delegates not to overturn the will of the people by endorsing the candidate with the lower number of pledged delegates. For someone who was supposed to stay out of the primaries because of her leadership position, this statement was seen as a veiled endorsement of Obama. But I agreed with her and it's not because I liked Obama. If Obama ended the primaries with a higher number of delegates than Clinton and also won the popular vote, would it not be damaging to the party if Clinton was still chosen as the nominee? If that happened, I did not see how the party could heal the rift that would certainly develop, in time to plan effectively for the general election season. If Obama was in Clinton's position, I would have said the same thing, although I think if that was the case, the calls for Obama to withdraw from the race would have been deafening.

The response to Nancy Pelosi's statement so shocked me that I had to remind myself that America was an established democracy and not an experimental one. A number of very powerful Clinton donors wrote to Nancy Pelosi, "urging" her to withdraw her statement and reminding her that they have been major contributors to the Democratic Congressional Campaign Committee. I could not believe it. They were not even trying to be subtle about it, it was an open letter! I knew in that instant that if the party did not get its act together quickly, they would be a divided party and ultimately lose an election in November that should have been a victory because of the massively unpopular incumbent Republican President. It was already bad enough that the Republicans had already wrapped up their nominating contest, but to have Democrats beating each other up was tantamount to a self-inflicted gunshot wound.

I just did not see how the establishment candidate, Hillary Clinton, would not be the nominee if it was down to the super-delegates to decide because a large number of them were friends of the Clintons. Also, a number of the ones that had worked for and with Bill Clinton were still loyal to him, in spite of what some pundits saw as a developing rift between Clinton loyalists and the more independent Democrats. That thinking changed a few days after Obama's speech because of an endorsement by a super-delegate, who had been courted by both campaigns for.

Bill Richardson, the Governor of New Mexico and the only Latino Governor in the US, announced his endorsement of Barack Obama! I was shocked when I saw this, because Bill Richardson was Energy Secretary and UN Ambassador during the Clinton Presidency. Since he dropped out of the race, a lot of people (including me) expected him to endorse Hillary Clinton. Bill Clinton even held a meeting with him just a few days earlier, to try to get him to announce his endorsement of Hillary Clinton. So for him to announce that he was endorsing Obama was a delightful surprise to me.

Even though I had never understood the importance of an endorsement because I just did not think it made any difference to voters on election day, I understood the importance of Bill Richardson's endorsement. First of all, and I think most importantly, he was a super-delegate. Second of all, he was a Clinton loyalist.

Pundits made a big deal about the fact that an endorsement by the only Latino Governor in the US would help Obama with Latinos, most of whom had voted for Clinton over Obama. I did not agree with this though because if I remember correctly, Bill Richardson did very poorly in polls taken in New Mexico when he was still in the race. Even though by the time the State held its primary, he had withdrawn from the race, it's highly unlikely he would have won there. This is a State where he was Governor and a State with a large Latino population. If he could not win there, how on earth could his endorsement help Obama with Latino voters?

Bill Richardson's endorsement was taken very badly by the Clinton campaign. Bill Clinton was so upset at this "betrayal", that in a meeting with some of the super-delegates, he had some choice words for Bill Richardson. When Bill Richardson told Hillary Clinton of his decision to endorse Obama, she allegedly said, "Don't waste your time endorsing him, he can't win in November". Bill Clinton's 1992 campaign manager and close adviser to Hillary Clinton, James Carville, called Bill Richardson, Judas! Basically, the Clintons were livid at the idea that a man who had made his name in politics as a result of Bill's Presidency, decided to endorse Obama over a Clinton. To be honest, I was actually surprised at the endorsement because I expected it to go to Hillary Clinton. The fact that the Clintons were as upset as they turned out to be, proved something that I had thought of throughout the primaries; Hillary Clinton or at least her supporters felt she should be the nominee because she is Hillary Clinton. There was this sense of entitlement to the nomination and I believe this was one of her biggest mistakes, because this sense was what made her fail to adequately plan beyond Super-Tuesday.

I think Bill Richardson's endorsement was even more important than it would have been because it opened the door to a floodgate of endorsements from other super-delegates, who were widely expected to endorse Hillary Clinton.

With Obama's chances of securing the nomination looking more and more likely everyday, the Clintons decided to try another strategy. They started putting forward the idea of a Clinton-Obama ticket. The first time I heard this, I thought it was a good idea, as their campaigns had generated an interest in politics not seen in America in generations. But I felt there was very little chance of this "dream ticket" becoming a reality because of how negative the campaign had been. Also, the Clintons were pushing for a Clinton-Obama ticket, rather than an Obama-Clinton ticket. If I was not mistaken, Obama was the one with the superior pledged delegate lead and was catching up in super-delegate endorsements as well, so how or why he should agree to drop out to become Clinton's VP was beyond me. As if echoing my thoughts, former Senate majority leader and Obama adviser, Tom Daschle, said, "This is probably the first time in history that the person in second place is offering number two to the person in first place".

Sometime in April, a statement Obama had made in San Francisco caused another controversy. It was a statement described as possibly his only mistake during the campaign.

It was of course no secret that he had trouble winning over "white working class voters". While trying to explain why this was, he said to a private audience, "You go into these small towns in Pennsylvania and like a lot of towns in the Midwest, the jobs have been gone now for 25 years and nothing has replaced them. And it's not surprising then, they get bitter, they cling to guns or religion or antipathy to people who aren't like them or anti-immigrant sentiment or anti-trade sentiment as a way to explain their frustrations"

Needless to say, there were a lot of angry people when

this statement was made public, not just in Pennsylvania, but across the country. The Clinton campaign jumped all over it, calling Obama an elitist and out of touch with the real America. The fact that John McCain had already secured the Republican nomination meant the daily attacks on Obama were now coming from both Clinton and McCain. The McCain campaign also attacked Obama on the guns and religion statement. That Clinton was going to win the Pennsylvania primary was a given, judging by her huge support in the state and her poll numbers. Obama's statement had now sealed that victory for Clinton. I was also worried that if Obama won the nomination, the statement could cost him such a crucial state in the general election.

While I understood the anger of the white working class voters after the statement, I think I also understood what Obama was trying to say, even though it could have been phrased better, as he admitted himself that it was a "boneheaded thing to say".

When people lose jobs, frustration setting in is a virtual certainty. But in the case of the small towns Obama was referring to, some of these jobs were actually shipped abroad, so they face the choice of starting a business, re-location or engaging in work that they do not necessarily like, but do anyway because it pays the bills. Because some of these jobs were shipped overseas or some given to minorities, it's only natural that frustration will evolve into resentment. The fact that successive administrations have not been able to help them, despite promises to do so has even worsened the situation. My feeling is that since the majority are decent people, and would obviously not go around venting their anger in lawless ways, the next best thing is their gun rights and religious rights. I believe it's almost like saying, "Everything has been taken from us, but these rights, you will not take from us". Of course I could be wrong, but that's what I think he meant.

The charges of elitism by both the Clinton and McCain campaigns were part of the ridiculous attacks made during the 2008 election cycle. Hillary Clinton grew up in an upper middles class home and attended elite institutions, with her tuition paid for. She is a former First Lady of Arkansas and a former US First Lady.

John McCain is the son and grandson of highly decorated military officers. He is married to a multi millionaire.

Barack Obama grew in a lower middles class, single parent home. He attended elite institutions with the help of student loans and scholarships, some of which he fully paid back only a few years ago.

How can anyone look at these three life stories and say Obama is the elitist? His statement about Pennsylvania was badly phrased, but to call him an elitist was just uncalled for.

Hillary Clinton won the Pennsylvania primary as expected. She won with 55% of the popular vote and 85 delegates, while Obama finished with 45% of the popular vote and 73 delegates. Ordinarily, this should have been and in fact was a huge victory for Hillary Clinton, but the fact that the delegate difference between them had shrunk by only 12 meant that she still had a lot of work to do if she was going to pull off a miracle or another Clintonesque comeback.

Just when I believed that the Reverend Wright

issue was forgotten, at least for the primary season, the controversy erupted again.

It started with Reverend Wright giving a series of interviews and explaining or trying to explain some of his fiery and controversial statements. He talked to the NAACP and National Press Club and made even more outrageous comments, like "The Government created HIV in a lab and intentionally infected African-Americans".

He said Obama had to condemn his statements and make the points he did in his "More Perfect Union" speech because he is a politician. What I saw, especially at the NAACP meeting was a man loving the attention he was getting and determined to milk it for as long as he could.

The only quarters in which Reverend Wright's re-appearance was greeted with glee was the press, especially FOX News. Just like when the clips of his sermons were first made public, they could not stop talking about his re-appearance.

Initially, I could not understand why he was even saying anything, just when it seemed like the first controversy had died down. Did he not know that these new comments would cause a problem for Obama, especially as Obama had refused to condemn him as a person? I began to get the feeling that something very sinister was going on and the more I thought about it, the more certain I became of this feeling.

I think it's obvious by now that Reverend Wright is an educated and intelligent man. So I think it's also obvious that when he decided to come out again to say the things he said, he knew it was going to hurt Obama, both as a person and as a Presidential candidate. If he knew this, why did he come out again and this time, with even more controversial statements?

Now, here is my main question: Is it possible that Reverend Wright was worried that his message that America is a racist society that has not and cannot change, had been challenged by the increasingly likely prospect of Barack Obama becoming the Democratic nominee for President? I know this sounds like a conspiracy theory, and believe me no one hates them like I do, but I've not been able to come up with any other logical explanations for his re-appearance.

First, I thought, or rather, I hoped he wanted to clear the air about the controversy generated by clips of his past sermons. Then, I thought he wanted to make sure his comments were not attributed to Obama. Lastly, I thought he just wanted to defend himself from the charges leveled against him and his church.

But instead, what I saw was a defiant man, who was determined to enjoy his time in the limelight. I'm 100% certain that he knew his re-appearance could not be good for Obama, but instead went on his press blitz. That, I think is the act of a self centered person. If he was such a fatherly figure to Obama, why did Obama's career come secondary to his 15minutes of fame? You could argue that some of the charges leveled against him were outrageous and he needed to defend himself and not Obama. My point is, he did not need to defend Obama. A preacher should be able to exercise more self control than Reverend Wright did in those interviews, especially his comments at the NAACP dinner.

The only good thing that came out of Reverend

Wright's latest comments was that it gave Obama the opportunity to finally severe the relationship. He denounced Reverend Wright's comments and this time, also denounce the man himself. I think it must have been a sad thing for him to do, judging from the pained look on his face when he made the announcement. For the first time, I actually saw Obama look angry, but I was glad he did it because it was obvious Reverend Wright was thinking about himself and not the career of his famous congregant. I hoped the rest of the country could finally draw a line on this whole issue, but knew it might only just be the beginning, as the Republicans had perfected the art of political attacks and guilt by association.

The candidates split the Guam caucuses on May 3rd, which meant that the delegate difference was pretty much the same as it was.

The next primaries were held on the 6th of May in the big States of Indiana and North Carolina. Both states showed the candidates were running almost evenly, but Clinton was expected to win both. Because of Obama's superior delegate lead, a Clinton win in both states would not change the difference by a lot, since he would also gain some delegates and Clinton's wins were not expected to be that big. But as this election had proved over and over, no one could have written the script of what happened next.

Clinton won Indiana as expected, but by only one percent! While I was jumping for joy at this unexpected result, I checked the result for North Carolina and saw that Obama won! Not only did he win, he won big, with 56% of the vote, to Clinton's 42%!

Once this happened, I knew it was over. There was absolutely no way Clinton could come back from this. The obstacles she had to overcome, if she was going to pull off a miracle and become the nominee had just been multiplied. Just by the sheer mathematics of the number of States left and the number of available delegates, it was impossible for Clinton to get anywhere near Obama's lead. To make matters worse for Clinton, the May 6 results led to a wave of super-delegate endorsements for Obama. I believe they had come to the same conclusion, that there was no way Clinton could overcome Obama's lead. Clinton's only hope now rested with trying to convince the party leadership to reconsider their stance on Michigan and Florida.

Both States had been stripped of their delegates as punishment for holding their primaries early. All the candidates had signed an agreement not to campaign in either State and Obama even took his name off the ballot in Michigan. Clinton won both States, but the results did not matter, based on the earlier agreement. However, the unexpected turn of events in the primaries had turned an all but certain victory for Hillary Clinton into an expected victory for Barack Obama. Consequently, the Clinton machine went into overdrive!

First, Hillary Clinton began stating that she had won more popular votes than Obama, IF Florida and Michigan votes are taken into account and if the caucus States are excluded!

Next she began advocating for the Florida and Michigan primaries to be ratified and for the delegates to be seated. She made the point that if the DNC decides to follow through on its planned punishment not to seat the delegates from both States at the convention, millions of voters would be disenfranchised.

Next, she made the point that she had won the primaries in big States and crucial "Swing States", which the Democrats would need to win in November, if the party was going to be victorious.

Finally, she made the point that super-delegates are not bound by their endorsements or votes and can change their minds.

I will take these points one by one.

First, the popular vote argument would have made sense if the primaries were being held in a country where popular votes actually count for much. The popular vote in the primaries and the general elections don't decide the nominee or the President. Besides, Clinton's mathematics and logic would have to "tortured", like Obama strategist, David Axelrod put it, for her to be ahead in the popular vote. She was including two States, where the results were invalid and neither candidate campaigned in, and Obama's name was not even on the ballot in Michigan! Clinton's argument that caucus States should be excluded from her popular vote calculation was probably the most ridiculous of all her arguments. Agreed, not a lot of people caucus or have the time to caucus, which was her central argument, but Obama was able to win almost all the caucuses because his campaign organization in these States was one of, if not the best in US primaries history. It was a known fact that the Clinton campaign conceded the caucus States to Obama early in the race because she felt all she had to do was win the big States and maybe a handful of the smaller States and it would be all over. So when Obama decides to organize a grassroots movement in the caucus States, which results in huge turnouts for him and then Clinton asks that the popular vote in these States be excluded, it simply defies logic.

Second, the argument that the Florida and Michigan primaries be included in the overall delegate count was another logic defying argument. ALL the candidates knew and agreed to the rules at the beginning and even signed an agreement to have the results of both States excluded if the primaries went ahead as early as planned. I think it was a silly rule to start with, since both States would be crucial in the general elections and the last thing the DNC needed was to anger people who would have their votes invalidated by the punishment. But the fact remains that both candidates were aware of these rules and more importantly, agreed to them. The people who turned out to vote were also aware of the planned punishments, but still voted anyway. I called up a friend of mine who leaves in Detroit and asked what he thought about what was going on. He told me that he and some of his friends who had been planning a volunteer effort for the Obama campaign in Michigan had decided to stay home, since they knew the votes would not count. He also said he knew quite a number of people who did not bother voting for the same reason. These are the ones I know about. Can you imagine how many more people did not bother to vote in both Michigan and Florida? If Clinton's argument was accepted by the DNC, it would not only be unfair to the voters who did not bother voting, it would be giving a pass mark to two States that were aware of, but still broke the rules.

I went on different blogs to get a sense of what people

were feeling. Unsurprisingly, the majority of comments were for the rules to be adhered to, but I there were also quite a few comments from people who said Obama was trying to disenfranchise them and that Hillary Clinton was the only one who cared about them.

How on earth was it Obama's fault that Florida and Michigan decided to hold their primaries early? If anything, the voters should have been angry at the DNC for imposing such a ridiculous rule, the Democratic Party leaderships in both States for deliberately breaking the rules and Hillary Clinton for insulting their intelligence by saying she was "fighting to make sure they are not disenfranchised".

The DNC decided to resolve the issue at a meeting of the rules committee at the end of May. Frankly, I did not see what there was to resolve because if Hillary Clinton was not in the position she was in, I don't believe there would even be a conversation about what to do with Florida and Michigan. But on the other hand, I could understand why this needed to be resolved amicably. It would be almost impossible for the Democrats to win the general election in November if they lost Michigan and Florida. To leave the issue as it stood would almost certainly have led to voter-alienation, which would be a recipe for disaster in November.

When the rules committee met, they decided to accept the results, but at half a vote. This made very little difference to the delegate count, as Obama's lead was too much for Clinton to even come close to.

The calls for Hillary Clinton to drop out the race, which had started as early as March, were now deafening. While I thought she or anyone else had the right to stay in the race for as long as they wanted, nothing prepared me for her explanation at the end of May, as to why she was still in the race.

She said, "My husband did not wrap up the nomination in 1992 until he won the California primary somewhere in the middle of June. We all remember Bobby Kennedy was assassinated in June in California".

There was an uproar when she made these comments! How could she have said that? Hillary Clinton has spent enough time in politics to know that people are quick to pounce on how a statement sounds, or the connotations behind a statement, rather than the actual statement that was made. In this case, her comment sounded like she was staying in the race, just in case Obama gets assassinated. I did not for a second, believe that she was saying this might happen, as most news outlets suggested, I just thought it was an incredibly silly thing to say. The fear of Obama being assassinated had been a constant throughout the campaign. It's not news that he received so many and sometimes serious death threats, that US Senate Leader, Harry Reid had to request Secret Service protection for him in June 2007, about a year and a half before the elections! For Hillary Clinton to have even allowed the possibility of such an insinuation to be made because of a comment that was not well thought out, was just another one of the unexplainable manner her campaign was run.

The remaining primaries were split by both candidates and it was down to Montana and South Dakota, where the last primaries would be held on 3rd of June. By now, the super-delegate endorsements were pouring in almost hourly for Obama. When he finally crossed that threshold of 2,117 delegates, I fell to my knees and was in tears. I mean that literally and not in any other way and I am not ashamed to say that. I felt like I had watched this guy's national career start from 4years ago and now he was the Democratic Party's nominee for President! I felt a rush of emotions I cannot describe. That this had happened! For the last couple of months, it had looked more and more like this day would come, but a little voice kept saying, "face reality". Reality now, was that Barack Obama was the Democratic nominee for President of The United States of America!

As I was listening to his incredible victory speech in Minnesota that day, tears began to roll freely down my face. In that moment, I wished I was in that auditorium where he was giving that speech. I wished I could walk up to him and tell him how much his candidacy and ultimately his life had affected and inspired me. Since that was not possible, my fiancée and I had to make do with watching and cheering from across the Atlantic. Just as I was about to say what an inspiring speech that was, my mobile phone beeped with a message alert. My cousin had sent me a text with the following, "Did you hear Obama's speech?!? Right now, I feel like I can pick up a gun and fight for America!"

That was the power of the kind of inspiration Obama commanded. I knew my cousin was obviously not going to "fight for America", even if given the choice, but I understood where he was coming from. The inspiration I felt listening to his speech, the inspiration I felt watching him all through the campaign, was something I never felt I could get from a politician. I had always admired Bill Clinton and I used to call him my role model, but I never felt the same kind of inspiration. If we as Nigerians felt this way, I could only imagine what his supporters in America felt when they said Obama inspired them. With speeches like that, it was easier to see why a generation of new voters got involved in politics for the first time in their lives and why some older voters got involved in politics for the first time in a very long time.

I must have pinched myself over a dozen times to make sure I was seeing what I was seeing. But it wasn't a dream, it was real. An event I never thought was possible even just a few short months ago was unfolding right before my eyes. A man I had first heard of and seen on TV only four years ago was now the standard bearer of the Democratic Party. A man who had been told by his own advisers when he decided to run for President, that America is not ready for a black President, but disagreed and said he would challenge that assumption. A man who had received death threats when his campaign started to do so well but decided he would not be deterred. A man who had come to the attention of the National Leadership of his Party only four years ago, was now their nominee for President. A man who had shunned the fast-track to fame and wealth by refusing to take up lucrative job offers after Law school was now the world's most popular person.

Barack Obama, the son of a black man from Kenya and white woman from Kansas, the self-confessed skinny kid with a funny name, was now just one election away from becoming President of The United States of America!

HOW IT ALL BEGAN

I guess the obvious question at this point is, How did this happen? While trying to answer this question, other questions arose:

1. How had a person go from a state legislator to a US Senator, to Democratic Party nominee for President in the space of 4years?

2. How does a 17minute speech turn a man from an unknown politician into a National phenomenon?

3. How had a politician, virtually unknown outside his home state just 4years ago, become the most popular politician in America and I daresay, in the world?

4. How had a freshman Senator knock down and knock out the most power political machine in the Democratic Party?

5. How had a politician become so popular that older and more experienced politicians seeking political office try to align themselves with him, to get elected or re-elected?

6. How had an African-American politician challenged the assumption that an African-American could never be president and put himself one election away from being just that?

To understand these questions, I decided to go back to the beginning. How it all began. I decided I would study his history and how he got to this position. I trawled through hours of material on him, from documentaries, to books, to internet sites. Some materials I found quite useful, some not so much, others, just plain ridiculous. There was one documentary I saw, with footage of Obama's trip to Kenya as a Senator in 2005, being passed off as the trip he made to Kenya just before he started Law school! I knew I had to be careful because there were all sorts of stuff on Obama all over the place and I wanted to get the most accurate picture possible. I trimmed my sources down to; CNN documentary, "Obama: Revealed", PBS documentary, "The Choice 2008", Obama's books, "Dreams From My Father" and "Audacity of Hope" and two websites.

After studying these in depth, I came up with his history the way I saw it and my own analysis of different events in his life. This was what I came up with:

Barack Obama was born on August 4 1961, to Ann Dunham and Barack Obama Senior. Barack Sr was a Kenyan student on a scholarship to the University of Hawaii. He had met Ann Dunham, a Kansas native and also a student at the same university in 1960, during a Russian language class. This unlikely couple soon began dating and eventually got married. They were an unlikely couple at that time because this was a period in American history, when segregation was the law of the land. The idea of a black man and white woman being seen talking together was not common place in most American states, much less getting married. As Obama put it in his book, "Dreams from my father", "There were states in the union where my father would have been strung from a tree, for just looking at my mother the wrong way".

This union did not last though, as Barack Obama Sr moved to Boston, Massachusetts to pursue a degree in Economics at Harvard in 1963. The distance led to a strain in the marriage and they were divorced the following year. Barack Jr was 3years old at the time. That was the last time Barack saw his father until he was 10years old.

His mother, by now 22years old, met Lolo Soetoro, a foreign student from Indonesia. They began dating and were married soon afterwards, against the objections of her parents. When Barack was 6years old, the family moved to Indonesia. While there, he attended a Catholic school and also a public school. His attendance of these schools in a country with the world's largest Muslim population led to questions during the course of the campaign about whether Obama attended Madrassas. The word, Madrassa actually literally means school and nothing else. Nowadays, Madrassa has been wrongly referred to as an Islamic school, usually where radical Islam is taught.

This distortion has led some to incorrectly and in some cases deliberately claim that Obama is a Muslim. An even more sinister reason (as I found from FOX News) why these questions were asked, was to insinuate that Obama had received radical indoctrination. While Indonesia has the world's largest Muslim population, it is important to note that it is NOT a Muslim country and is in fact one of the most religiously tolerant countries in the world.

The schools Obama attended had students of all faiths and were affordable. As Obama said in an interview, "I was going to an Indonesian speaking school, because we could not afford to send me to a fancy international school".

In 1971, when Barack was 10years old, his mother sent him back to Hawaii to live with her parents, while she stayed back in Indonesia. This separation from his mother was a very difficult experience for both mother and son. Obama said in a CNN interview, "I always knew that I was the centre of her world. I've always believed that if kids know they are loved, if they know that in their parents' eyes, they are special, that can make up for a lot of instability". I think that is such a powerful statement! That there was instability in young Barack's life was a given. From a father, to no father, to a step-father and then a move a new country. Then, just as he is getting used to his new life, he moves back the US, this time without his mother. From his statement, it was obvious that the relationship he had with his mother made these constant changes easier to deal with than they might have been for the young boy.

Something else happened in the young boy's life when he moved back to Hawaii. His father, Barack Sr came back to see him. According to Obama, his father's presence was strange because he never really knew him and just as he was starting to get to know him and trying to accept who he was, his father was gone again, this time forever.

Obama got a scholarship to study at the Punahou school, a private school in Hawaii. Even then, he was a popular kid in school. He was known for his basketball prowess and nicknamed Barry. He was hardly a straight A student then, but did well enough. A former school mate of his, Kelly Furishimo, said the first time she noticed political inclinations in the young Barack was when the students wrote pieces for a literary magazine. According to Kelly, "while other students wrote about butterflies and music, the last line of his poem went something like; walking a straight line in a crooked world"! I was quite dazed when I saw this. How could a kid be so deep? I believed a kid being able to articulate words like that was most likely an indication of a mind with a million unanswered questions. My guess is that these questions had a lot to do with his identity as an African-American. As Suzanne Malveaux put it in the CNN documentary, "Obama: Revealed", Obama was "a mixed race child, raised by his white grandparents in a largely white school, he struggled with his own identity". This struggle led to stormy teenage years, during which Barack turned to drugs. According to him, "I experimented with drugs, didn't apply myself at school and in some ways, I think I was conforming to some of the stereo-types of an African-American". That is the sad reality of the African-American experience. For a lot of African-Americans, doing well in school is seen as acting white. Being a "bad boy" is a way of getting along with peers and usually, serious students are outcasts. Obama himself said that he was lucky he was in Hawaii because it was a multicultural environment and there was no large black population. I believe the existence of a large black population in Hawaii at the time would have further driven him to try to conform to the negative stereotypes of a young African-American man.

After High School, he was accepted to Occidental college in Los Angeles. After two years there, he transferred to Columbia University in New York and graduated with a B.A in political science.

After a few years in New York, he moved to Chicago to become a community organizer. He worked in this capacity until 1988, when he decided to go to Law school. He was accepted into Harvard Law School, but before starting his studies there, he decided to take a trip to Kenya to meet his father's family and to try to understand his father, who had died in a car accident in 1982.

He got back from Kenya, according to him, with a better understanding of his father and some ways, himself.

Life as a Harvard Law School student was next for the young Barack. It is interesting to note that in 1988, the same year that Obama was to start Law School, Joe Biden was running for President!

At the time, Harvard was a racially and politically divided institution. This situation was made worse by the fact that most of the liberals were African-American, while most of the conservatives were white. While Obama was a liberal, he was seen as a middleman because according to a documentary, "he was able to win arguments without losing friends".

At the end of his first year, he went for a summer internship at a powerful Chicago law firm, Sidley & Austin. It was while there that he met Michelle Robinson. Michelle Robinson was also a Harvard Law School graduate and had now been assigned to be Barack's mentor at the law firm during his internship. Michelle has said the first time she was told that she would mentor a Law School student named, Barack Obama, her first reaction was, "What kind of name is that?" They began dating soon afterwards.

Barack Obama returned for his second year and ran for President of the Harvard Law Review. He won the race and became the first black President of the Review. Because of the prestigious nature of the Harvard Law Review, his historic win was reported in national newspapers and came with the usual lucrative job offers. I believe his Presidency of the Law Review was a precursor to the kind of leader Obama would be. As I said earlier, one of the ways Harvard was divided was politically, between liberals and conservatives. Obama was seen as a middleman in this conflict, which was partly why he was elected President of the Review. On becoming President, the liberals expected him to give them the top editor jobs at the review, either because Obama was also a liberal or because he was also an African-American. But Obama did not do this. My belief is that he decided he was the President of the Harvard Law Review, not the President of the Harvard liberals or the President of the Harvard African-American society. He chose people he believed were the best for the job, regardless of race or political affiliations. This, needless to say, did not go down too well with his liberal colleagues, but as usual, Obama managed to win that argument without losing friends.

Upon graduation from Law School, Obama was expected by friends and associates to take up one of the lucrative six figure salary job offers he had received or even go for a Supreme Court clerkship, which according to his friend Hill Harper, "was the next big power move" for Harvard Law School graduates. Obama did neither. Instead, he moved back to Chicago to continue his work as a community organizer, work as a civil rights lawyer and to teach constitutional law at the University of Chicago. He and Michelle Robinson got married in 1992.

His first book, "Dreams From My Father", which was mostly an autobiography, was published in 1995 to a moderate reception. It was re-released in 2004 though and became a bestseller.

While working as a community organizer, Obama spearheaded the most successful voter registration drive in Chicago history. Within a period of a few years, his organization registered hundreds of thousands of new voters. This and other work he did in the city began to build him a reputation as a public figure to be reckoned with in Chicago.

In 1996, a highly respected Illinois State Senator, Alice Palmer decided to run for the US Congress. She offered her State Senate seat to Obama, who was just starting out as a politician. Unfortunately, Alice Palmer lost the US Congressional race very badly to Jesse Jackson Junior and decided she wanted her State Senate seat back. Obama, who was already campaigning for the seat promptly refused to withdraw from the race. Because of Alice Palmer's standing in Chicago, the top African-American politicians in the city appealed to him to drop out of the race. His refusal to do so proved one thing to me; he had a spine of steel. Some would have seen this refusal as political suicide for someone who was just starting out. A new politician, who was not even a native of Chicago, was being asked to withdraw from the race by some of the most respected people in the city, people he would obviously need support from to be a successful politician in the state. Conventional wisdom in that circumstance would have dictated for him to withdraw, if only to earn favors from these respectable people. He was after all still young and could run again, this time, with the support of these power brokers. But Obama stood his ground and Alice Palmer got into the race to challenge him for the seat she had vacated.

There is a strategy in Chicago politics, in which signatures of candidates on election petitions are challenged as being inauthentic. The Obama campaign challenged Alice Palmer's signatures, and guess what? She got booted out of the race as a result of the inauthentic signatures! The Obama campaign then decided to go after the other candidates in the race. One by one, they were booted out of the race on account of their signatures. At the end of the day, the only one left in the race was Obama! He had won his first political race by playing dirty, although you could argue that he followed the rules and took advantage of the fact that the others in the race did not.

He quickly distinguished himself in the State Senate and became a very popular figure. In 1998, his first child, Malia, was born.

Even though he was now a well known State Senator, Obama had his eyes on bigger things and decided in 2000 that it was time to make a run for the US congress from the Southside Chicago district. His challenger was incumbent Congressman, Bobby Rush. Bobby Rush had been one of the most revered politicians in Chicago for decades and still was. Obama definitely had his work cut out for him and before he had time to settle into his campaign, the race turned nasty. Obama was accused of being an outsider and not understanding the hearts and minds of black people, since he was "not black enough". He was painted as an Ivy League product, who was only running for political office because he thought he was better than everybody else. The Rush campaign also made the location of Obama's house an issue, as he lived in a sub-urban area of Chicago, with mostly rich, white neighbors. Unfortunately, these attacks struck a chord with the electorate. What probably finally ensured that Obama would lose the race, was a radio address by President Bill Clinton, during which he endorsed Bobby Rush. Needless to say, Obama lost the election and lost very badly. Friends have said in interviews after that election that the most painful thing for Obama was not the loss, but the personal attacks leveled against him. Obama soon recovered and continued his work in the state senate. He had his second child, Natasha (Sasha) in 2001.

In 2002, Obama made another politically risky move. President Bush was making his case for the war in Iraq. The war was supposed to be part of the war on terror and was one of the few issues that had bi-partisan support, as most politicians sided with the President on it. The war on terror had tremendous support with the American people, as the painful feelings from the nightmare of September 11 were still fresh. For a politician to oppose the war was seen as political suicide, since the premise of the war was that Saddam Hussein possessed weapons of mass destruction and could either use them on the US or her allies or even give them to terrorists. But Barack Obama was one of a handful of politicians to oppose the war. In front of a crowd of anti-war protesters, he gave an impassioned speech on what he called a dumb war. Most politicians across the country, regardless of party, would never have risked such a move, because of the expected fallout of opposition to such a popular war. This also proved what I already believe from his refusal to withdraw from the race for state senator; Obama had a spine of steel.

The strange thing that happened after his speech was that his popularity seemed to increase! (A full transcript of the speech of the speech is at the end of this book).

The 2004 election season was fast approaching and the ever ambitious Obama decided to run for the US Senate. Friends and advisers were skeptical about this move because of how badly the loss in 2000 had affected him. Close friend and adviser, Valerie Jarrett, said she felt if he lost another election so close to the last one, his political career could be over. It was while launching his campaign that he enlisted the help of a man who was to become possibly his most important and most respected adviser for years to come, David Axelrod.

In the race for the Democratic nominee for the US Senate, there were seven candidates and Obama was the least likely to get the nomination. But it appeared that fate was on his side. The frontrunner, Blair Hull's chances of securing the nomination were dealt a huge blow, when allegations of domestic abuse surfaced. Against all odds, Obama secured the nomination with over 52% of the vote. The amazing thing about this victory was that his closest rival, Daniel Hynes was about 29% behind him! This big win brought him to the attention of the national leadership of the Democratic Party, who began to see him as a star for the future.

Next, he faced the Republican candidate, Jack Ryan. It was in the course of this campaign that Obama's appeal to young voters and educated voters across racial lines, became evident.

As the race was heating up, a sex scandal involving Jack Ryan and his ex-wife, Hollywood actress, Jeri Ryan erupted. The scandal became so damaging that Jack Ryan withdrew from the race. Obama was now effectively a candidate for the US Senate, without an opponent!

John Kerry had been elected as the Democratic nominee for President in 2004 and was getting ready for the convention in July. According to PBS documentary, The Choice, "convention organizers were looking for someone to deliver the keynote speech, preferably a minority politician who could excite a crowd". Obama's name was floated around and he eventually got the nod to deliver the keynote address at the convention.

No one could have predicted what happened next. Obama's speech at the convention took only 17minutes, but in that time, his life was changed forever. People were cheering, crying, applauding, praying; it was unbelievable! His campaign manager, David Axelrod, said, he had obviously read the speech before the convention, but still when he heard it that night and saw the crowd's reaction to it, in his words, "I knew his life was never going to be the same again". I heard of a woman in the crowd who was crying loudly and kept repeating, "This is history!"

There were all sorts of comments from analysts and reporters after the speech. One said, "Anyone who missed this speech has missed a piece of history". Another said,

"In Illinois, people talk about him openly as the first black President." Another said, "We've heard tonight from a transcender". And another said, "It's amazing that he's only still a State senator!"

Everyone had an opinion about the speech, but one thing was clear: A 17minute speech had turned Obama from an Illinois State senator into a national phenomenon! (A full transcript of the speech is at the end of this book).

In August, the Republicans put forward Alan Keyes as their candidate to challenge Obama in the US Senate race. Alan Keyes was a colorful and controversial character, who had run for President in 1996 and 2000. He had also run for the US Senate as a Maryland resident in 1988 and 1992. Before long, his character was evident. Among other interesting statements he made on the campaign trail, he said, "Jesus Christ would not vote for Obama"!

The elections were held on November 2 2004 and Barack Obama won by a landslide, with 70% of the vote. No one was surprised by the result, but it was still amazing that a non-incumbent had run a campaign so powerful that it resulted in such a large victory margin. Alan Keyes, in keeping with his colorful nature, refused to congratulate Obama on his victory.

Obama arrived in the US Senate as the star and some said the future of the Democratic Party. His speech at the convention a few months before meant that everyone knew who he was. But the fact remained that he was still a brand new Senator and so had to work hard to make sure the buzz surrounding him turned into political clout.

His second book, "The Audacity of Hope" was released in 2006. While on tour to promote the book, he also campaigned for Senate colleagues, who were seeking re-election. Before long, people began to notice a trend. Anywhere Obama went to campaign, there was more attention on him than the people he was campaigning for. People then openly began asking him to run for President! At every single event he appeared in, he was mobbed by people who asked or sometimes begged him to run for President. According to chief adviser, David Axelrod, "It was the closest thing to a draft I had ever seen". Whether this was what made him begin to consider a run in 2008 or if that had been his original plan, only he and his close advisers would know, but before long it became obvious that he was considering it.

He began asking more experienced friends for advice. Senate colleague, Richard Durbin said, "I told him that in this business of politics, sometimes you pick the time and sometimes the time picks you. This is your time".

Former Senate majority leader, Tom Daschle said, "I told him not to assume that another opportunity would present itself if he passes off the one he has now".

The rest, as the saying goes is history.

Of everything I read and watched about Obama's life, two decisions he made struck and amazed me more than anything else.

The first was his decision to return to Chicago after law school. He had just graduated near the top of his class from Harvard law school and was also the president of the Harvard law review. He had received lucrative job offers from prestigious law firms around the country; accepting one of them would have been a fast track to wealth, if not necessarily fame. He could have applied for and most likely gotten a Supreme Court clerkship, which would have been a fast track to power. He did neither. Instead, he returned to Chicago to continue his work as a community organizer and practice civil rights law! This struck me because I don't know a lot of people who would have such options and pick the last one, especially not someone who came from a lower middle class background and went to school with the help of loans and scholarships. But then again, maybe that was exactly why it was easy for him to turn down the more logical career paths.

The second thing that struck me was his refusal to withdraw from the Illinois State senate race, when asked by Alice Palmer and other revered Chicago politicians. This refusal could have ended his political career at a time when it was only just starting. Even though he ended up winning that race by default, I don't believe he knew that Alice Palmer or the other candidates would have problems with their signatures, which means he could easily have lost that race. Obviously, we'll never know what would have happened if the signatures were okay, but I believe if he had lost that race, it would have been difficult, if not impossible for him to have re-started his political career.

These two decisions he took, I believe ultimately propelled him to where he is today and I can only imagine what or where he would be on 3rd June 2008 if he made the decisions everyone else expected him to at those turning points in his life.

WHY HILLARY CLINTON LOST

Next, I wanted to understand how and why Hillary Clinton lost a race that she seemed not just likely, but also destined to win. Why did her campaign crash and burn so badly? Here are three reasons why I think she lost the nomination:

1. **Overconfidence**: I think this was Hillary Clinton's biggest mistake, because almost every other mistake she made sprouted from this one. Most Democrats, or maybe I should say most people in the country believed Hillary Clinton would win the nomination. There was this air of entitlement that surrounded her candidacy and unfortunately, she bought into it. This led to an overconfident candidate who ended up making costly errors. First, the decision to spend a huge chunk of her campaign funds in the first few States to hold their primaries, so that the race would be over by Super-Tuesday was ill-advised. True, she was the front-runner, but the speed with which Obama was closing the gap in those months and weeks leading up to Iowa should have put paid to such a strategy. How could she expect to land

a knock-out blow to someone who was catching up with her almost everyday in the polls and was raising more money than she was? That strategy would only have made sense, if she maintained her once substantial lead, going into Iowa. It was this same mindset that led to inadequate funding for a race beyond Super-Tuesday. Secondly, the decision to practically cede the caucus States to Obama was not only a costly error, it was also a baffling one. The primaries are all about the delegate math and the caucuses are a good way to add up those delegate numbers. Instead, Clinton concentrated on the big States, believing that if she won enough of them and some other smaller ones, that would be sufficient. Even though she won quite a number of the big States, more than Obama did, Obama's campaign organization in the caucus States led to a string of victories and delegate totals that Clinton was never able to catch up with. The outcome might have been a lot closer or even different, had she put the same efforts she put into the big States, into the caucuses.

2. **Negative campaigning**: There is no doubt that Clinton's attacks on Obama turned off a lot of voters. While you could argue that both candidates attacked each other, it seemed to me that most of Obama's attacks were in response to attacks from Clinton. The painful and frustrating thing about these attacks was that she had given the Republicans ammunition for the general

elections. No one is better than the Republicans when it come to political and personal attacks. So, for Hillary and in a lot of cases, Bill Clinton to have attacked Obama so relentlessly, knowing fully well that the Republicans were most likely taking notes, I think was to her disadvantage, especially since the attacks only started after Obama became the front-runner. Statements like her saying that she and John McCain would bring lifetimes of experience to the White House, while Obama would bring a speech he gave in 2002 or telling Bill Richardson that Obama cannot win in November went way too far. I also believed that in addition to anything else he might consider, the depths of the attacks would prevent Obama from naming her as his running mate, not because he wanted to be vindictive, but because of how ridiculous it might have looked after months of personal and political attacks.

3. **Wrong campaign theme**: I believe this mistake was almost as costly as the first one. In a year when voters were obviously looking for change, Hillary Clinton was running a campaign based on experience. Because of the missteps of the Bush administration, it was obvious that the voters wanted not just something new, but a complete course reversal. They wanted something that did not have the stain of Washington on it. Hillary Clinton had effectively been a Washington insider since her husband was elected President in 1992 and the last thing voters wanted to hear was

someone who had been at the top in Washington for that long touting her experience, when they wanted the exact opposite. In the change versus experience debate, change had obviously won and even John Edwards, who did not go that far in the race was seen more as an agent of change than Hillary Clinton. Some of her supporters argued that electing a woman President would represent change, but her critics argued back that while this was true, Hillary Clinton as a person does not represent change and it would be business as usual, if she is elected. Whatever the case, Hillary Clinton's experience campaign was a very serious strategic blunder.

In all, I believe Hillary Clinton was supremely qualified to be the Democratic nominee for President, but I also believe she did not expect to win the nomination as a result of this. She expected to win just because she was Hillary Clinton.

THE CHOICE

Each Party had now made its choice and what they represented was a crystallization of the debate that had been raging since the beginning of the year.

Barack Obama, the youthful freshman Senator from Illinois, against John McCain, the older and more experienced Senator from Arizona. If ever there was a debate on change versus experience, this was it.

This debate that had started during the primaries in both the Democratic and Republican races was now raging even more because of the stark differences between the two nominees.

Senator Obama had started his political career in 1996 as an Illinois State Senator and was elected to the US Senate in 2004. Even though he had first featured in national newspapers in 1989 when he was elected President of the Harvard Law Review, he did not achieve national prominence until his speech at the Democratic Convention in 2004.

Senator McCain had started his political career in 1977, first as Navy liaison to the US Senate, was elected to the US House of Representatives in 1982 and US Senate in 1986. He had shot to national prominence and was first featured in national newspapers in 1967, following his capture in Vietnam.

I thought about past US Presidential elections and tried to remember if there had ever been any, where the electorate was faced with two such contrasting views from two very different candidates. The fascinating thing I remembered was that every four years, the differences are usually so stark that there is always a debate about what the candidates represent.

In 2004, it was all about National Security and the war on terror. The electorate had a choice between a popular "war-time President" who favored pre-emptive action over diplomacy and a former soldier turned Senator who favored tough diplomacy over pre-emptive action.

In 2000, it was all about integrity and leading America into the 21st century. The electorate had a choice between a popular Vice President and an equally popular Texas Governor.

In 1996, it was all about maintaining the huge cut in the budget deficit and finally balancing the budget. The electorate had a choice between a very popular 50year old incumbent President and a 73year old conservative Senator.

In 1992, it was all about getting rid of the budget deficit, getting the economy back on track and preventing Saddam Hussein from developing biological weapons. The electorate had a choice between an unpopular but experienced incumbent President and a popular but inexperienced Arkansas Governor.

I thought about these two concepts; Change and

Experience. If I was voting in these elections based solely on one of them, which would I go for?

The need for change, in a general sense, usually comes when things are not going very well. The need for change comes when there is a desire for things to be better than they are. In the context of the view of a non-American following the 2008 elections, the need or prayer (since I cannot vote in the elections) for change has been brought about by the kind of President the country has had for the last 8years. President George Bush's policies have obviously affected Americans, either positively or otherwise, but I don't think Americans realize how profound an effect they have had on the rest of the world. For the last 8years, President Bush's "for us or against us" policies have so shocked and angered the whole world, that change could not come sooner. At this point, I think the rest of the world would gladly have settled for anyone, as long as the surname is not Bush. Politicians from Britain to Pakistan always tried to downplay their personal relationship with George Bush. Never in my lifetime had I seen or heard of a US President so reviled both by a huge majority of Americans and the rest of the world. I remember telling my fiancé that regardless of what happens in this election, the whole world will heave a sigh of relief when George Bush is gone. An American colleague of mine at work, said, "For the first time in my life, when I go to gatherings, I try not to let anyone know I am American. There was a time when it was a thing of pride to be American. For the last 8years, America has been seen as part of the problem in the world, rather than part of the solution, as we are accustomed to being."

The funny thing is that in terms of Africa policy,

President Bush has actually done more than most past US Presidents. An example is in the area of combating HIV. Unfortunately for him, he has ultimately been judged by his actions and decisions on other issues. Issues like, the Iraq war, the war in Afghanistan, the economy, global warming, the incarceration and treatment of prisoners in Guantanamo Bay, torture, prisoner abuse in Iraq, blatant abuse of power by his staff, blatant abuse of power by Vice President Dick Cheney and his staff. Sometimes, it seemed to me that President Bush and Vice President Dick Cheney believed they were monarchs, rather than a democratically elected leadership.

For example, just after the September 11 attacks, it seemed President Bush believed he had a blank cheque to do exactly what he wanted, regardless of the consequences. Even though the majority of Americans were behind him, obviously because of the devastation caused by the attacks, the ones who did object or even just asked questions was labeled, "unpatriotic". Any country that opposed the resulting unilateral foreign policy approach was deemed as not friendly to America! I can understand that after such a terrible event, America, like any other country, wanted those responsible brought to account, but I don't think countries disagreeing with certain aspects of how to go about this makes them unfriendly or terrorist sympathizers. Since when did it become wrong for friends to disagree?

The terrorists on September 11 killed almost 3000 people, which of course is a tragedy of unspeakable proportions. But I don't believe killing was their only intention. I believe they also intended to create an atmosphere of fear which would lead to suspension of civil liberties, turn America against other nations and ultimately turn a government of and for the people into a government feared by the people. The resulting quasi-suspension of civil liberties, disagreements with other nations, wanton arrest of Arab-Americans, the invasion of Iraq and ultimately, the massive unpopularity of the Iraq war provide proof.

The reason the terrorists were unable to go beyond killing Americans, and were also unable to negatively affect the structure of the American society, is due to the incredible spirit of the American people. America is not just a country; America is a way of life. America is an ideal. America is a mentality. You cannot defeat a way of life, an ideal or a mentality by killing or plotting to kill the people who possess them! These concepts are much too strong and I think that is one thing terrorists have never understood. After September 11, the average American would say, "You can make us afraid, you can bring down our tallest buildings, but you can never bring down our spirit!"

This mentality is one of the reasons why America is the most powerful nation on earth. Where I believe President Bush got it wrong and what I don't think he was able to grasp during his 8years in office is that America's awesomeness is not in its military might or in its ability to wage war, but in its strength to be gentle. Now, don't get me wrong, I'm not saying that America should be gentle on terrorists; OF COURSE NOT! My point is that America is too powerful a nation to unleash its power without properly thinking it through and weighing the consequences of such an action. For example, America did not need to go into Iraq! There is a reason why, when

President Bush decided to attack Afghanistan, the whole world rallied behind him. In the same way, there is a reason why, when he decided to attack Iraq, almost every country, including the ones that ended up going in with him, was skeptical. Even though most of America was with him when the decision to go into Iraq was made, it is important to note that the American people agreed with him because they trusted their President when he said there were weapons of mass destruction in Iraq. They trusted their President when he said they would go in, kick Saddam Hussein out and secure the weapons on mass destruction. When no weapons were found and the body count of American troops started rising, the country knew what a lot of other countries knew: The US should never have gone into Iraq.

With regards to Afghanistan, it was justified, which was why there was hardly a dissenting view when America decided to attack. With regards to Iraq, it was a different story. President Bush has never seemed to understand that any country that disagrees with him is not necessarily a terrorist sympathizer, or an unfriendly nation. He has never seemed to understand that in the same way his number one responsibility and priority is the American people, leaders of other countries also have a first responsibility and priority to their citizens ahead of American interests. That America is the world's most powerful nation is not in doubt, but that does not mean every nation has to agree to America's demands in detriment to their own national interests. For the Bush administration to label such countries as unfriendly for this reason is part of why I think he has never understood the meaning of "the strength to be gentle". If a country decides to make enemies of America, then it would most likely be to that country's detriment, but America is too powerful to make enemies of countries as easily as President Bush did. This is why it is so important for an American President to be one who thinks issues through and gets the best advice before acting and not just a "shoot from the hip" mentality. Other countries can afford that, but not America. I once heard somewhere that, "With great power comes great responsibility".

I know I seem to have drifted away from my initial point, but I deliberately wanted to highlight why the whole world was clamoring so much for a change from George Bush. You might argue that the rest of the world should have no business in how America votes, but I beg to differ. The last 8years have shown exactly why the world feels like it has a stake in these elections. Whether a country likes or hates America, one thing is certain; America is and has always been the mirror with which the world looks at itself. President Bush and his policies had effectively shattered that mirror and change would be the only hope for restoration.

Obama said during one of the debates, "The one good thing Bush and Cheney have done for us is that they have given their party a very bad name".

On the American side, from what I saw and read during the primaries, young voters were the most vocal and passionate about the need for change in America, and I could understand why. I felt that in a lot of ways, they probably had the most to lose and the most to gain in this election because the worse the situation in America gets, the less chances they would have at the kind of future they had dreamed of.

Unsurprisingly, the most vocal calls for experience over change came from older voters. The reasoning behind the experience over change calls was that at a time when the economy is in distress and the country is involved in two wars, an experienced hand is needed. Senator McCain has been in one way or the other involved in the military for decades, first as a Navy Pilot, then Navy liaison to the US Senate and finally as a member of the Senate Armed Services Committee. Senator Obama was a member of several committees including the Senate Foreign Relations Committee. The pro-experience movement believed that it was smarter to entrust the reins of government to someone who was proven and tested, rather than someone who according to a voter in Texas, "still has a lot to learn". The only problem with this argument was that polls showed that a majority of the voters had become so disillusioned with anything Washington including "Washington Experience" and wanted a complete reversal of course for the country. There was the argument that George Bush was inexperienced when he was elected in 2000 and relied on "on the job training", which is one of the reasons that the country is in the state it is. While that is a valid argument, I don't think any President ever really comes in with experience unless he or she was President before. Decades in the Senate or decades as a Governor, does not automatically make a good President. What a good President needs is to surround himself/ herself with competent and experienced advisers and have the good judgment to decide what is best, based on the advice given. I define competence in this context as the ability to do the job you were elected or appointed to do. President Bush surrounded himself with experienced advisers, but their competence is something that is open for debate. This sounds harsh but look at the facts: When George H Bush was President in 1993, Dick Cheney was Defense Secretary and Donald Rumsfeld and Condolezza Rice were senior advisers. The country ended up with a war, stationed troops in Saudi Arabia and Kuwait, left a huge deficit in the budget and left the economy in ruins. When Bill Clinton took over, he brought in his own team, balanced the budget and left a surplus for the next President. Now that George W Bush is President, Dick Cheney is Vice President, Donald Rumsfeld was Defense Secretary, Condolezza Rice was National Security Adviser and now Secretary of State. As George Bush is getting ready to step down, the country is involved in two wars, the budget is in a huge deficit and the economy is back in ruins, this time even worse that 1993. Even though George H Bush and George W Bush are two different Presidents, they had almost exactly the same advisers and the results were almost exactly the same. My point? The same team that dragged the country into a war that led to troops being stationed in the Middle East for years and also ruined the economy is the same team that has done exactly the same thing, only it's a different President and it's over a decade later.

This goes to show that experience and competence are two completely different things and a man's experience does not necessarily make him competent. I'm not at all implying that John McCain would make an incompetent President, what I am saying is that the fact that he is experienced does not mean he would be a competent President.

Before I move on, I want to point out that I have left

out Colin Powell, even though he served as Chairman of Joint Chiefs for President George H Bush and Secretary of State to George W Bush. Now, before Rush Limbaugh fans start getting testy, I did not leave him out because he is black. I left him out because in both administrations, he was the moderate voice, who believed war should be a last resort. As a General, he was called, "The reluctant General" because of this doctrine. As Secretary of State, he was the dissenting voice in the room when the "Hawks" were clamoring for an attack on Iraq and possibly Iran and North Korea.

Since even the most partisan polls showed that the pro-experience movement was vastly outnumbered by the pro-change movement, it was obvious that the candidate who could convince the electorate that he could deliver change would most likely be elected President.

So the question was now; "Which candidate represents change?" Not just a rhetorical change, but the kind of change that will make a difference in the lives of Americans.

On the surface, Obama looked like the one who represented change, while McCain looked like the consummate Washington insider. Apart from the fact that it had been Obama's main campaign theme, he had not been in Washington long enough to be considered a Washington insider. While some saw this as a reason why he was unqualified to be President, others saw it as the exact reason why he should be President. Like Anderson Cooper said, "Senator Obama, your supporters say you are different, your critics say you are inexperienced."

But a closer look at McCain shows that this issue was

not that clear cut. When the primaries started, I told my fiancé that regardless of who the Democratic nominee is, it will not be as easy as everyone seems to think for Democrats to win the general elections, if John McCain is the Republican nominee. I said this because I had always known John McCain as one of the Republicans who had a lot of support from Democrats and Independents. This was because of his moderate views on certain issues, his ability to work with Democrats and disagree with his own party leadership on a variety of issues. Also, the fact that he and President Bush had never been the best of friends didn't hurt. However, when I started listening to John McCain, I was surprised at some of the things he was saying. Gone was the Republican most feared by Democrats because of his appeal. That John McCain had been replaced by a barely recognizable "conservative", who suddenly began to reverse positions he had held for decades, positions that had made him possibly the most popular Republican in the country. The two issues that stuck with me more than any other were his reversal on tax policy and immigration. The reason these stuck with me was because I remembered when he actually stood against his party on these two issues, years ago.

I remembered listening to him in 2001, when he described George Bush's tax plans as "fiscally irresponsible, unfair to the middle class and only benefits the wealthy". That "fiscally irresponsible" tax plan had now become the backbone of McCain's economic plan!

I also remembered that he was one of the most vocal Senators, when it came to immigration. He, along with Senator Ted Kennedy, spearheaded a move to set up guest worker, amnesty and path to naturalization programs for certain eligible illegal immigrants. Of course at the time, this was hugely unpopular with Republicans, but it was generally supported by the American public. This issue further enhanced John McCain's appeal with Democrats and Independents, because Republicans are usually seen as being anti-immigration. Now, John McCain was saying that none of these programs were in America's best interests! I could not believe it! Apparently, he had been saying these things since last year and all through the primaries, but I did not really take notice because I was more engrossed in the soap-opera style primary battle between Barack Obama and Hillary Clinton.

What had happened to the John McCain that I had always admired because I did not know any other Republican who had that kind of appeal? Even one of his closest friends, Republican Senator Chuck Hagel said that John McCain is a lot smarter than some of the things he's saying! As I watched, read and studied a bit more, I began to understand why he had reversed his positions on these and other issues.

While his willingness and ability to work with and appeal to Democrats and Independents was seen as a good thing by a neutral observer, it made his own party members very weary of him. Some believed this ability meant he was not a true conservative. "Conservative" activist, Ann Coulter once remarked that if the general election is between John McCain and Hillary Clinton, she would campaign for Clinton because even she is more conservative than John McCain. When McCain ran for President in 2000, he lost the Republican nomination to George Bush, mainly because he was seen as too liberal. His criticism of "conservative" icons, Jerry

Falwell and Pat Robertson was an unforgivable sin for a Republican candidate and he was severely punished for it. His campaign for President in 2000 was based on his standing as the Republican who could appeal to people of any party. What he either did not realize or chose to ignore, was that these qualities are not very welcome in the Republican Party.

In 2008 though, John McCain had learnt his lesson. He knew that if he was going to be the Republican nominee and also count on their votes in November, he would have to start talking about issues conservatives care about and stop trying to appeal to people of all parties.

Now, here is what I have never understood about the Republican Party: What exactly is wrong with a Republican being able to appeal to other parties? If a Democrat appeals to Independents and Republicans, he becomes popular within his party. With a Republican, the exact opposite is the case. It is this kind of attitude that has made so many people see the party as intolerant.

Now, McCain had pledged to run an honorable campaign, without negative ads, personal attacks or animosity. Considering the fact that these kinds of attacks are part of what Republicans are known for during campaigns, it would be interesting to see if their nominee for President could pull this off. If he had been the nominee in 2000 and had made that pledge, I would be inclined to believe he could pull it off, but in 2008, I knew John McCain had become a different man or at least he was now playing by a different set of rules.

Even before the general election season started, Obama and McCain's strategies were already obvious.

Obama would tie McCain to President Bush, while McCain would paint Obama as inexperienced and risky to entrust the country to.

Two very sound strategies if they got them right, but I believed Obama had the easier task because of how much McCain had changed positions and fallen in line with President Bush's policies. Also, the fact that McCain had been one of the most vocal Senators in support of the now unpopular Iraq war was an advantage for Obama.

In McCain's case, his strategy was not as easy because of lessons from history. Three of America's most popular Presidents were once described as inexperienced, too young and not ready to be President.

During the 1960 elections, the Republicans, led by incumbent Vice President Richard Nixon, tried to paint John Kennedy as inexperienced and too young to be Commander in Chief. It was at a time of economic uncertainty and National Security concerns. Kennedy won the election and even though his Presidency was cut short, he is regarded as one of the most popular Presidents in US history.

During the 1992 elections, the Republicans, led by incumbent President George H Bush, tried to paint Bill Clinton as too inexperienced and too young to be Commander in Chief. It was also at a time of economic uncertainty and the new President also had to deal with the issue of stationing US troops in the Middle East, following the Gulf war. I remember a comment President H Bush made during that campaign, that his dog had more foreign policy experience that Bill Clinton. Clinton won the election by a landslide and left office as once of the most popular US Presidents ever.

I decided to leave Abraham Lincoln till the last because his story is not as straight forward as the first two. Abraham Lincoln, like Obama, decided to run for President after a few years in the state legislature and one term in the US Congress. Like Obama, he was an incredibly popular politician at the time and was considered too young to be President, (he was 51). He won the 1860 elections and is today named among the best, if not the best ever US President.

If history was going to be a crystal ball, Barack Obama would be on his way to being the 44th President of The United States.

From the moment it became obvious that John McCain would be the Republican nominee, I knew there was going to be a debate on foreign policy and National Security. The Republicans could not hope to win with a debate on the economy, job creation, the mortgage crisis or even Iraq. The Iraq question was not helped by John McCain saying during the primaries that the US would be there "for 100years if necessary". Considering the fact that the Iraq war was now very unpopular, that was an incredibly strange thing to say. The economy was obviously the number one issue for most Americans, but I knew John McCain would try to change the topic to National Security. He also pointed out that the economic issue is a National Security issue. I did agree with him though, that the economic crisis is a National Security issue because all through history, no militarily powerful nation has been able to maintain its power when its economy hit a downward spiral.

Throughout the primaries, Obama, who had opposed

the Iraq war from the start, had called for a withdrawal of US combat troops from Iraq within 16month of taking the oath of office. The basis for this argument was that the Iraqis had to start taking responsibility for their own affairs. He further opined that it was inexcusable that the US was spending about $10billion a month in Iraq on a war that should never have been started. I agreed that there was no justification for spending that kind of money at a time when the US economy was in a downward spiral and owing China billions of dollars. However, while I subscribe to the view that the Iraq invasion was a bad decision, I believe just picking up and leaving would be an even worse decision. The sporadic violence, absence of an organized military, a new government and a host of other issues, I felt obliged the US to sort out or at least oversee the sorting out of these problems before leaving. Leaving Iraq in the state that it is in would result in unimaginable chaos, and the ripple effects of that kind of instability in an already unstable region would probably bring the US back again anyway. So, in my opinion, for the sake of peace and stability in what is already a volatile region, they would do best to sort the mess out first before leaving. Like Obama said, "As President, I will make sure we are as careful going out as we were careless going in".

America might be the world's most powerful nation, but even she cannot solve the Iraq problem alone. The worst part of it though, is that no other country will help! A lot of other countries could have been very helpful in rebuilding both the physical and governmental infrastructure of Iraq, but President Bush has so alienated them that it is not even an option at this point. The old saying, "You broke it, now fix it" comes to mind.

Meanwhile, John McCain, who was a vocal supporter of the war from the start, was calling for a "victory" in Iraq before leaving. The problem with that argument though, is that he failed to define what exactly a victory in Iraq would entail. The problem with defining victory in Iraq was that the objectives of going into Iraq in the first place had changed. With the Iraq war, like any other thing in life, every new objective comes with a new definition of victory. When the US invaded Iraq in 2003, the objective was to rid Saddam Hussein's regime of weapons of mass destruction. Victory for that objective would have been finding, securing and destroying these weapons. No weapons were found and the Bush administration said it did not matter, since Saddam Hussein "retained the intent" to develop weapons of mass destruction. After the failure of the first objective, the military was given a new one; liberating the Iraqi people from a despotic ruler and establishing a democracy. The definition of victory for that objective would have been getting rid of Saddam Hussein, stabilizing the country and turning it into the Middle East's latest democracy. As this goes to print, only the first part of that objective has been realized. Even though Iraq now has an elected President and Prime Minister, I believe it was an election born out of a lack of options, rather a firm choice.

Obama's timeframe for withdrawing from Iraq was heavily criticized by the Republicans, who pointed that out as further proof of his inexperience. He was accused of a lack of understanding of the issues on the ground, since he had not made a trip to Iraq since January 2006. Their argument was that he needed to go to Iraq to see things himself before talking about a timeframe for withdrawal. This point made sense, but I don't think Obama needed to be on the ground in Iraq to know that a timeframe needed to be set, because the US stay cannot and should not be indefinite. As Obama was the Chairman of the Senate sub-committee on European affairs, a committee which had oversight of NATO, he was expected to have held hearings on Afghanistan and made fact finding trips to Iraq. He was accused of being too busy planning his campaign to care about his day job. The Republican National Committee actually had a live digital counter on their website, counting the number of days that have gone by since Obama's last trip to Iraq! Some said he could only give a great speech, but would be out of place in a meeting with world leaders, as he had no experience. He was accused of being ready to talk to Iranian President Mahmoud Ahmedinejad, but not with US military leaders about Iraq.

On the other hand, since John McCain secured the Republican nomination, he had made trips to Iraq, Afghanistan, Israel, England and France and held meetings with the leaders of these countries. Whether or not it was this goading that made Obama decide to schedule a trip abroad or if it was already planned, we'll probably never know, but when he announced his itinerary, it was suddenly the most anticipated trip by a US politician in years. The press could talk of very little else and it became the newest topic on blogs. Even the obsession with guessing who the running mates for both candidates would be, suddenly took a back seat.

Obama started his trip abroad with visits to Iraq, Jordan, Afghanistan and Israel. Not only did he meet with the leaders of these countries and the American military, he actually looked very Presidential, which was the worry of some of his supporters. The press coverage of these trips and meetings was unprecedented! If a visiting President had received the kind of coverage and public attention Obama's Middle East trip had, it would have been too much, so what made this even more amazing was the fact that he was not even President yet!

While in Israel, he dropped a prayer at the Western Wall. Within a few days, his prayer was front page news! I know Obama was a fresh face in public, but I thought pasting his personal prayer all over the news was crossing the line. I've always subscribed to the notion that a public figure should not expect any privacy, but something like that was going a bit too far.

After the Middle East leg of his trip was over, he moved to Europe and it was there that his popularity became the most evident. He was mobbed by reporters in France and England and it was only the Secret Service cordon around him that prevented supporters and fans from doing the same. His Germany trip though, was incredible! He addressed a crowd of over 200000 (two hundred thousand) people. Even Rock concert organizers would have been envious of a crowd of that size!

To be honest, I was a bit worried at the kind of reception Obama had gotten in these countries, because I knew the Republicans would try to play up the idea that he was more concerned with his rock-star status around the world than with the problems back home. Even though this was obviously not true, I felt the picture of 200000 people in Germany cheering a US Presidential candidate could be a turn-off at home. Already, his speech in Germany was being described by FOX News, the RNC and the McCain campaign as presumptuous, since he was not President. According to John McCain, "I would like to give speech in Germany, but I'd rather do it as President".

The McCain campaign even released an ad, with clips of the crowd in Germany shouting Obama's name. He was described in the ad as one of the world's three biggest celebrities, along with Britney Spears and Paris Hilton. Even for the McCain campaign, and the RNC that had written the playbook on dirty politics, this was a new low. Comparing Obama to Britney Spears and Paris Hilton? That was really not necessary. I think by now, we had all accepted that McCain had ditched his pledge to run a honorable campaign, but ads like that were still shocking. Polls showed that the ad was very well received by Republicans, but it turned off independents, who McCain was trying to attract.

I think the problem with Obama's overseas trip was that McCain and the Republicans did not expect it to be as successful as it turned out to be. The fact that American voters saw Obama looking comfortable and relaxed with other world leaders was a problem for McCain, because of his argument that Obama could not handle being on the world stage. I knew the criticism of Obama's "presumptuousness" was only because their argument that he would be out of place had been completely shot down. If he had indeed looked out of place, there would have been no "presumptuousness" argument; instead, it would have been, "You see, he cannot even face world leaders. How can you entrust the country to him?"

Not long after Obama's return from his successful trip

abroad, John McCain was handed a chance to exhibit his expertise; foreign policy.

A conflict, which had been brewing for several months between Georgia and the Russia controlled region of South Ossetia finally turned into a full blown war. The Georgian President, Mikhail Saakashvili had ordered his troops to attack and capture the capital of South Ossetia, Tskhinvali. This move was met with overwhelming force by Russia, who pushed the Georgians back and decided to move into other parts of Georgia. The force employed by the Russian military was so much that it seemed like Russia actually planned a full scale invasion of Georgia. The International community roundly condemned Russia for what it saw as an over-reaction. John McCain, who had always been a fierce critic of Russia and Vladimir Putin in particular, was all over the situation. He strongly condemned Russia's actions and called for a complete withdrawal of Russian forces, both from the disputed South Ossetia territories and from the new positions captured by Russian forces. He saw this as his opportunity to show himself as the candidate who would be ready to protect America and stand up to Russia. During one his town hall meetings in the middle of the crisis, he said, "Today, we are all Georgians".

Barack Obama instead had a more measured approach. He called for both sides to show restraint and not allow the situation to escalate any further than it already had. Needless to say, this response was criticized by the McCain campaign. They claimed that they expected a much tougher response from Obama and pointed this out as further proof that Obama is inexperienced and not ready to be President.

Now, the criticism from the candidates, the US Government and the rest of the International community of Russia, was swift and uncompromising.

What no one mentioned though, was that it was Georgia that had actually escalated the conflict.

What no one mentioned was that when Georgian President, Mikhail Saakashvili ordered his troops to attack and capture the South Ossetia capital, he had broken the terms of a 1992 ceasefire agreement with Russia.

What no one mentioned was that the decision by Saakashvili had turned Russian citizens living in that region into targets.

I think the decision of the Georgian Government to launch that attack was one of the worst strategic miscalculations ever made by a world leader. The reason I termed it a miscalculation is because I believe Georgia made the decision to attack because they expected to be backed up by the US, the European Union and NATO. Not militarily, but in terms of pressure on Russia to either show restraint or possibly even pull out of South Ossetia. Russia is a very powerful and very proud country. Russia and Georgia have never really had the best of relationships. Russia, like any other powerful country, listens or takes counsel from the International community only when it is in its national interest and there is something to be gained from such counsel. In this case, the only thing Russia stood to gain was humiliation on an international scale. How on earth could the Georgian Government even for a second, flirt with the thought that Russia would not retaliate? What made the Georgian Government think the US, the EU or NATO could put the kind of pressure on Russia that would make them show restraint in the face of an attack by a former satellite State of the Soviet Union? I get the feeling that if a country attacked an area, region or State under US or any other country's control, they would not just accept it lying down either. If the US or Britain or France will not accept it, why does everyone expect Russia to accept it? I think the problem is that the US, under President George Bush, has made it a policy to condemn actions by nations that are not close allies and either turn a blind eye or at least refuse to publicly criticize their ally. Don't get me wrong; I actually think the Russian response was a gross overreaction. I even think the Russians were either expecting or hoping the Georgians tried something like that, just so that they could prove a point. Georgian President, Mikhail Saakashvili actually said in an interview, that the Russian reaction was proof that Russian President, Dmitry Medvedev and Prime Minister, Vladimir Putin were just looking for an opportunity to make a move against Georgia. My question to Mr Saakashvili is this, "If you knew that, why did you give them the opportunity?"

I also thought the criticism of Russia by the US and the rest of the international community's criticism of Russia was a bit hypocritical. In 2006, two Israeli soldiers were kidnapped by the Hezbollah group. Israel proceeded to launch an offensive, which lasted for 34days. At the end of the conflict, lives had been lost, including 200 Israelis and people had been displaced. The two captured soldiers were not found or released. I thought this was an overreaction, but apparently, most of the international community did not seem to think so, as there was almost no criticism of Israel's actions. Don't get me wrong, if Hezbollah fighters had been the only ones who lost lives and properties, that would have been a more than fitting response to the madness of kidnapping Israeli soldiers, but my point is, how do you react to the kidnap of two of your citizens by starting an action that kills many more? I'm not saying Israel should have sat back and done nothing, what I am saying is that a mission to recover or revenge the kidnap of two citizens and getting many other killed in the process makes very little sense to me. If the goal of the Israelis was to make an example, which would serve as a deterrent for other would be kidnappers, then it was a job very well done because somehow, I don't see anyone attempting to kidnap Israelis if they understand the consequences of such an act.

In the Russia-Georgia case, I thought Russia overreacted, but if the goal was for this response to be a deterrent, then it worked very well, because I don't see Saakashvili trying anything along those lines, now or in the future.

Whether the world likes or agrees with Russia or not, the fact of the matter is that, it is a proud and powerful country and deserves to be accorded that respect. I don't mean turn a blind eye when Russia misbehaves, but quit acting like anytime Russia is involved in a military conflict, it must have done something wrong. Russia, like any other nation has a right to protect its citizens and its interests.

As for the candidates' responses to the Russia-Georgia crisis, I think it showed the stark differences between the candidates.

John McCain's response mirrored President Bush's usual cowboy rhetoric. I don't believe he even had all the facts before condemning Russia's "aggression" towards Georgia. If John McCain had criticized Russia's overreaction and also criticized Georgia's leaders for escalating an already toxic situation, I would have been very impressed. But his response was typical of the unwritten George Bush policy on Russia; If Russia is involved, Russia is at fault.

Barack Obama's response, even though he condemned Russia's actions in stronger terms after getting all the facts, was an insight into the kind of leader he is and the kind of President he intends to be. Get all the facts first and be careful about your public reaction and criticism. The world has had 8 years of an American President with a "shoot from the hip" mentality and I think that is about enough. What is needed now is a thoughtful leader, who is tough when he needs to be and not when he is expected to be, but who also knows when to take a step back and reveal a softer side. A man of steel and velvet.

THE RUNNING MATES

After both candidates secured their parties' nominations, attention turned to who their running mates would be. All sorts of names were put forward as likely running mates for both parties. The most ridiculous of all the speculation I heard was that Condolezza Rice was campaigning to be John McCain's running mate! If I remembered correctly, she had repeatedly said that at the end of the Bush administration, she would go back to being work at Stanford University. How the press went from that, to her "actively seeking" the Republican number two slot because she attended a Republican meeting she usually does not attend was baffling. Anyway, she shot down that idea personally, before it could gain much traction.

I felt it would be particularly interesting to see who Obama would pick because I knew he had to walk the fine line between his campaign for change and the need to have someone with experience running with him. At a time when the country's military is stretched in two wars and the economy in a downward spiral, I felt the best thing for Obama to do would be to pick someone with Washington experience who could compliment him. His intelligence, tenacity and judgment were not in doubt. What he now needed was someone who could shore

Omololu Elegbe

up the areas in which he was weak or at least perceived as weak. This area was obviously foreign policy. Unlike what the analysts said, I did not think experience was the only ingredient needed to run a successful foreign policy. It has to be a combination of experience and good judgment. Obama had proved he had the judgment. What I think he needed now was someone with the right kind of experience.

True, this would be viewed by pundits as backing down on his change theme. The change versus experience debate had raged right from the primaries and it was now raging in Obama's running mate selection process. There were those who felt he should pick someone like the popular Governor of Virginia, Tim Kaine, which would really represent change. I believed such a move would be too risky for American voters. I believed the jury was still out on the experience issue of Obama's candidacy and selecting a running mate with little experience would give the pro-experience voters a much louder voice.

I thought about these issues and decided that Obama would most likely pick one of three choices:

Governor Tim Kaine of Virginia: a very popular Governor, who had endorsed Obama as early as February. On paper, I thought he was a good choice, but I believed Obama would only select him if he decided to go for change, rather than experience.

Senator Evan Bayh of Indiana: The little known Senator, who was quite popular in Democratic circles. He had been the elected Governor of Indiana at the age of 33 in 1988. He had been a US Senator since 1998 and a member of several powerful Senate committees, including the Armed Services Committee and the

Intelligence committee. Of all the names put forward, he was the one I believed Obama would pick. He was relatively young, had been a hugely successful Governor and was now one of the most respected US Senators, despite his youth. But when I began reading up on him, I saw that he was one of the most vocal proponents of the Iraq war. If there was going to be a problem with Obama picking him, I believed this would be the issue. For a candidate who had touted his early opposition to the Iraq war, picking a running mate who had been very vocal and visible about his support for the war would be counter-productive. Even though a lot of Senators had supported the war at the time, few received the handshakes and photo sessions Senator Bayh did in the White House Rose Garden with President Bush and Senator John McCain.

Senator Joe Biden of Delaware: Senator Biden had been in the Senate for over 30 years and was obviously very experienced. He was a member of powerful committees, including the Foreign Relations committee, of which he was chairman. I also thought he was a good choice, but he had a legendary tendency to talk quite a bit. This tendency meant if he was picked, he could end up saying things that may be at odds with the campaign. I remembered a documentary I saw; the Senate Foreign Relations committee was holding a confirmation hearing for Condolezza Rice as Secretary of State. During the hearing, Joe Biden talked so much and for so long that Obama, who was also a member of the committee, passed a note to an aide saying, "Shoot me, please shoot me now!"

The media had a lot of other names, including Hillary Clinton, John Edwards and Al Gore. I frankly did not think any of these three had a chance of being VP nominee for the following reasons:

Hillary Clinton: Even though press reports stated that she was interested in the role, I did not think she stood a serious chance of being selected. True, she had "suspended" her campaign and endorsed Obama, but I felt the bitterness and the depths of the attacks during the primaries would have made it ridiculous if he picked her. They had spent the last year attacking each other and it had only gotten worse as the months progressed. For Hillary Clinton to be running mate to someone she had practically endorsed John McCain over would just not have looked right. On the "Democrats Divided" issue, I did not subscribe to the view that Hillary Clinton supporters would not vote for Obama if she was not the VP nominee. I believed that regardless of the animosity and emotions during the primaries, Democrats would eventually unite behind Obama. A lot of people threatened to vote for McCain, but I think that was back when they thought he was still the same person they had known and admired for decades. His new found conservatism meant that he was not a viable alternative and I knew it was only a matter of time before the threats would dissipate.

John Edwards: While Obama and Edwards obviously had chemistry and looked good together, I did not see Obama choosing him because I believed John Edwards was even less experienced than Obama. The biggest criticism by Obama's opponents was that he was inexperienced, so for him to bring in someone with even less experience would have played right into their hands.

Besides, Edwards had been running mate to John Kerry in 2004 and I did not think he was up to another shot at being running mate, just in case it ended in another loss.

Al Gore: Of all the names put forward, I think Al Gore's was the most ridiculous. He had been Vice President for 8years and the 2000 Presidential election was practically snatched out of his hands. Since he left public office, his profile had risen even more as a result of his global warming campaign, he had won an Oscar award for his film about global warming and he had also won the Nobel Peace Prize. So why on earth would he want to spend the next four or possibly eight years as Vice President again? He had endorsed Obama, but I don't think he did it to be considered as running mate. Besides, Al Gore had said himself a number of times that if he ever went back into politics, it would be to run for President and nothing else.

On the Republican side, I believed and was almost certain that John McCain would pick Mitt Romney. He had quite a following during the primaries and having started a successful financial company, I thought he would shore up McCain's weakness on the economy. After all, McCain admitted early in the primary that "the issue of economics is something I've never understood as well as I should". To be honest, I actually give him a lot of credit for making that statement. Nobody, no matter how smart, has a monopoly on knowledge. Of course, it was probably not the smartest thing for a Presidential candidate to say, especially at a time of economic downturn, but that kind of honesty is what made people admire and respect John McCain. On the flip side of that, I don't know how exactly John McCain expected voters to trust him to deal with their number one concern, after a statement like that.

I believed picking Mitt Romney would have assuaged the doubts of voters who were worried about McCain's weakness on the economy.

There were also two very popular Governors, Tim Pawlenty of Minnesota and Charlie Crist of Florida, who were mentioned as possible running mates for John McCain. I thought John McCain would have an easier time with his running mate pick than Obama would, because he did not have to choose between experience and change. He was experienced, he was 72 years old, so it was unlikely he would pick someone older or more experienced in Government. I felt since National security was his forte, he should pick someone with economics credentials, possibly a Governor, since he or she would have both executive experience and experience trying to balance budgets.

Based on these, I thought his running mate pick should be Mitt Romney (he was the former Governor of Massachusetts), Governor Tim Pawlenty or Governor Charlie Crist. Speculations went into overdrive, when McCain invited these Governors and their spouses to a barbeque at his Arizona cabin. The invitation also included Louisiana Governor, Bobby Jindal. Bobby Jindal has been described as the Republican Obama because of his ethnicity (he's Indian-American) and charisma. At age 36, he is also the youngest current Governor in the US.

The day Obama was to announce his pick was the

same day of the men's Olympics football final, between Nigeria and Argentina. Due to the time difference, the match was to be shown at 5am British time. I wanted to watch the match and also wanted to find out who Obama would pick, so I decided to sleep until 5am, even though I knew that by then, Obama's running mate would have been announced.

When I stumbled downstairs with swollen eyes and switched on the TV, I saw that Obama had picked Joe Biden to be his running mate. I wasn't sure if I was surprised, but I was pleased that he had decided to go with experience. I changed the channel to FOX News, to listen to their view on this pick. I was expecting a very colorful view and as usual, I was not disappointed. According the FOX News, Obama's pick of Joe Biden proved that Obama had no confidence in himself. Their argument was that he had picked an obvious foreign policy expert to shore up his foreign policy weakness. The McCain campaign noted that Joe Biden was one of the most vocal critics of some of Obama's plans. They also described his pick as hypocritical, since he had run his campaign on the promise of change and had now picked as his running mate, a man who had been in the Senate for 30years.

What FOX News, the RNC and the McCain campaign failed to mention was that even though Joe Biden had been a Senator for over three decades, he had never lived in Washington and actually took the train home to Delaware every night! To hear that a Senator as powerful as Joe Biden took the train home every single night was something I found fascinating. This showed Omololu Elegbe

me that while he worked in Washington, he could not be considered a Washington insider.

The argument that Obama's selection of Joe Biden to shore up his foreign policy weakness meant he lacked self-confidence was not just silly, it was also a sad one. It was a sad reminder of what exactly is wrong with the Republican Party. Not that the argument was not true, of course he selected Joe Biden mainly because of his foreign policy credentials, but one of the qualities of a good leader is to seek the counsel of experts in areas where he is not an expert. I believed his selection of Joe Biden actually showed that he was confident enough to pick someone who knew more about foreign policy than he did and not be intimidated by that fact. It showed that he was ready and willing to listen. Even though, as the McCain campaign pointed out, Joe Biden was a vocal critic of Obama during the early stages of the primaries, did it not occur to them that, that may be one of the reasons Obama had actually picked him? A good leader does not need "yes men" around him. He needs people who will tell him the brutal truth, whether he wants to hear it or not. Joe Biden has been described as someone who always speaks his mind, sometimes to a fault. I believe Obama picking him "despite" that, shows a level of confidence that only exists in great leaders.

The next thing I was looking forward to was the Democratic Convention. Just before the convention though, the author Jerome Corsi, was at it again. He was the author, whose book, "Unfit for Command: Swift Boat Veterans Speak out against John Kerry", many Democrats believe derailed John Kerry's chance of being elected President in 2004. It was a book filled with lies and exaggerations, but John Kerry's defense came too little too late. This time, his book was about Obama and titled, "The Obama Nation".

Like the John Kerry book in 2004, "The Obama Nation" was filled with lies, innuendos, exaggerations and distortions. Writing the book about Obama, Jerome Corsi obviously knew the contents were false, but that did not matter, since all he had to do was "put it out there" and let the voters decide what is true and what is not. Even if voters realize what the book is filled with, the contents would still be enough to sow seeds of doubt or create more doubt with people who were still not sure about Obama. Obama did not make the same mistake John Kerry made though. He pushed back on the lies immediately with his truth squad. He used this team to answer any false remarks or rumors flying around. And there were nasty rumors; like he's a Muslim, he was not born in the US, he renounced his US citizenship when he lived in Indonesia, he does not sing the National Anthem, he's a closet radical, he probably still uses drugs and a lot of other unnecessary stuff. His truth squad did its job though, as not a lot of people took Jerome Corsi book seriously, except of course, Sean Hannity and friends at FOX News.

Attention now turned to the Democratic Convention and I could not wait for it to begin. I wanted to hear what Hillary and Bill Clinton would have to say. I wanted to hear Barack Obama's acceptance speech. The strange thing though, was what I actually looked forward to the most. I wanted to watch all the speeches to see if there would be another 2004 Obama type speech. The keynote address was being delivered by Mark Warner, who had been rumored to be a possible Vice Presidential nominee for Obama and a future Presidential candidate. I hate to say this, but his speech was like watching paint dry!

Michelle Obama's speech, especially the end, when her two lovely daughters came on stage was touching, passionate but calm. Former Presidential candidate, Dennis Kucinich also gave a passionate speech, but I thought the delivery, with him bouncing up and down was weird and probably explained why his campaign did not go anywhere. There was quite a buzz before Jesse Jackson Junior's speech, but it ended up being quite boring.

Hillary Clinton's speech was impressive, but I thought Bill Clinton's was phenomenal! I will never forget a line in the speech when he said, "The world has always been impressed by the power of our example rather than the example of our power". With that speech, Bill Clinton showed why 16 years after he was elected President and 8 years after he stepped down, he is still one of the most popular Presidents in recent US history.

Joe Biden's speech was also impressive, although I thought his son's speech was more brilliant.

On the last day of the convention, it was time for Obama's speech. As usual, the time difference meant I needed to stay up very late, but I did not mind. I knew that his speech would be great and I wanted to hear it live. I thought again about the last two conventions, 8 years ago and 4 years ago and I was amazed at how far Obama had come in that time. In 2000, he could not even get a floor pass to the convention and had to go back home. In 2004, he was the keynote speaker and by the end of the convention, he was a superstar. Now it was 2008 and the convention was all about him. Spectacular rise would be a gross understatement.

I listened to his speech and did not get up for a second or even move. After it was over, I prayed again, "Please let this man be President". It was a speech for the history books and I was glad I listened to it. According to The Daily Show's Jon Stewart, "Obama gave the latest greatest speech of his life".

I think the reason why Obama's speeches are always so effective, apart from the powerfully charismatic delivery, is that he talks about things you usually never hear from politicians. He talks to people like he is one of them, so he understands what their issues are. The politicians that do that, often times lack the charisma to go with it. In his case, he has the charisma and he knows the issues. The result is what we all marvel at whenever he opens his mouth.

After the convention, I was looking to see if he would get the usual bump in the polls, which usually comes after a party's convention. The poll bump was slight and analysts began predicting that Obama's campaign might be in trouble if he could not get a big bump from the convention. The Republican convention was a few days away the general thinking was that if John McCain got a big post-convention bump, then Obama might really be in trouble.

I now turned my attention to who John McCain would pick as his running mate. By now, it was clear that it was not going to be Mitt Romney or Bobby Jindal.

On the day the announcement was due to be made, I logged on to the Drudge report website and saw that McCain's pick might be Alaska Governor, Sarah Palin. The McCain campaign had not officially announced it, but according the Drudge report, a private jet carrying a man, woman and children landed at an airport not too far from where McCain was going to hold a rally with his new running mate and were whisked away in a convoy of tinted glassed vans. The guess was that the people on board were Sarah Palin, her husband and their children.

I had heard of the Alaska Governor a couple of times and I remember thinking she looks nice, but nothing prepared me for her selection as Vice Presidential nominee for the Republican Party. When it was finally official, I decided to read up on her, since I knew next to nothing about her.

I called my wife and said, "Guess who John McCain picked as his running mate? A 44year old, Hollywood looking Governor!" My wife said she believed John McCain probably picked her to be able to appeal to bitter Hillary Clinton supporters. I had thought about this as well and was worried that if this was McCain's reason for selecting Sarah Palin, it might actually work. I was less worried though, after I watched her first rally with John McCain. I could not put a finger on it, but there was something about her that just seemed off. She was good-looking, so it was not her appearance; she was well dressed, so it was not the dress; she gave a good speech, so it was not the speech. When I had racked my head for long enough without successfully figuring out what it was about her that seemed off to me, I decided to let it go and told myself that if there is something, it will come to me as the campaign goes on and I continue to watch and hear her speak.

I think FOX News was the most excited about the Sarah Palin pick, since she is considered a very conservative Governor. They saw her selection as a chance to rally the base of the Republican Party, some of whom had never fully accepted John McCain. His moderate stances in the past, his willingness to work with liberals and his bitter battle with George Bush for the Republican nomination in 2000 were still fresh in the minds of the extreme right wing of the party, who saw him as not conservative enough. The thinking was that an ultra conservative like Sarah Palin might just be enough to prevent them from staying home on election day.

The press, as usual, began scrutinizing Sarah Palin and the more stuff that was released, the more it seemed like John McCain's Vice Presidential choice might have been a mistake. It was revealed that she was under investigation by the authorities in Alaska for firing a state trooper who had refused to fire her former brother in law. It was revealed that her husband, Todd Palin, was a member of a secessionist movement that believed Alaska should be separate from the United States. It was revealed that her 17year old daughter was pregnant for her 18 year old boyfriend.

She was attacked almost daily by the press and they even started to question her qualification and readiness to be Vice President, a job that required the holder to also be ready to be President, in case anything happened to the President.

I thought some of the attacks were unnecessary and

frankly over the top. Some, I believe were legitimate criticisms or questions.

The issue surrounding Todd Palin's membership and Sarah Palin's support for the Alaska Independence Party came as a bit of a surprise to me because I believed something like that would have been vetted by the McCain campaign and not become such a major issue. I don't like taking the word of the press for it, so I decided to do my own research.

The Alaska Independence Party was formed by Hal Volger in 1978 to push for a vote on whether Alaskans want to remain a part of America. Today, the party's website states that its goal is one of four options:

-   Remain a territory;

-   Remain a separate and independent nation;

-   Accept commonwealth status;

-   Become a state.

The argument of the McCain campaign was that there was no evidence that Todd or Sarah Palin supported secession, but I think if you join a party with these sorts of clearly articulated goals, you don't need to declare publicly or otherwise that you support the goals. Membership of the party, I think is proof enough. But then again, Todd Palin may have been a member to support the other issues on the party's platform, without necessarily subscribing to the secessionist goals. He could have been the dissenting voice on the secessionist movement, although we'll probably never know for sure. Of course the extent of his involvement with the party was played down by the

McCain campaign, the Republican National Party and my favorite news station, FOX News. Even though I thought this was a non-issue after my research, I found it curious, disingenuous and hypocritical that FOX News was playing it down. This was after all, the same news channel that criticized African-American preachers' black consciousness preaching as advocating secession.

The issue surrounding Sarah Palin's teenage daughter's pregnancy, I thought went too far though. It was and should have been a family issue, although I thought the Republican and conservative argument that Bristol and her boyfriend planned to get married in the future was a lame defense. They should have simply left it at, "Every family has its challenges and less than ideal situations. This is ours".

In both the secession and the Bristol Palin pregnancy issues, I could understand the arguments of hypocrisy leveled by the public and some in the media. The Republicans and conservative media have always believed that they have the monopoly on issues like family values, morality and Christian values. Obviously, a parent can only train a child and then pray that they become better people. I don't think Sarah Palin or any other parent would be happy at the fact that her teenage, unmarried daughter was pregnant. But I can bet everything I own that if Obama had a 17 year old pregnant daughter, the "outrage" from the "conservatives" would have been deafening. It is this kind of hypocrisy that makes right thinking people so weary of the Republican Party. What did Obama do about the controversy? He said he believes Sarah Palin or any other candidate's family should be off limits and refused further comment on the issue. Show me a Republican who would have said that if the tables were turned and I will show you someone who is baffled by his/her party's hypocrisy.

What I admired about Sarah Palin was the graciousness with which she took all the criticism. She never commented on the issues and instead concentrated on campaigning and getting ready for the Republican convention. I was so impressed with her response (or non-response) that I actually started to believe that McCain had actually made a brilliant choice. I believed she was a different kind of Republican politician and feared that this might appeal to a lot of Independents, which would be a problem for Obama.

My attention was now on the Republican convention and I was looking forward to three things;

- John McCain's speech;

- Sarah Palin's speech;

- What President Bush and Vice President Dick Cheney would have to say (They was going to be absent from the convention, which was unprecedented).

I was especially looking forward to hearing President Bush because of the care with which the McCain campaign had made sure that the two men were not seen together. It was incredible to think that a sitting President could be so unpopular even in his own party, that his appearance at the convention could become an embarrassment. His non-appearance had made official something everyone already knew; he had become a liability to the Republican Party.

The devastation caused by Hurricane Gustav meant that the convention or at least the beginning had to be scaled back. When it eventually began in earnest, the speeches crystallized exactly why the Republican Party is where it is politically.

Speech after speech, Obama and the Democrats were pilloried with all sorts of criticism, both true and untrue. None of the speeches were memorable in the sense that it was the same old Republican attacks. However, Rudy Giulliani's speech was quite interesting. I think in the few minutes he spent on stage, he showed exactly why he ran such a poor campaign, considering the fact that he was the early front-runner in the race to be the Republican nominee.

When I watched Sarah Palin's speech, all the admiration and respect I had for her evaporated. The viciousness of her attacks came as a complete surprise to me and in a sudden foreboding moment of clarity, I realized that Sarah Palin was just like most Republican politicians. The ferocity of her attacks showed that she would now revel in the "attack dog" role that is usually the terrain of Presidential running mates.

John McCain's speech, was unsurprisingly unmemorable. At the end of the convention, I thought back at the tone of the speeches and knew that the race was about to take a very nasty turn.

THE LAST 60 DAYS

Sarah Palin's addition to the Republican Presidential ticket was a boost for a campaign that seemed amateurish and headed for a big loss in November. Suddenly, John McCain rallies were drawing the kinds of crowds that had hitherto been more commonplace with Obama rallies. McCain's poll numbers actually began to rise dramatically and he eventually overtook Obama! This got me so worried that I actually started to think that the unthinkable might happen. This election was tailor made for the Democrats. John McCain was not even supposed to be polling close to Barack Obama, much less, polling ahead of him. President Bush and Vice President Cheney had messed things up so badly for the Republican Party that they were practically guaranteed to lose in November. From the economy, to Iraq, to unemployment, to gas prices, to allegations of abuse of power, to politicizing the Justice Department. There were so many things the voters were angry at the current Republican administration for, that it was almost impossible for another Republican President to win the White House in 2008. I knew it was not because John McCain was seen as a different kind of Republican because throughout the campaign, he had become like any other Republican. As much as I tried not to, I had to admit that the resurgence of John McCain's campaign was down to the arrival of Sarah Palin. Obama had always been said to have rock star status. Sarah Palin had become the Republican rock star. She became an inspiration to working women because of her ability to juggle her role as Governor with being a mother of five children, including a special needs son. My confidence that disgruntled Hillary Clinton supporters would still end up voting for Obama, began to waiver. To make matters worse, John McCain held a fundraiser in Chicago and raised $5million! In Obama's backyard! The race had been turned on its head and I was not sure if it would change again.

When I heard that CBS reporter, Katie Couric was going to interview Sarah Palin, I could not wait to watch it. The only time I had heard her speak was at rallies and I wanted to see a more one on one format. I had seen her interview with FOX News's Sean Hannity, but the questions were so obviously leading that it was almost sad to watch. I had watched Katie Couric a few times and she did not strike me as someone who would patronize Sarah Palin or anybody else.

Nothing, and I mean that literally, prepared me for what I saw in the interviews. Day after day, as clips from the interview were released, I stared incredulously at the screen and said out loud, "You've got to be kidding me!"

Never had I seen a Presidential level candidate so unaware of what is going in the country and in the world. Her answers to the questions showed a complete lack of understanding of the issues facing Americans and the rest of the world. Her responses were worse than how a layman would have answered the questions. When asked about one of the most important case laws in US history, Roe v Wade, it was so obvious that she knew little or nothing about the case. I'm not licensed to practice law in America, neither am I a US citizen, but I'm sure my response would have been way better than hers. When asked about US Supreme Court decisions, she talked for a few minutes about the Supreme Court, but could not mention one decision! The most shocking answer came when she was asked what she meant by saying she had foreign policy experience due to Alaska's proximity to Russia. She said, "It's very important when you consider National security issues with Russia. If Putin rears his head and comes into the airspace of the United States of America, where do they go? It's Alaska. It's just right over the border. It is from Alaska that we send those out who keep an eye on this very powerful nation, Russia, because they are right there, they are right next to our State." When asked if she had been involved in any negotiations with the Russians, she stated that Alaska and Russia have trade missions back and forth!

I could not believe what I was hearing. I called up my brother, my cousin and a good friend of mine, who is a fellow scholar of International Law. I asked each of them if they saw the interview and specifically the part about Russia. When they said they did, I asked, "Was she serious or was she joking?" I watched it again and asked my wife to watch it with me this time. When she finished, she asked, "Was that a real interview or was it Punkd?"

How on earth does Russia's proximity to Alaska qualify as foreign policy experience? If that is the case, every Governor of a State that borders a country automatically has foreign policy experience. I know all politicians try to embellish their records, but what Sarah Palin said was not just ridiculous, it was irresponsible. I thought her comments were insulting to the voters' intelligence. A State does not have to border a country for trade missions to exist. In Nigeria, most States have trade missions to other countries; I don't think the Governors of any of these States would claim to have foreign policy experience as a result.

While trying to get over the shock, I heard one of my favorite CNN personalities, Fareed Zakaria, talking about the interview with Wolf Blitzer. The way he broke it down was so incisive that I went to watch the interview again, just to put what Mr Zakaria was saying into perspective. His most interesting comment was that the scariest answer in Sarah Palin's interview was not the question on foreign policy. According to him, the foreign policy answer was funny, rather than scary. He said the scariest answer was the one about the economy. I could understand exactly where he was coming from. My shock at the foreign policy answer had made me completely forget her other answers. The US was in the middle of the worst financial crisis since the great depression. One of the oldest investment banks in the country had just declared bankruptcy. The Government was in the middle of negotiating a $700billion dollar bailout package to stimulate the economy. When Sarah Palin was asked about the bailout package, she talked for almost five minutes, but nothing she said had anything to do with the bailout! When pressed further, her answers were even worse. One thing was made abundantly clear during that interview. I'll use Fareed Zakaria's words to illustrate what that was.

He said, "It's not that she did not know the right answers, it's that she clearly did not understand the questions!" Fareed Zakaria could very easily have taken the words right out of my mouth, because watching the interviews, it was so clear that she did not have a clue about most of the questions she was asked. The ones she did answer seemed more like rehearsed speeches.

How on earth can anyone be running for Vice President of the United States of America and not understand the issues surrounding the most serious financial crisis in recent American history? The opposing argument would be along the lines of, "Well, she's not running for President, so as Vice President, she can study and learn the issues, in case she needs to assume the Presidency". Fair enough, but what if she needs to assume the Presidency before she has finished learning and studying all she needs to? Considering the fact that John McCain is a 72 year old man, with a history of illnesses, his Vice President's readiness to assume the Presidency should have been taken a lot more seriously than I believe it was. At a time of economic uncertainty, if John McCain is elected President and is incapacitated, does anyone seriously think Sarah Palin would be the best person to sort the mess out? I had heard the theory that John McCain picked Sarah Palin, just because she was a woman. I had even subscribed to that view, admittedly without proof. The Katie Couric interview provided that proof. If that was not the reason, I could not come up with any other reason. If he was bent on picking a woman, was he trying to say that Sarah Palin was the most qualified woman in the Republican Party? I'm 100% certain that there were better qualified women in the party than Sarah Palin. If he was bent on picking a State Governor, was he trying to say that Sarah Palin was the most qualified Governor in the Republican Party? I'm 100% certain that there were better qualified Governors in the Republican Party.

Anyway I looked at it, one thing was clear; John McCain's pick of Sarah Palin was a mistake. She might have excited the Republican base of the party, but she had scared the very people the Republican Presidential ticket needed to appeal to; Independents. Call me naïve, but I don't think John McCain needed a candidate to appeal to the Republican base. Regardless of their dislike or mistrust for John McCain, there is no way they would vote for Obama on election day. What John McCain needed was a Republican with conservative credentials, who also appealed to Independents and even Democrats. That choice may not excite the party base into the kind of frenzy that Sarah Palin did, but at least it would ensure that they did not decide to stay home on November 4. True, finding such a Republican would probably have been difficult, but considering the fact that McCain wrapped up the nomination in March, he had the advantage of starting a more thorough search than Obama. John McCain always accused Barack Obama of not putting the country first, but I think in both candidates' choices of running mate, it was obvious that John McCain did not put the country first. If he truly believed in his heart that he put his country first when he picked Sarah Palin, then he probably has the most flawed judgment of any Presidential candidate I have ever seen.

With the revelations of the Katie Couric interview, I could not wait for the Vice Presidential debate. If

Sarah Palin could not handle an interview with one of the less confrontational journalists, how exactly did she expect to handle a 90minute debate with one of the most experienced senators in the country?

Before the Vice Presidential debate, the first Presidential debate would come first. I wondered how the debate was going to fare. It was supposed to be a debate on foreign policy and National Security, which were supposed to be John McCain's strong points. However, the economic crisis meant a portion of the debate was going to be on the economy. For a candidate who had admitted to not knowing a lot about the economy, I'm sure he would have preferred to have a debate only on foreign policy.

Two days before the debate, he did something else that further proved to me that his judgment is not just strange, but scary. Scary, because if the judgment of the President of the world's most powerful country is so flawed, the world could be a far more dangerous place than it already is.

The White House was in the middle of negotiating a massive $700billion economic stimulus package with Congress. The House of Representatives was due to vote on it, but it was not looking good. John McCain then decided he would suspend his campaign and fly to Washington to try to rescue the package! He also called for a postponement of the first Presidential debate. It was supposed to be one his "putting the country first" moments. When I first heard the news, I thought, is McCain kidding? Suspending his campaign and calling for a debate postponement! It was so obvious that this was a publicity stunt that I wondered how McCain and his advisers did not see it. When Obama was asked about it, he said, "This is exactly the time when America needs to hear from the person, who in approximately 40days will be responsible for this mess". When asked if he would consider postponing the debate, he said, "A President should be able to do more than one thing at once".

This is what I have so admired about Barack Obama. His ideas are so simple that I sometimes wonder how no one says these things before he does. If John McCain wants to be President, he would need to learn that crises don't hold on for one to finish before the next one starts. About 10 different things, all important, could happen at the same time; if it was impossible to suspend one or more to concentrate on another, what would a President McCain do then?

McCain eventually flew back for the debate, since he felt enough progress had been made in the talks for the economic rescue package. This back and forth behavior by McCain led to TV ads from Obama that McCain is erratic! The worst part of the whole episode was that his flight to save the day was as unsuccessful as it was a complete waste of time because The House of Representatives, led by the Republicans, rejected the package. The way I saw it, John McCain had just put himself out there and shown the whole world that he had little or no influence with his own party because if he had flown all the way to Washington, held face to face meetings with his party members and still ended up with nothing, then he cannot be that influential in his party. That's a very sad reality, considering the fact that as the Presidential nominee, he's effectively the leader of the party.

On the day or rather night of the debate, I set my alarm to 2am as usual and went to bed. When my alarm went off, I got up, stretched and made my way to the stairs. About two seconds later, I was downstairs. Not because I was running down the stairs, but because I fell from the top all the way down! My wife heard the noise and woke up. She switched on the lights and said, "Why did you leave the lights off? I don't care who's debating, if you break your legs, it's not worth it!" I replied, "You were sleeping and I didn't want to wake you. I'm sure the debate will be fantastic. Sorry to have woken you, why don't you go back to bed?" She replied, "I'm watching it with you so you don't fall over the TV!"

The debate turned out to be quite interesting. McCain obviously tried to paint Obama as naïve and inexperienced about foreign policy, while Obama tried to paint McCain as just another George Bush. I thought Obama was lucky in the sense that he did not have to try that hard to link McCain to George Bush. John McCain, intentionally or otherwise, was doing a pretty good job of that all by himself with statements like, "We'll be in Iraq for 100 years if we have to", which he sought to explain during the debate.

At a time when almost the whole United States and even the Iraqis want the US out, John McCain's 100year statement was exactly what they did not want to hear. It sounded to me like the sort of thing that George Bush would say. He had actually said something like that before, except that his version was along the lines of, "We will stay in Iraq for as long as necessary". Not quite 100years, but I guess "as long as necessary" is close enough.

Statements like, "The fundamentals of the economy

are strong", which he also sought to clarify during the debate. Even his chief economic adviser implied the crisis is not that bad when he said, "The US is suffering from a mental recession and we have become a nation of whiners!" It does not take an economist to be able to tell that the fundamentals of the US economy are anything but strong. I know McCain has admitted in the past to not knowing a lot about the economy, but that "fundamentals" statement was still a baffling thing to say! It sounded to me like the sort of thing that George Bush would say. He had actually said something like that before, except that his version was along the lines of, "This economy has made great progress".

What economy is he talking about? The same economy in which unemployment is skyrocketing every month? The same economy where people are losing their homes everyday? The same economy in which banks have no more money to lend and some are even closing down? The same economy that requires almost a trillion dollars stimulus package from the Government? The economy that has been so badly damaged that it has affected so many other countries?

FOX News analysts seem to take issue with that last point because they feel that the global economic recession has nothing to do with the US. When British Prime Minister, Gordon Brown, announced the British stimulus package, he noted that the recession had started in the US and spread to other countries. One FOX News reporter, Bill Hemmer, was so upset at that statement that I could see the veins in his head bobbing when he was shouting for the British to take responsibility for their own financial mess and stop blaming America. What I think Bill Hemmer failed to understand or chose to ignore is that the US economy drives the world's economy, so any problems with the US economy automatically affects every other country. I think that's just simple logic.

Back to the debate, John McCain's embrace of President Bush's policies were so surprising that sometimes, I wondered if he was aware that George Bush is the most unpopular President in recent US history and one of the most hated figures in the world. I wondered how John McCain could be aware of these facts and still say the kinds of things he was saying. It occurred to me that if John McCain was elected President, America would have another President who wantonly ignores the facts when they are not in line with his policies or ideas. I say this because I have a very hard time understanding how, in the midst of what is the worst financial crisis in our lifetime, anyone, never mind a US Presidential candidate, can say that the fundamentals of the economy are strong! Americans and the rest of the world are so tired of President Bush that January 20 2009 could not come sooner. Yet, John McCain expects to win the election by effectively vowing to continue George Bush's policies! Using the debate to explain why these policies were best for America was almost sad, but definitely scary to watch. What was obvious to me in that debate was that John McCain kept trying to shift the talking points to foreign policy and National Security, because that was supposedly his area of expertise. My opinion was that a candidate who wants to continue most of President Bush's failed foreign policies, cannot be much of an expert. But the fact of the matter was that the economy was the most important issue to Americans and not Iraq, Al Qaeda,

Afghanistan, Iran, Syria, Cuba or North Korea. One of his advisers even went as far as saying a terror attack on the US at the moment would be a great advantage for him.

After the debate, polls showed that Obama convincingly won the debate, as he was the candidate who showed a greater mastery of the issues that were most important to Americans, most of which centered around economic policies. A CNN poll showed that 51% believed Obama won, to McCain's 38%. I decided to amuse myself a little bit and switched over to FOX News to see what their polls were saying and also listen to the post debate analysis. As usual, I was not disappointed. According to FOX News polls, 84% believed McCain won, to Obama 14%! I was rolling on the floor with laughter when I saw this. I said aloud, "Are they talking about the same debate or a different one?" Do they really believe that or do they just do stuff like this anyway? Even if Obama showed up for the debate and kept quiet throughout the 90minutes, McCain could not have won by 84%! FOX News is just an amazing news channel. I have never and I mean never seen a more biased news channel in my life. The venom that is spewed out daily on this channel is reminiscent of a TV channel in a country where a dictator exists. But then again, a TV station in a country with a dictator is better because at least, they are forced to pander to the ruler's views. But FOX News is an American TV station! The bias is mind boggling. Obama is constantly insulted and called all sorts of names by FOX News reporters and analysts, that I wonder how anyone takes them seriously. I once heard a FOX News analyst call Obama a baby-killer because he does not support a ban on abortion.

What the analyst did not mention was that Obama's actual view on abortion is that it's a tragic situation that nobody wants, but he believes people who are pro-life and pro-choice should be able to find common ground in order to reduce unwanted pregnancies by providing options for adoption and helping single mothers who decide to keep their babies.

The Vice Presidential debate was held a few days after the first Presidential debate and I noticed that Sarah Palin had kept a low profile. She was supposed to be getting ready for the debate. I just kept wondering to myself how she was going to deal with 90minutes with Joe Biden, who has a reputation for being talkative and sometimes brash. She had obviously been in debates before, since she was a Governor, but not anything on this level and not against a veteran. Even my wife said she was going to wait up to watch this debate!

When the debate started, I was almost cringing at what she might say. But as the time went, I felt, she was actually doing okay. Not okay in the sense that she answered the questions well, but okay in the sense that she sounded better than she did during the Katie Couric interviews. She started doing her "folksy" talk, which I thought was just silly, but that is supposed to be part of her appeal, so good for her. One thing was still obvious to me though, as the debate went on; Sarah Palin was clearly not ready to be Vice President and by extension, President. The only questions she answered were the ones that had to do with energy policy, which was not surprising, considering the fact that she is Governor of Alaska, an oil producing State. All the other questions she was asked, she kept running around in circles, most likely rehearsed answers, and they ended up having little or no bearing to the question asked. My wife turned to me and said, "Is it me or is she not answering any of the questions?"

Sarah Palin must have noticed everyone knew she was not answering the questions, so she said, "I know I'm not answering the questions the way you want me to, but I'd rather talk to the American people directly." And then she gave a wink and continued with the "folksy" talk! I thought, does this woman realize she is running for Vice President of the United States of America? I have nothing against folksiness, but in her case it seemed more like a ploy to distract from the fact that she was not answering the questions.

At the end of the debate, I switched to FOX News to hear what they had to say and again, I was not disappointed! The analysts were salivating at how "brilliantly" Sarah Palin had handled herself during the debate. According to one, she stood toe to toe with a 30year Senate veteran and even came out on top! Even though I had come to expect stuff like that from FOX News, that still took me by surprise. In their view, the debate was a success for Sarah Palin.

I actually agreed with FOX News that the debate was a success for Sarah Palin, but not because she did well or answered the questions she was asked in a way that gives the impression that she understood the issues. I thought the debate was a success for Sarah Palin, because she succeeded in not looking or sounding as funny, scary and clueless as she had looked during the Katie Couric interviews. She succeeded in doing this and even managed to sound likeable without being too scary. If this was a measure of success, then she succeeded. That measure pointed out one thing, though; Sarah Palin was clearly not ready to Vice President and by extension, President of the United States of America.

Polls after the debate showed mostly that Joe Biden won, but also showed that some people were turned off by Sarah Palin's folksiness, while some liked it because it showed she was one of them. I was very worried about people liking her folksiness. I thought, hasn't America learnt its lesson? Don't Americans remember what happened the last time a folksy and likeable Governor was entrusted with the welfare of the country? The last eight years happened! When George Bush first ran for President in 2000, one of the ways he appealed to voters was because of his folksiness and Texas charm. According to CNN's Jack Cafferty, "In 2000, we made the mistake of voting for someone we would like to have a beer with."

The McCain-Palin stock rose considerably after the Vice Presidential debate and their rally sizes continued to swell more and more. Unfortunately for them though, this coincided with the meltdown of major US financial institutions. Polls showed that Obama was starting to open up a gap on McCain because most voters saw Obama as being the candidate capable of dealing with the economic mess. Obama's attack on McCain as being erratic had struck a chord, as the last thing people worried about their jobs and losing their homes wanted was an erratic President who had admitted that the economy was not his strongest and point and still insisted that the fundamentals of the economy are strong. McCain had been inconsistent and changed his positions on the economy too many times to convince voters that he had a clear grasp of what was going on and that he had a definite plan to sort the mess out. The only thing that was clear was that he intended to continue what President Bush had been doing. Since the economy was in a free-fall and had been for most of Bush's Presidency, to win the election, McCain would have to come up with a reason why Americans should vote for an extension of the Bush economic plan.

Obama on the other hand had been consistent throughout and had remained as calm as ever while the financial crisis unraveled. This kind of calm and thoughtful approach suddenly made people who were hitherto skeptical about him start to look at him differently. This, and of course the economic meltdown, I believe were responsible for his rapid increase in poll numbers. McCain had also shot himself in the foot by his answer to a question by Pastor Rick Warren during the Civil Forum on the Presidency in August. He was asked how much a person should be earning to be considered rich/middle class. His answer was, "Anyone making above $5million a year!"

That was an incredible thing to say, considering the fact that 90%-95% of Americans make $250000 and below a year. This answer fed into one of Obama's criticisms of McCain; that he was out of touch with the issues Americans face everyday.

The McCain campaign decided to change tactics again, but this time I could not have predicted the change of tactics that was coming.

A McCain adviser said if they keep talking about

the economy, they would lose the election. So instead of talking about the economy, instead the McCain campaign would talk about Obama's ties to radicals, step up the attacks on his inexperience and paint him as a risky choice! When I heard this, I said, "Are these people joking?" To have the audacity to say that in public was astounding. The fate of the economy was obviously the most serious concern for most Americans and what the man who wants to be the next President wants to do, in the middle of the greatest financial crisis in recent history, is talk about his opponent's ties to radicals? It was beyond belief. Polls showed that even the most vocal Obama critics thought this move had ensured that McCain would lose the election.

Even though the McCain campaign had vowed to step up their attacks on Obama's character, judgment and relationships, I was still caught off guard by the ferocity and depths of the attacks that came next.

During a campaign event in Colorado, Sarah Palin said of Obama, "This is not a man who sees America as we do, the greatest force of good in the world. This is a man who sees America as so imperfect that he's palling around with terrorists who would target their own country".

She was referring to his "relationship" with former domestic terrorist, turned distinguished professor, William (Bill) Ayers.

Bill Ayers was a member of the radical group, the weather underground, which targeted public buildings in a campaign of bombings around the US in the 1960s. I think it is important to note that while Bill Ayers was engaging in all this craziness, Obama was an eight year old kid! His connection to Bill Ayers was as a result of their membership of the board of directors of the Chicago Annenberg Challenge, an organization that helps secure funding for local schools. They also served on the board of the Woods Foundation, an anti-poverty organization. Obama and Bill Ayers also lived in the same neighborhood in Chicago. The McCain campaign's version was that the relationship between the two was much deeper than that, but there has been no proof to substantiate that claim. Major news outlets had investigated the ties between Obama and Ayers during the primaries and discovered nothing out of the ordinary.

What scared me about Sarah Palin's comments wasn't just the fact that she was linking Obama to a domestic terrorist, it was in saying that Obama does not see America as "we" do. I knew statements like that had the dangerous potential of re-igniting the flame of divisiveness and hatred that American has tried for decades to move forward from. By implying that Obama does not share American values, the only thing that could come out of that was a deeper polarization at a time when the country needed to unite. She continued this line of attacks and before long, her supporters began saying exactly the same thing. FOX News also got in on it and began talking about Bill Ayers every night. It was such a sad thing to watch. How could this be what some consider important at a time when people are losing their jobs, losing their homes, shutting down their businesses, and financial institutions are going bankrupt? Playing the politics of fear is something Republicans are generally very good at. Karl Rove had used it so effectively with the George Bush campaign in 2004, that I could not help but ask myself if it could actually work this time. But the more I thought about it, the more something very interesting started to occur to me.

In 2008, the Republicans and Democrats were actually both playing the politics of fear. Both Obama and McCain were playing the politics of fear, but in two very different ways and using two very different substances.

John McCain and the Republicans were playing the politics of fear by trying to make the voters afraid of Obama, both as a person and as a politician. They were also throwing in his relationships as proof of a lack of good judgment of Obama's side. As pointed out in the earlier chapter, the general idea was to paint Obama as a risky choice for President.

On the other side, Obama and the Democrats were playing the politics of fear by trying to convince voters that the present economic problems would never be resolved and could even get worse if John McCain is elected President, since his economic policy mirrors President Bush's. As pointed out in the earlier chapter, the general idea was to tie John McCain and George Bush together.

The difference between the two strategies was that while John McCain's was predicated on inciting (knowingly or otherwise) divisiveness, hate and intolerance and trying to use polarization to get votes, Obama's was predicated on the fact that the economic policies being proposed by John McCain were almost exactly the same as President Bush's. I could actually argue that Obama's strategy is a legitimate policy issue and called for legitimate policy debate. Part of the job of the US President is to set economic policy and the one set by President Bush has been an obviously bad one. The one being proposed by

John McCain was the same. Obama disagreed with these and explained to voters why his was the better idea and why they needed to be afraid of McCain's.

On the other hand, McCain's politics of fear had absolutely nothing to do with policy differences. Rather than talking about why the voters should choose his policies over Obama's he was talking about why Obama's was wrong without explaining why they should expect different results, if he enacts the same policies as President Bush. Not understanding the economy is one thing, but I sometimes got the feeling that either John McCain did not think the economy was as bad as reported or he did know and decided since he did not know how to fix it, he would make the race about anything but the economy.

I knew a lot of voters were still unsure about Obama, and I thought all the nonsense about William Ayers might even make them that more unsure about him. But when I looked at the polls, what I saw made me heave a huge sigh of relief. Not only had Obama's lead increased, majority of the people polled actually believed the William Ayers line of attack was unnecessary and was turning voters off the McCain-Palin ticket. The polls also showed that women were being turned off by Sarah Palin's incendiary language and constant attacks on Obama. I thought this would make McCain and Sarah Palin especially, ease up on the attacks, but if anything, the attacks only intensified.

Next, the McCain campaign decided to go after the Association of Community Organizers for Reform Now (ACORN), for what he called, "one of the greatest frauds in voter history, maybe destroying the fabric of democracy".

What John McCain did not seem to understand or chose to ignore is that there is a huge difference between voter fraud and voter registration fraud. Before going into that, I'll start from the beginning.

ACORN is a group that advocates for mostly low income earners on issues, like housing, health care, and voter registration, and other social issues. As a former community organizer, Obama had obviously done work with them in the past. He had also paid ACORN to help with a "get out the vote" effort (not voter registration) during the 2008 Democratic primaries.

In the last couple of years, the voter registration department of ACORN had problems because some employees were submitting voter registration forms with details of non-existent people. This became apparent when ACORN tried contacting the non-existent people as part of the registration process. ACORN itself alerted the authorities to this problem and some ACORN employees were subsequently indicted. However, the authorities have repeatedly stated that they have found no evidence that this voter registration fraud was being perpetrated in order to commit voter fraud. Instead, it was a case of employees of ACORN's voter registration department, trying to get paid for not doing their jobs. They got paid (some as little as $8 per hour) to find people who are not registered to vote and submit the details to ACORN, who would then contact and register them. For whatever reason, some of these employees made up names of unregistered voters and submitted them. None of the fictitious names have ever appeared at any polling booth. As the prosecutor investigating the ACORN affair said, "The only thing ACORN is guilty of, is a lack of proper oversight of its employees".

By the way, the prosecutor who made that statement is a Republican.

Even in light of all these, the McCain campaign continued with its Obama/ACORN link. FOX News did multiple reports on the "relationship between Obama and ACORN.

Sometimes, I find it hard to believe or even understand how people can so easily disregard readily available facts, just because it does not fit into whatever case they are trying to make. I'm certain that if I had access to the research I did on the ACORN issue, the McCain campaign and FOX News probably had better access, but chose to ignore the facts because an Obama/ACORN link seemed like a more productive thread to follow. Of course, what they did not mention was that not long ago, John McCain gave a speech, complimenting ACORN on their good work!

This line of attacks continued all the way into the next debate.

The town hall setting for the next debate was supposed to favor McCain, since most of his campaigns had been in this format. The candidates would take questions from the audience and the moderator, Tom Brokaw, would also ask questions.

The debate followed the usual tactic of both candidates trying to draw a sharp contrast between their policies. It was obvious that Obama was more in command of what was going on with the economy. Not long into the debate, McCain attempted to make a comeback, but it backfired very badly.

He claimed that Obama had announced that he would attack Pakistan if elected President. He cited this as irresponsible talk by Obama and one of the reasons why voting for Obama would be a dangerous risk. I thought to myself, Obama did not say that. Just as I was trying to remember what Obama actually said about Pakistan, he himself clarified what he had said. He never said he was going to attack Pakistan or any other country. What he did say was that if the US has reliable intelligence that Al Qaeda leaders are hiding somewhere in Pakistan and the Pakistani Government is unable or unwilling to go after them, then the US should. He then mentioned John McCain's singing songs about bombing Iran and calling for the annihilation of North Korea. I wondered aloud if McCain really thinks peoples' memories are that short. Here he was, talking about talking responsibly, yet he was singing, "Bomb, Bomb, Bomb Iran". The worst part of it was his response to Obama's chiding. He claimed when he was singing that song, he was just joking! I think it would have been best if he did not say anything at all. How can you expect to achieve peace with a country that you made jokes about bombing? Are the lives of the innocent Iranians who would die in the crossfire worth just a laugh? How many people find songs about bombing another country funny?

What I don't think John McCain realized is that so many of his statements sounded too much like the kind of stuff George Bush would say. That was why I made the point earlier that Obama did not have to do much to link

McCain to Bush, since McCain was doing a very good job of that all by himself.

After the debate, most polls again showed Obama had convincingly won. To amuse myself, I decided to switch to FOX news. Again, I was not disappointed! This time FOX News polls showed that 86% believed McCain had won the debate! I just could not stop laughing. How do these people do it? Do they just make themselves feel better by coming with these ridiculous data? I noticed my good friend, Sean Hannity, was having a heated debate with Obama's communications director, Richard Gibbs. Richard Gibbs so cornered Sean Hannity that Hannity was obviously angry and agitated. By now, I was on the floor and holding my stomach because I had never seen Sean Hannity in such a position. I actually felt sorry for him at one point, but then I thought this is exactly how he makes people feel when he invites them on his show and then shouts and insults them. Seeing him that flustered was refreshing and actually very funny.

The third and final debate was about a week after the last one and I was not even sure I was going to be able to watch it because my wife was due to give birth at any moment. So all that week, I was not as attentive to what was going on as I had been previously, although I still checked CNN ticker and the Cafferty file everyday.

My lovely little girl was born on the day of the final debate, October 15. I spent the whole day in hospital and by the time I got home, I was too happy and too tired to stay up to watch the debate, but recorded it anyway. I woke very early the next morning and decided to watch the debate first before checking the internet because I wanted to form my opinion without any distortions from the talking heads. Prior to the debate, Obama had challenged McCain to be brave enough to bring up the Bill Ayers issue to his face instead of always talking about it on the campaign trail. I think that challenge pretty much guaranteed that McCain would bring up Bill Ayers during the campaign.

McCain did bring it up and I was actually glad he did, because it gave Obama a chance to clarify on the record his relationship or non-relationship with Bill Ayers (even though he had done that a number of times in the last year). I loved what Obama said to McCain after clarifying the Bill Ayers issue. He said, "Bill Ayers has been at the forefront of your campaign for the last few weeks. I think that says more about your campaign than it says about me".

The main talking point of the debate was the multiple references to an Ohio plumber named, Samuel Joseph Wurzelbacher, nicknamed Joe the Plumber. He had met Obama during a campaign rally in Ohio and told him that he had saved up enough money to buy the plumbing business he had worked in for a long time, but was worried that Obama's tax plan meant he would be paying more than he is at the moment. Obama explained his tax plan to Joe and the rationale behind his paying more than he was at the moment. Finally, he said, "......my attitude is that if the economy is good from the bottom up, it will be good for everybody...........and I think when you spread the wealth around, it's good for everybody".

John McCain pounced on this and spoke directly to Joe to assure him that his plumbing business would not be taxed extra under his tax plan. Obama then spoke directly to Joe to assure him that his business would not suffer as a result of his tax plan. And so it went. Joe the Plumber was mentioned quite a number of times throughout the debate as a symbol for working class Americans.

The debate was another reminder of the stark differences between the two candidates. One obviously had and showed respect for his opponent, while the other was almost condescending to his opponent. One seemed to be interested in finding solutions to deal with the crises engulfing the country, while the other seemed bent on questioning his opponent's ideas and offering the same ideas that had gotten the country into the problems in the first place. That was why when McCain pointed that out that he was not George Bush and that if Obama wanted to run against Bush, he should have run four years ago, Obama's response was that their plans are so similar that it is very easy to mistake one for the other.

At the end of the debate, the polls showed again that Obama had won convincingly. Some polls however showed that the winner of the debate was Joe the Plumber!

After the last debate, I knew two things with a reasonable degree of certainty;

1. Barack Obama was going to win the election;

2. Joe the plumber was going to become an overnight celebrity.

As I suspected, Joe the Plumber became an instant star. Journalists camped outside his home to interview him and it soon emerged that he would be campaigning with John McCain. When I watched his first rally with McCain and Palin, I was disappointed that instead of talking about the tax and economic issues that got him on the campaign trail in the first place, he indulged in the same silly negativity with which the Republican ticket was running its campaign.

During a campaign stop, a voter told Joe the Plumber that he believed a vote for Obama was a vote for the death of Israel! I'm not sure if I was more shocked by the question or by Joe's response when he said he knew what the man was talking about and agreed with him. Joe the Plumber was asked what he meant by this during an interview with Neil Cavuto of FOX News. Joe said he would leave the viewers to make their own decision as to what he meant. Neil Cavuto was visibly disturbed by the whole episode and actually said some of the stuff that gets thrown around by the McCain campaign is just scary sometimes. If someone from FOX News of all places was that appalled at some of the McCain campaign tactics, I think that says a lot about the kind of campaign McCain was running.

What was the McCain campaign's response to this? Intensified attacks against Obama! It seemed to me like McCain had figured out that he could not win the election by convincing Americans that he was the right person for the job, so he resorted to trying to convince the voters that Obama was the wrong man for the job.

As a result, the character and associations attacks continued and most came from Sarah Palin. The only time she sounded confident was when she was on the attack. The attacks began to get as nasty as I had believed it would get because of all the inflammatory rhetoric coming from the McCain-Palin campaign. At campaign rallies, people were openly yelling, "kill him!" and terrorist, whenever Obama's name was mentioned. At one of McCain's town hall meetings, people in the crowd were shaking with anger and rage at the fact that all the polls were predicting a big Obama win on November 4. They still chanted the "kill him" and "terrorist" whenever Obama's name was mentioned, but this time the rage with which these chants came was unprecedented in a US Presidential campaign history. I read about a Pastor who put a sign outside his church saying, "Obama, Osama – Are they brothers?" A Pastor put that outside his church! What kind of message does such a Pastor preach in his church? I honestly felt very sorry for his congregation.

In another attack, an African-American radio talk show host, James Harris begged McCain to keep up the negative campaigning by continuing to talk about Bill Ayers and also bring up Reverend Wright!

In yet another attack, a woman said she does not trust Obama because he's an Arab! Even though McCain corrected the woman, I felt it was too little too late.

Obama was called a socialist for his "spread the wealth around" response to Joe the Plumber's question.

In the middle of all this, I saw what I thought was one of the silliest TV interviews I had ever seen. It was an interview Joe Biden gave Barbara West of WFTV in Florida. First she asked Joe Biden if he was not embarrassed that Barack Obama had ties with ACORN; next, she asked him if Obama was not being a Marxist for telling Joe the Plumber that wealth needs to be spread around. To defend the second point, she cited a recent poll in which 84% of Americans did not want Government to spread their money around or redistribute it. Finally, she asked if Biden's comments that should Obama be elected

President, he would be tested early in his Presidency, meant that the days of the US as a superpower were over. At a point Joe Biden actually had to ask her if she was joking! Consequently, the Obama campaign refused any further interviews with the news station and cancelled an interview with Joe Biden's wife. There was outrage from "conservative" quarters, cheer led by the always entertaining FOX News. They wondered why Joe Biden was angry at being asked "tough questions"!

First of all, the issue regarding ACORN had already been dismissed as a non-story by the person who had the responsibility for investigating the voter registration fraud, Republican attorney, Dan Satterberg.

Secondly, comparing Obama's comments on wealth redistribution to Karl Marx, was one of the most audacious charges I had heard leveled against Obama. It's difficult to believe that Barbara West is an educated person, because I was taught as far back as when I was in primary school, that Tax, in its most basic definition, is redistribution of wealth. When you delve into the issues behind different tax policies and why some people pay higher rates than others, it starts to get complicated. But that is the simple definition of taxation. I did not school in the US, but it's hard for me to imagine that she was not taught something so simple. As for the poll she cited, I was surprised the number was not more than 84%, because no one likes to pay taxes, so of course they would tell Government to get their hands out of their pockets!

Finally, I must say Barbara West's last point confuses me, even till now. Where is the connection between Obama being tested if he is elected President and America's days as a superpower being over? Joe Biden's point was obvious to any right thinking person, unless they just decide they will not bother to think. His point was obviously that any new American President would always be tested, dangerous times or not. There are countries or people that would always want to test the mettle or tolerance levels of the new leader of the world's only superpower. If John McCain is elected President, he will also be tested. The point is that the test will not come because Obama or McCain is President, the test will come because America has a new Ppresident. I think that is just simple logic.

The Republican reaction to why Joe Biden was angry at being asked "tough questions" was another reason why I thought the Party had a lot of issues to resolve among its members. Don't get me wrong, there is nothing wrong with asking tough questions, especially of politicians, but Barbara West's questions were not tough questions, they were silly questions. They were obviously asked to evoke a reaction which the press would then jump on to generate another controversy. What is sad is that they came from a respected reporter. But then again, with the kind of journalism exhibited by FOX News this election cycle, maybe I should not have been as surprised as I was.

While reading some comments on FOX News website about the Barbara West interview, I looked up at and saw a picture of Obama. I was just about to smile in surprise at Obama being on FOX News' home page, when a caption came up under the picture. The "almost smile" vanished and it turned to a cross between incredulity and sadness. The caption said, "FOLLOW THE OBAMA CAMPAIGN ALL THE WAY TO ITS BITTER END ON NOVEMBER 4"!

Incredulity, because even by FOX News standards, that was amazing. Sadness, because I had never seen a mainstream news outlet exhibit this kind of bias that bordered on hatred!

Meanwhile, Sarah Palin was making ridiculous statements about how small towns are the real and patriotic America and the other parts, not so much. She called reporters who were not favorable to the McCain campaign the liberal media, which resulted in reporters being verbally and in at least one case racially abused at some of her rallies. She continued talking about Bill Ayers, even though the only people listening were the people at her rallies and FOX News. According to Sean Hannity, "Obama's connection to Bill Ayers is in the hearts and minds of all Americans!" I was amused at the fact that he actually said that with a straight face!

In interviews, Sarah Palin said she wanted to also talk about Reverend Wright, but because McCain had said early in the campaign that he would not use that line of attack, she could not.

I believe these attacks were one of the reasons why the Republicans found themselves in the position they were just weeks before November 4. The ferocity and incendiary nature of some of these attacks were triggered by Sarah Palin's comment that Obama was palling around with terrorists and does not see America as "we" do. I knew at the time she made that statement that the only thing that could come from it, was an encouragement for Republican supporters to ratchet up the attacks on Obama. But even I did not expect the rage with which these attacks came. The question, "Who is the real Barack

Obama?" was repeated over and over again and at the rallies, the reply was always, "Terrorist!"

The amazing thing was that while all this was going on, the economy was getting worse and people were still losing their jobs and their homes. In the middle of these, the Republicans running for President and Vice President were talking about anything but the economy! I had always believed the Republicans wrote the book on negative campaigning, but I think the McCain campaign, especially Sarah Palin took it to another level. In all this, FOX News was acting as the cheerleader for the Republican attack machine. Sean Hannity's comment that Bill Ayers is in the hearts and minds of Americans was one of the most ridiculous things I have ever heard from a reporter. It was more like Bill Ayers was being rammed down the throats of Americans. FOX News did a show titled, "Ties that bind", which "examined" Obama's relationship with certain colorful characters. As usual, the idea behind the show was to put the information out there and allow voters to decide by themselves if it was a legitimate criterion for deciding who would get their vote. However, the polls showed that this was not the kind of nonsense Americans wanted to hear about, just a few days before election day. The really comical part was that Cindy McCain actually said that Obama had run the dirtiest campaign in US history! What McCain, Palin, Joe the Plumber, FOX News and the so called conservatives did not seem to get was that the only people that attached any seriousness to all the garbage they were spewing were mostly ignorant people who could not see past their frustration. Frustration, that the "conservatives" seemed to be losing the election. Frustration, that most of the country seemed to be more concerned about keeping their jobs and their homes than who Obama spoke to or did not speak to decades ago. Frustration, that America seemed to on its way to electing a black President.

On the flip side, Obama kept on talking about solutions for the economy. He laughed and joked about the Republican attacks. Instead of going on the offensive, he quoted the McCain adviser who said if they kept talking about the economy, they would lose the election. So while John McCain was flying from State to State to recue the bailout package and attacking Obama relentlessly, Obama had remained calm all through, looked totally in control and offered solutions to fix the economic issues, which was voters' main concern. His message was obviously getting through because his poll numbers kept going up everyday and he even began to pull ahead in some traditionally Republican States. Because he had a lot more money than John McCain did, he was able to outspend him in battleground States like Florida, Pennsylvania, Ohio and Michigan. He actively campaigned in typically Republican States and he was soon pulling ahead in States like Virginia that had not voted for a Democratic candidate for President in over 40years. Even in John McCain's home State of Arizona, Obama was starting to close the gap! In Sarah Palin's State of Alaska, he was endorsed by the State's biggest newspaper, Anchorage Daily News!

I tried very hard not too much attention to the polls because if they were always reliable, the general election would have been between Rudy Giulliani and Hillary Clinton.

Another major endorsement came Obama's way just before November 4. For months, reporters and analysts had been trying to predict who former Secretary of State, Colin Powell would endorse. Colin Powell has been one of the most respected people in America, across party and racial lines, for decades. He himself had considered running for President during the 1996 elections, but his wife's concern about his safety had put paid to that plan. I sometimes wonder what might have happened if he had run in that race twelve years ago.

When he did make the announcement, his decision to snob John McCain, his party's nominee, and endorse Obama instead came as no surprise to me, and not because they are both African-Americans, as Rush Limbaugh suggested. I had always thought of Colin Powell as one of the most thoughtful and rational people in the Republican Party. If the well liked and well respected John McCain, the John McCain of 2000, the one who promised to run a honorable campaign had been the one in the race, I have no doubt that Colin Powell would have endorsed him. But I just did not see how Colin Powell was going to endorse the person John McCain had become. Endorsing him would have been like giving a stamp of approval to the kind of campaign that John McCain had run and the kind of candidate he had picked as his running mate.

In explaining his reasons for endorsing Obama, he, among other things, made it clear that he was disheartened at the kinds of things that have been said by the McCain campaign and the Republican National Committee. He also mentioned the fact that McCain's running mate was obviously not ready to potentially be

President. I especially liked his comment on the rumors about Obama being a Muslim. He said, "Obama is not a Muslim, he's a Christian, he's always been, but the real right answer is, what if he is? Is there something wrong with being a Muslim in this country? Is there something wrong with a 7 year old American Muslim kid dreaming of one day being President?"

Personally, I thought in those few words, Colin Powell showed exactly why he is one of the most respected people in America and why he was the only one who wasn't demonized following the Iraq misadventure.

His endorsement was seen as a very big deal in the media and I was finally able to understand why there is so much emphasis on endorsements. I saw that Colin Powell's endorsement was not just a scathing criticism on the Republican Party, it was also thumbs up to the way the Obama campaign had been run and how he had managed to remain calm all through the financial meltdown and the constant attacks from the Republicans. For the first time, I actually believed an endorsement could help sway undecided voters. Colin Powell was such a revered figure that I believed his decision not to endorse his own Party's nominee would make some voters who were still unsure about Obama consider voting for him. I pictured some of these voters saying, "If one of the most respected people in the country, who happens to be a Republican, chose to endorse the Democratic nominee, maybe he's the one to lead the country at this difficult time".

I could not wait to hear what the Republicans had to say about the endorsement. I was expecting a declaration of "Colin Powell bashing", but I was genuinely surprised at the reaction. They actually took it quite well! There were no tantrums as I expected, except from Rush Limbaugh, who suggested that Colin Powell endorsed Obama because they are both black. Even FOX News did not attack Colin Powell over the endorsement! I think the reaction of the Republicans showed just how much respect Colin Powell commands in America.

John McCain attempted to play down the significance of the endorsement, but ended up shooting himself in the foot. He pointed out that five Secretaries of State had endorsed him (even though he could not remember the name of one of them), so Colin Powell's endorsement of Obama was not such a big deal. Of course, that was not the point. The endorsement was not significant for Obama because Colin Powell was a former Secretary of State. It was significant because Colin Powell was a prominent Republican who had decided to endorse a Democrat for President. The Secretaries of State McCain named were all Republicans, so I guess in the same vein, Obama could have named a number of Democratic Secretaries of State who had also endorsed him.

As November 4 approached, it was looking more and more likely that Obama was going to win the elections. Even with undecided voters, it was clear to me that it was more of a referendum on Obama, than a consideration of John McCain. Whatever the reason was for this, one thing was obvious: It would be a shock if Obama did not win on Election Day.

November 4, 2008 and I was seated in front of the TV with my wife, my three week old daughter and my mom. We were all waiting to see the outcome of possibly the most important US elections in our lifetimes. I kept pinching myself and thinking is he actually really going to win? Will this really happen? Will America actually have its first African-American President? Could the Bradley effect happen again? Would the Republicans try any of their dirty tricks, like trying to jam the Democrats' phone lines as they had done in the past? Would the voters decide that change was too risky and go for experience instead?

All these questions raged in my mind and I could hardly sit down for a minute.

As the polls started to close, I finally sat down and started to take count in the race to reach the magic number of 270 Electoral College votes.

As each State was announced, Obama's Electoral College votes kept increasing. It quickly became obvious that Obama was on his way to a big win. He won in all the critical battleground states like Ohio, Pennsylvania, Florida and Michigan. He also won usually Republican leaning states like Indiana, Virginia and North Carolina. It was clear which way the race was heading, but I did not want to start jumping and celebrating yet, since he had not yet reached the 270 Electoral College votes he needed to be named President-Elect.

As 4pm British time drew closer, I was certain that it was over. California and a few other States would be announced at 4pm and John McCain was never going to win California. The state's 55 Electoral College votes would take Obama past the 270 he needed. As that reality hit me, I started to have goose pimples. I had prayed and dreamt and hoped that this day would come, but was it really just a few minutes from being a reality?

At 4pm, Obama won California as expected and was named the 44th President of the United States of America!

It was funny, because I had always thought if Obama won the elections, I would jump and dance for joy. But I did neither. Instead, I sat still and just kept staring at the TV. I switched to FOX News, just to make sure that they did not try to pull a George Bush, like they did in 2000. The headline was the same as every other news channel; Barack Obama elected 44th President of the United States of America.

I had this feeling that I'm not quite sure how to describe. It was a cross between euphoria, shock, disbelief and that feeling you get when reality hits you. I looked beside me and saw that my wife and daughter had both dozed off. I woke my wife up and whispered in her ear, "He's won". She got up and said, "I prayed he would win, but somewhere deep down, I thought it would be taken away from him". My mom just kept laughing and cheering. It was not until I listened to John McCain's concession speech that I cheered for the very first time. But I was not cheering because John McCain was giving a concession speech. I was cheering because the man that gave that speech was the man I had known before the start of the 2008 election season. I felt sorry for him and could not help but wonder what might have been had he stayed the same person. One thing was certain: If he had, the race would have been a lot closer than it turned out to be. Obama would probably still have won because of how badly President Bush had messed things up for the Republican Party, but not by the huge margin with which Obama won.

I switched back to FOX News to hear what they had to say, but was pleasantly surprised at what I heard. There was unanimous praise for Obama and the way he had run his campaign, which was drama-free and consistent. Juan Williams, who is black, was trying very hard to fight back tears while talking about the significance of Obama's win.

As I waited for Obama's victory speech, I cast my mind back to July 2004, when I first heard his speech at the convention. I remembered how I thought his name all but guaranteed he would not win the Senate seat. I was glad to be proved wrong.

I then cast my mind back to October 2006, when I saw the Time Magazine article, "Why Barack Obama could be the next President of The United States" and I how I started asking myself if it was possible.

Finally, I cast my mind back to February 2007, when he announced his candidacy for President. I remembered how I hoped he would win, but deep down, did not really think he could. I thought of how far he had come in that period and all the drama and intrigue in between. Again, I was glad to be proved wrong.

It all seemed like a really long soap opera, which sadly was now about to end. But then I thought, it's the beginning of a new administration, so maybe the soap opera is only just beginning.

When the President-elect and his family eventually stepped onto the stage in Chicago's Grant Park, it was an image I don't think I will ever forget. The image of the new first family of The United States of America. An

African-American family. Never did I think I would see such an image in my lifetime. When Obama gave his victory speech, I heard it but I'm not sure I listened to it. I was still trying to tell my mind to get used to the fact that Barack Obama is now President of The United States.

Getting to this point was the result of a combination of factors. There was the obvious charisma of Obama, his intelligence and political genius. There was also the element of luck. Most people may not agree with this, but let me explain why I stated that.

I don't think Obama's increase in the polls just before the elections would have happened had the economy not been in the state it was in. If I remember correctly, Obama and McCain were practically running neck and neck in the polls until the economy went into an even sharper decline. It gave Obama a chance to show Americans that he could stay calm and still be in control while in the middle of a national crisis. If the economy was okay and other issues were at the forefront of the campaign, Americans might not have had the opportunity to see a candidate being calm under pressure. They were given the opportunity to see him in this light and compare that calm, thoughtful approach to John McCain's frightening similarity to President Bush's handling of crises.

Another very important factor is the incredible ability of America to constantly redefine itself in its quest for a more perfect union. The world view of America had changed in the last 8years and was getting worse by the day, but it took an election to turn that around again. The world respects and wants to look up to America. The last 8years had made that difficult and even impossible in some cases. The similarities between John McCain's proposed policies and the ones in place under President Bush meant that a McCain Presidency would effectively have been an extension of the last 8years. Americans recognized this, not just in terms of foreign policy, but in terms of fixing the economy and restoring America's place in the world as that last beacon of hope.

The most important factor though, was the way the Obama campaign was run. Before I say anything else about how he ran his campaign, I want to quote my cousin on this issue. She said, "Decades from now, when politicians talk about how they want to run their campaign, they will talk about the Obama Model of 2008".

Barack Obama's campaign was one of the most effective campaigns ever run by a US politician for any office. It is interesting to note that when he ran for the US Senate in 2004, his campaign was described by analysts as one of the most powerful campaigns ever run by a non-incumbent candidate for the US Senate. Even critics, including FOX News, were in awe at the level of professionalism and discipline with which his campaign was run.

Press leaks, which had hitherto been a constant in politics, was conspicuously absent from the Obama campaign. Again, even FOX News gave the Obama campaign credit for this, because it is generally not known to happen.

Another point that I think is worth mentioning, because it's very easy to forget, is the meticulous planning and simple, but effective strategies he employed in his campaign. For example, his decision to actively campaign in States considered Republican territory was pure genius.

Democratic candidates usually make lackluster efforts in these States because they were seen as impenetrable Republican fortresses. The result of this simple but audacious plan was wins in States like Virginia, North Carolina, Indiana and Nevada, where no Democratic candidate had won in decades (Apart from Bill Clinton). He also won critical States that President Bush had won in 2004, like Florida, Pennsylvania and Ohio.

When Obama first decided he was going to run for President, some of his advisers were skeptical. Not that they did not think he was qualified or capable enough, but because they were not sure America was ready for a black President. But as he had done for most of his life, he challenged the assumption, because he knew something that only a few people knew at the time and that everyone now knows; America is color blind to excellence. Obama knew that if he could show Americans that he was the person best equipped to deal with the myriad challenges facing the country in the 2008 election cycle, his race would be the last thing on voters minds. He knew there would be those who would not vote for him because of his color, but he also knew that if he could show himself as the candidate who could change the direction the country was heading, such people would be in the minority. This at the time, sounded like a naïve idea, but I believe it was this idea that helped him build the large support base he was able to, including people who did not even like him! I remember reading about a woman in Pennsylvania who said she did not like Obama because she disagreed with him on a large number of issues and because she felt he was arrogant. But she also said that she would still vote for him because she believed he was the best available candidate to deal with the economic situation in the country.

Obama ended up winning the election with over 69million votes (52.9%), to McCain's 59million (45.7%). This margin was the largest ever by a non-incumbent US Presidential candidate and the sixth largest in US history.

He needed 270 Electoral College votes to win, but ended up with 365, while John McCain ended up with 173.

One interesting thing I noted though, was that John McCain was the first US Presidential candidate in history to get up to 59million votes and still lose the election. I'm not saying that to disparage John McCain in any way, but to point out the level of participation in the 2008 Presidential election.

A lot has been said about the fact that a record number of African-Americans voted for Obama. Some have said, if so many African-Americans had not voted for him, he would not have won the election. That theory, I find quite ridiculous. Let me try to put that into perspective. In the 2008 elections, African-Americans made up 13% of the electorate, which was only 2% more than the number of African-Americans that voted in 2004, so first of all, the turnout was only slightly higher than it was in 2004. In 2008, even though 95% of African-Americans' votes went to Obama, that could not have won win him the election. Even if the entire 13% had voted for him, it still would not have been enough.

The statistic I find more intriguing is that 47% of the voters on November 4 were aged 40years old and below.

Of this number, about 65% voted for Obama! His ability to inspire an entire generation was evident even before the primaries started, but the number of youths that turned out to vote for him was still amazing. It is even all the more amazing when you consider the fact that young people are usually the most cynical when it comes to politics. Obama's relative youth and his appeal to the youths of America meant that his election victory was not only a change of direction in terms of policies, but also a generational change. At age 47, Obama is one of only 9 US Presidents who were less than 50years old when elected. Apart from his obvious charisma, I believe his youth was one of the reasons the youths of America were able to relate and respond to him they way they did.

For those who were worried about the Bradley effect on election day, the reverse happened. A reverse Bradley effect. It turned out that thousands of people who had stated in opinion polls that they would vote for John McCain, ended up voting for Obama instead! Some analysts have dubbed this, "The Obama Effect".

From all this, it was obvious to me that when Americans saw Obama, they did not see a black man running for President. They saw a political genius, who was running for President and just happened to be black. Like the woman in Pennsylvania, all Americans wanted was a President who could lead them out of the condition the country was in and it did not matter if he was black, white, brown, blue or green. The question they asked was, "Can he do the job?" The answer, I think was a resounding yes. Or to quote a popular US politician, YES WE CAN! Or to strictly answer the question, YES HE CAN!

All that being said, I wondered about an argument I had heard after the election. It was an argument that if the country was not in as bad a shape as it was, if President Bush was not as unpopular as he was, if the last 8years had been like the Clinton years, would Americans have looked beyond Obama's race? Obama's message of change and hope was music to the ears of anyone who wanted a new course for the country, but what if the economy was stable and the country was in generally good shape at home and abroad?

Personally, I think one of the reasons Obama decided it was time to run for President was because of the state the country was in. He believed in his ability to inspire people not to lose hope and bring people together to work towards reshaping America, at a time when America badly needed it. A wise man once said that there is nothing more powerful than an idea whose time has come. Barack Obama was an idea whose time had come, so it did not matter if he was black or white. I remember the story of when Obama told Senator Richard Durbin that he was considering running for President. Senator Durbin said, "Sometimes you pick the time and sometimes the time picks you. This is your time".

Having said that, I believe if the circumstances were different, Obama would have had the right message for whatever time it was. His ability to inspire and get people to find common ground would still have captured the imagination of Americans, as he pulls them together to tackle the challenges the country might be facing. Besides, the country was not in as bad a shape as it is now in 2005, when people had already began trying to get him to run for President. Most of these people were white and I'm certain they were aware of his race.

WHY MCCAIN LOST

As for the reasons why John McCain and the Republicans lost not just the Presidential race, but also a number of Senate and House races, I believe there are too many of them. The main reason though, was the Presidency of George W Bush.

The 2008 elections were always going to be a tough election for Republicans, John McCain or not. After the last 8 years, any Republican candidate for President had to face the fact that he or she was running in a race where the Party's leader is the most unpopular politician in the country. That would have killed any Republican's chances, but I believe John McCain could have challenged that assumption. An Obama adviser said after the elections that, "the John McCain of 2000 would have been a lot harder to beat than the John McCain of 2008".

Personally, I believed it was a lot harder for Obama to beat Hillary Clinton than John McCain.

John McCain was destined to lose this election from the moment he strayed from principles he had held for decades, principles that led to his being labeled a maverick. The same principles that almost made him quit the Republican Party a few years ago to join the Democrats. He basically hit the campaign self destruct button when he started trying to convince his Party base that he could be as "conservative" as they wanted him to be.

Even after he won the nomination, the Republican Party base, made up of staunch "conservatives" and "evangelicals" was still unsure about him and there were fears that they might decide to stay home on Election Day.

You may have noticed that all through this book, I put the word conservative in quotes. The reason I have done that is because I believe that the word conservative has been distorted by the Republican Party of today and at no time has this been more evident than in the 2008 elections. The word used to mean a support for the philosophies or ideologies of the status quo or in lay man's terms, "not wanting things to change from how they used to be".

Unfortunately, whenever the word conservative was used during the 2008 elections and probably well before, the first word that sprang to mind was intolerance. The same is true of what the word evangelical has now become. I put those words in quotes because I don't believe there is anything wrong with being conservative or having conservative values. I don't believe being an evangelical means you are intolerant. But the problem with the Republican Party of today is that the people that spew the most hate and divisiveness are usually self-described conservatives and/or self-described evangelicals. From what I have read about the history of the Republican Party, these are not the principles it was founded upon.

The word evangelical becoming synonymous with intolerance is even sadder, because as far as I am aware, the Bible teaches tolerance. In 2004, Pastors were telling their congregations that it would be a sin to vote for John Kerry, because George Bush was supposed to be an evangelical! But the so-called evangelicals of today are the same ones who send death threats to abortion doctors and use every profanity imaginable to describe gay people and talk about how the US needs to exterminate Arabs! The really unfortunate thing is that when they say and do things like this, they believe that they are defending God. What no one mentioned to them is that God does not need defending. He is God whether anyone believes or accepts that fact or not!

In the 2008 elections, so-called conservative analysts, radio and talk show hosts used the stage they had to propagate so much hate and divisiveness with incendiary and oftentimes, outrageous comments. FOX News specifically and people like Sean Hannity, Ann Coulter, Bill O Reilly and Rush Limbaugh, to mention a few. The fact that people like these have millions of viewers and listeners who hang on to their every word is one of the reasons the Republican Party has become so reviled in America today. These people have turned the Republican Party from a Party of principles and integrity to one of intolerance and divisiveness. They got on the air everyday and showed just how ignorant they were and invited equally or even more ignorant people to analyze and give "expert" opinions. I once heard an "expert" on FOX News talking about Obama and saying something along the lines of Obama being successful because he is a black guy who has surrounded himself with white people! As sad as that comment and others like it are from these "conservatives", the even sadder part is that there are those who actually take these people seriously!

Colin Powell remarked in a recent interview with CNN's Fareed Zakaria that for the Republican Party to move forward, they would need to stop listening to people like Rush Limbaugh. I would add the aforementioned names to that list as well.

One of John McCain's biggest mistakes was that he decided that to be President, he needed to get these people on his side, even though all through his career, he had showed that he had fundamental disagreements with them. His pick of Sarah Palin, a staunch "conservative" Governor, was another example. I personally think he picked her for two main reasons;

-   She was a woman;

-   She was conservative enough to give his campaign credibility with the Republican base.

Obviously, there must have been other reasons, but I believe these two informed his decision more than any other.

Her incendiary comments which led to some of the most hateful things ever said in public in America since segregation was just the tonic the "conservatives" and "evangelicals" needed. What I think they forgot though, was that this was 2008 and not the 1950s or 1960s. I believe the McCain campaign scared millions of voters who wanted to move forward from the hate and divisiveness of the past, but saw that Sarah Palin and John McCain were dredging up these issues again. From the moment Sarah Palin said Obama "palled around with terrorists" and "he does not see America as we do", the floodgates opened. A line that the McCain campaign was never able to return from, had been crossed. It is one thing to have a policy debate and question Obama's experience which would have been fine, but to get to a point where supporters started calling a US Senator and Presidential candidate a terrorist was just over the top.

The Republican Party needs to take a step back and do some serious soul searching. They need to understand that attacks and polarization as a tool to gain political power will probably always backfire now because of the times we live in.

Recently, the scandal involving Illinois State Governor, Rod Blagyoevich was not even a few days old, when the Republican National Committee (RNC) had already released an attack ad showing pictures of the Governor together with now President-elect Obama. When I saw that, I thought, "Didn't these people learn anything from their catastrophic losses on November 4?" This, at a time when Obama had just started forming his new cabinet and was trying to look for ways to sort out the economic mess. From that ad, it was obvious to me that the party had still not understood that these kinds of attacks turn people off and makes them look at the party as one that uses its energy to point fingers and promote divisiveness instead of looking for ideas and solutions to better the lives of Americans. Even former Republican Speaker of The US House of Representatives, Newt Gingrich, who was well known for negative politics, criticized the attack and advised the Party to be looking for ways to help Obama move the country forward instead of resorting to unnecessary attacks.

While trying to recover from the shock of that attack,

I saw that a candidate for the leadership of the RNC had sent a Christmas CD to RNC members as a gift. Among other songs on the CD, was one titled, "Barack the Magic Negro"! Again, I don't think that was even the sad part. The sad part was that there were people ready to jump to his defense, calling it a political satire and criticizing anyone that did not see it as such! There were also songs featuring the Jeremiah Wright controversy. I thought very sadly that all this came from someone running to be the next head of the party. I think that crystallizes the depth of the problems the party has.

Also, the fact that some polls show that Sarah Palin would be the top Republican choice to be nominee in 2012 is another example of what is wrong with the Republican Party.

Since the elections have been over, the kinds of things Sarah Palin has been saying, have shown that people who were worried about the prospect of her being a heartbeat away from the Presidency were justified in their fear. In one of her first TV interviews after the elections, with CNN's Wolf Blitzer, she was still talking about how she is "still concerned about Obama's relationship with Bill Ayers"!

She's also spent a lot of time accusing the media and the McCain campaign for how she was portrayed. She accused Katie Couric of asking her trick questions during those disastrous interviews. She accused the McCain campaign of allowing her to continue the interviews, after the first day went badly. She even accused the media of giving Caroline Kennedy, who was campaigning to replace Hillary Clinton as the junior US Senator from

New York, an easier ride than they did her because of a class bias.

Sometimes, I think or maybe hope is more appropriate, that Sarah Palin is joking when she says some of the stuff she says. How on earth is it even remotely possible for a candidate for a US Senate seat to get the same level of scrutiny as a Vice Presidential candidate?

Regarding the Katie Couric interviews, I think the questions asked were some of the most direct and straight to the point questions I've ever seen asked of a US Presidential or Vice Presidential candidate. If Katie Couric had been interviewing Joe Biden or John McCain or Barack Obama, I suspect the questions would have been a lot tougher. I heard one of her supporters recently ask why she was not allowed to be interviewed by more friendly reporters. Has it occurred to Sarah Palin's supporters that she was running for Vice President of The United States? She probably preferred the interview format with FOX News's Sean Hannity, whose questions were so leading that anyone could have answered them. But it is not the job of reporters to make politicians feel good. It is their job to ask tough questions of the people who are asking a whole nation to entrust their welfare to them. Like a CBS reporter asked, "If she cannot hold her own against a TV journalist, how should the American people expect her to hold her own against world leaders?"

Personally, I think if Sarah Palin were to become US President or even the Republican nominee for President, it would set the country back by decades because she does not seem to realize that this is the 21st century.

As for John McCain, what I don't think he understood

was that the 2008 elections were never going to be about which candidate could attract the most Republicans or Democrats. It was always going to be about who could attract the most number of Independent voters. Sarah Palin's addition to the Republican ticket and the resulting explosion of incendiary language effectively scared off Independents and even some Republicans that may otherwise have supported John McCain. When you also add the fact that Sarah Palin was obviously not ready to be Vice President and potentially President, you begin to understand why her presence on the Republican ticket was more of a liability than an asset.

But after the elections, John McCain's comments have shown that he is back to being the man who puts politics aside when he believes in something. And if my instincts are as good as I want to believe they are, mark my words, if in 2012, Sarah Palin decides to run for President and says the kinds of things she said in 2008, John McCain will either publicly criticize her, or he will endorse someone else over her without necessarily criticizing her.

As for the Republicans, I think Newt Gingrich realized something a lot of them still have problems understanding or accepting and that is; we live in a very different time and in a very different world from the one "conservatives" think we still do.

The other thing I believe they need to understand is that younger voters are getting more and more involved in the political process and majority of them are more concerned with how they can move the country forward. Of course there are a few ignorant young people out there, but generally speaking, most do not care about a lot of things the older generation of Republicans seem to care about. As I pointed out earlier, the younger generation of voters, Republicans, Democrats or Independents, have the most to gain or lose from the current direction and the direction the country is turning towards. That probably explains why 47% of the voters on November 4 were young voters. And if I know anything about the determination courage and commitment of youth, I know that they will fight for their voices to be heard. The sooner the Republican Party can understand these simple concepts and channel their energies accordingly, the brighter future the party will have.

FINAL ANALYSIS

So what does the election of the first black President mean for African-Americans?

For African-Americans, the election of the first black President was the realization of a dream by a preacher 45years ago, when he said, "I have a dream that my four little children will one day live in a nation where they will not be judged by the color of their skin but by the content of their character".

Martin Luther King's dream had become a reality in a lot of different ways in America, but the election of a black President was surely the crown of it all, at least for now.

I think Obama's election is a chance for African-Americans to reflect on how much the country has changed. How much they need to move forward from the horrors of the past, look past the bitterness of the present and concentrate on the goals for the future and that of their children. Obama won the election with over 50% of the vote, majority of which were from white people. The reason that was able to happen was because they saw Obama as a voice for the kind of forward movement America should be pursuing and they responded to him. While I'm not naïve enough to think that Obama's election victory signals an end to racism or racially motivated discrimination in America, it does show that another barrier has been knocked down in America's quest for a more perfect union. It is a chance to move forward and stop blaming every failure on racial discrimination. While I accept that not everyone can be President, I sincerely believe that anyone can be anything they decide they want to be if they can just keep their focus.

According to conventional wisdom or the general assumptions, there were a lot of reasons why Obama should not have won this election; a lot of reasons for him to have lost his focus, even before the primaries started. First and foremost was his skin color; then there was his name, which reminded everyone of his African roots; then there was his Arabic middle name. I suspect Obama knew all these things, but like he said during his convention speech in 2004, his parents gave him his name because they believed that in a tolerant America, a name is not a barrier to success. If an African could say that about America almost 50years ago, what excuse do African-Americans have not to succeed? You could argue that Obama's father did not really understand America, but then I would ask this question, "Has he not been proven right 47years later?"

Obama could have lost his focus when death threats against him became so serious that the Senate Majority Leader, Harry Reid, had to request Secret Service protection for Obama and his family, as early as July 2007; something that had never happened that early in a Presidential race.

He could have lost his focus when the Jeremiah

Wright controversy erupted or when he was called every name under Heaven by the Republicans.

But he did not, because his eye was on the ball and he chose to be the bigger person. November 4 2008 was his reward.

During his victory speech that night, he talked about Ann Nixon Cooper, a 106 year old woman from Atlanta, who had voted in the election. I can only imagine the memories that were going through this woman's head when she cast her vote on November 4.

She was alive during both world wars;

She was alive when black people and women were not allowed to vote and when the laws preventing them from voting were abolished;

She was alive when segregation was the law of the land and when it was abolished;

She was alive when Martin Luther King delivered his "I have a dream" speech;

She was alive when Martin Luther King and John Kennedy were assassinated;

She was alive when the first African-American ran for President;

She was alive when Colin Powell became the first African-American National Security Adviser, Four Star General, Chairman of the Joint Chiefs of Staff and Secretary of State;

She was alive when Madeline Albright became the first female Secretary of State;

She was alive when Condolezza Rice became the first woman to be named National Security Adviser and the first African-American woman to be Secretary of State.

Finally, she was alive and even voted in the election that produced the first African-American President.

Anyone who thinks the plight of African-Americans has not changed needs to have a conversation with Ann Nixon Cooper.

On the night of November 4, there was a reason why Jesse Jackson, Oprah Winfrey and Colin Powell cried and why Condolezza Rice was as ecstatic as a little kid in a candy store. I believe it is people like these, who grew up when things were so much different, who can really appreciate the significance of a black man as President. Even with their achievements, I get the feeling that they did not expect to see a black man being President in their lifetimes. Maybe in their children's lifetimes, maybe in another few decades, but not now. I remember a recent interview I saw with Colin Powell. He was talking about how much America had changed and he gave a very profound example. He said when he was a teenager, he was hanging out with some friends one day and they heard that a black driver had been allowed to drive a certain bus route somewhere in the South. He went further to say that when they heard the news, they all looked at each other and sighed in astonishment. The first one to find his voice then said, "I hope he doesn't have an accident, because you know what those white people are going to say".

So when someone like that, who went on to achieve so much, is still as emotional as he gets every time he talks about November 4, I can understand exactly why.

How did Obama succeed where Jesse Jackson and Al Sharpton failed? I believe the first thing was that Obama never saw himself as the black candidate running for President. He saw himself as the American candidate running for President, who just happens to be black. To paraphrase Colin Powell, "Obama was so successful because he made his race a secondary issue".

The problem with Jesse Jackson and Al Sharpton's candidacies was that they were running as the black candidates. Almost all their proposed policies had to do with making life better first for African-Americans and secondly for the whole country. Even though they did not actually put it in those words, that was the feeling I got from studying their policies. They failed to grasp the concept that to be elected President of the United States, the issues facing Americans should be the priority, not the issues facing a particular group of Americans, African-Americans or otherwise. That is not to say Obama or any other President should ignore or deny the fact that racial discrimination still exists, but rather to challenge victims of this kind of discrimination to rise above it and not allow it to become a stumbling block in their path to success. Obama knew that America did not need a candidate who reminded them of a past they wanted to forget. America needed a candidate to show what was right with America, not what was wrong with America. America needed a candidate to show how far America has come and how far America can go, not a candidate to show why America has not gone further. My belief is that Obama represented that hope for anyone who was ready to move on, whether they be black or white. Like Obama said in an interview during the primary season,

"I'm rooted in the African-American community, but I am not defined by it".

I wrote in the introduction to this book, that asking if America is ready for a black President was the wrong question. The right question should be, "Is there a black person who is ready to be President?"

A candidate who sees himself as an American leader and models his life and campaign on that premise, rather than a candidate who sees himself as a black leader before anything else.

Unfortunately, some black people saw this mindset in Obama and, accused him of pandering to white people. Some went as far as forming a group called, "Blacks against Obama", and tried on at least one occasion, to disrupt his campaigns, before they were marched out by Secret Service agents. They saw Obama as insensitive to "African-American issues" and more concerned by "white issues".

Some said his candidacy had been endorsed by the Ku Klux Klan (KKK), no doubt referring to the endorsement by Senator Robert Byrd. Never mind the fact that Senator Byrd is a 92year old man, who joined the KKK when he was 24years old and has since disavowed the group, attributing his membership to the time and place in which he had been raised and has advised young people to avoid groups that prey on hate and division.

Some said Obama talks down to black people and feels like he is better than them. I remember having this argument with a friend of mine, who was one of those who believed that Obama talks down to black people. I pointed out that I totally disagreed with that notion because what I think Obama does, is that he tells black people brutal truths that a white politician cannot tell them, for fear of being called racist.

An example was when Obama stated that he did not support financial reparations for slavery. He went further to state that he only supported reparations in the form of new schools and new infrastructure in deprived African-American communities. Groups like this did not take kindly to this statement and pointed that out as proof that Obama is not black enough. Obama was once asked about this and he responded that, "Unfortunately, we black people are still locked in this notion that if you appeal to white people, you must be doing something wrong".

I think the problem with these peoples' line of reasoning is that it allows black people to use racially motivated discrimination as an excuse not to succeed. America is not perfect, but America is still the only country where regardless of your skin color, you can have a dream, any dream, work towards actualizing your dream and see your dreams come true. Unfortunately, I think these people are more interested in playing victim, instead of looking for ways to move forward and better their lives.

Nobody doubts the fact that racially motivated discrimination still exits, but even if Obama had not been elected President, I would still have said that race relations in America of today is not a barrier to success.

As President, I am confident that Obama will take on racially motivated discrimination, but he will not do it because he his African-American, he will do it because he is President of The United States.

I think he followed the advice given by Democratic

strategist, Donna Brazille after he won the US Senate seat in 2004. She said at the time, "Obama does not have to become the next black leader. He needs to become a great Senator from the State of Illinois."

His Presidential campaign showed that he has become so much more than that.

The other aspect of Obama's election victory that I think is worth mentioning is the powerful imagery involved. The Obama family, not just Barack, had become role models for an entire generation of people all over the world.

I remember hearing about a 14year old boy in America, who said, if he had been asked a year ago who his role model was, he would have said Michael Jordan. But now, his role model is Barack Obama.

I heard of young ladies who were interviewed in Britain and said that seeing the Obama family had made them raise the bar in terms of the kind of man they want to marry. I heard a bit of back and forth on this particular issue. There was a particular argument I heard between a young lady and her boyfriend. She asked why all men could not be as responsible as Barack Obama. Her boyfriend responded that Obama was as successful as he was, because he had a very supportive wife; so his question was, why could all women not be as supportive as Michelle Obama. His girlfriend then responded that Michelle Obama was able to be supportive because Barack Obama was a responsible husband to start with. And on it went for a about an hour, before they both decided that they were not Barack and Michelle in each other's lives, so they would break up and try to find them!

I read about a 22year old man in South Africa who had been wasted most of his life on drugs and alcohol because he did not think there was any point trying to be responsible or successful since, "a black man's life is always going to be about chaos and drama" (that is a direct quote from him). While in high school, he had always been described as having "raw analytical talent". Obama's election so inspired him that he has quit the lifestyle he was living and has now decided to go back to University (he had previously dropped out after a year).

I'm used to seeing actors, actresses, musicians, sports stars and maybe a couple of politicians as role models. Considering the fact that people are generally cynical about politics and specifically politicians, seeing one who is almost universally regarded as a role model for the younger generation and a symbol of hope to every generation, is awe inspiring.

I also believe that the election of the first President of the United States, who happens to have African roots, represents a unique opportunity for Africans, especially African leaders to take a long hard look at themselves. On the night of November 4, all the votes had not even been counted, when the whole world already knew who won the election. Apart from a handful of cases, including the recent Ghanaian elections, I don't remember an election in Africa that has been straight forward. There are almost always intrigues; from opposition intimidation to banning of political opponents by incumbents, to election related violence and assassinations, to vote rigging, to frivolous court challenges.

The post-election violence in Kenya at the beginning

of 2008, that led to the deaths of over 800 people and left over half a million people displaced is a glaring example of the level of work that still needs to be done in Africa.

In Nigeria, the last Presidential election was held in April 2007, but as at 2008, the losing candidates were still vowing to get the Supreme Court to annul the results.

In Zimbabwe, the refusal of Robert Mugabe to step down after 3 decades in power is another sad, but brutal reality of the mindset of African leaders.

I think the reason there is so much dishonesty and violence and why African elections are such a do or die affair is because politicians see whatever post they are vying for as a business, of which they intend to be CEO and the profits would be theirs. Consequently, when a politician spends millions of his own money on his campaign, like any good businessman, he obviously expects a return on his investment. If he loses the election, his priority at that point is not a concession speech or making sure his supporters get behind the winner; it's getting his money back. So when he decides to drag out his opposition to the results, it's most likely in the hope of being offered some sort of post within the new administration; a post where he will make his money back and much more.

I've heard some arguments that it has taken America over 200 years to get to where she is today and that it's taken slavery, a civil war, segregation, assassinations and a host of other social issues to get here. The argument further goes that most African countries achieved independence around the 1950s and 1960s, so it's unfair to compare America's progress with Africa's.

That's a fair argument, but I think the point that is being missed by its proponents is that it might have taken

America over 200 years to get here, but each decade was far more progressive than the one preceding it. So while it was a 200 years rife with one issue after the other, it was also one in which the progress being made was visible. So even in 2008, while it is obvious that America is not yet perfect, no one can deny the progress that has been made.

That being said, I must say that in several cases with regards to Africa, progress has been made. For example, Nigeria is listed by the International Monetary Fund (IMF) as one of the fastest growing economies in the world.

According to the Central Intelligence Agency (CIA) world fact book, 12 of the 20 fastest growing economies in the world are African!

I hope and pray that we can sustain this rate of growth because if we can, Africa will eventually become relevant on the world stage. I say this because as it stands now, Africa's opinion is considered a formality, rather than a necessity. And to be honest, Africa, rather than the international community, is to blame for this.

Our legitimacy when it comes to important policy issues, is almost always called into question, but what do we expect when Governments are rife with corruption and electoral systems are so flawed. The really unfortunate part of this is that when Africa gets frozen out of these important issues, we scream about racism and how the international community does not respect Africa. But the fact of the matter is that we Africans need to show ourselves as being ready to be relevant in the international community.

We need to show ourselves as ready by reforming our electoral systems.

We need to show ourselves as ready by seeing Government as an opportunity to serve, rather than an opportunity to rule.

We need to show ourselves as ready by dealing with eruptions of violence all over the continent, instead waiting for the international community to tell us how to resolve them.

To be brutally honest, as long as we don't buckle up in these and other areas, Africa's role in the international community will continue to be a formality and not a necessity.

Obama's election should be an opportunity to correct these failures, not in terms of what Obama can or will do for Africa, but in terms of Africans seeing that the whole world is moving forward and Africa is in danger of being left behind. The reason I made this point is that following Obama's election, I heard a lot of commentaries on how America's election of a black President would mean more aid for Africa. I think that is exactly the problem! We need to be trying to partner with America and other developed countries, instead of trying to get aid from them. Besides, I think the expectation overdrive that Obama's election brought should have been along the lines of partnership and not aid. What a lot of Africans do not seem to understand is that if we don't deal with these failures or at least show that we are trying to deal with them, there is very little Obama will be able to do for Africa that would be different from past American Presidents. Obama might be black and have African roots, but first and foremost, he is President of The United States.

COULD THERE EVER BE A BLACK
BRITISH PRIME MINISTER?

It was not only Africans who were guilty of going into an expectation overdrive.

In Britain, Obama's election victory led to talk of if and when there would be a black Prime Minister. It was a debate that had started subtly after Obama won the Democratic Party nomination in June. The events of November 4 turned the heat up on that debate. Obama's claim that, "in no other country on earth is my story even possible", was seen in some quarters, including Government, as inaccurate.

I sat and thought about this idea for a very long time. I believed deep down that it would take decades for Britain to have a black Prime Minister, if ever. I had a variety of reasons why I thought so, but I wanted to get a different view, someone to challenge the reasons why I believed this so strongly. I asked colleagues, relatives and friends, including one very good friend of mine, who has a British father and Irish mother. The strange thing, or maybe not so strange thing, was that even though they all had different reasons, none of them believed that Britain could ever have a black Prime Minister. I was looking for a dissenting view, but found out that my view was probably the most optimistic, even if only slightly so, or maybe I should say the most naïve, since I believed that if it could happen at all, it would only be in the far future, but almost everyone else I spoke to thought it could never happen.

Like I pointed out, there is a variety of reasons why I think the likelihood of a black British Prime Minister is something that could only happen decades from now. I've grouped these reasons into two main points:

1. Class;

2. Political Systems;

To explain the first point, I will look back in history and examine how black people came to be in both societies.

In America, most black people arrived in the country as slaves. Needless to say, they had little or no rights at the time and even after the abolition of slavery, segregation became the law of the land. Their rights were limited until segregation, but they were still considered American citizens. Following the end of segregation, African-Americans had all the rights enjoyed by white people as enshrined in the Constitution.

A now desegregated America opened the door to an emerging African-American middle class, as black people were now able to compete for the same jobs and were given the same opportunities as their white counterparts (at least in theory). So when this emerging African-American middle class was allowed full access to the American political and economic systems which generally allow for upward mobility, the result was a powerful African-American middle class. Consequently,

African-Americans began to make inroads into positions of authority, both economically and in Government. As long as they could prove themselves as ready and capable, their color was not an issue, at least in most cases. I need to mention here though, that this did not happen overnight, it took decades after the end of segregation for talent and ability to become more important than race.

The American constitution is based on the principles of freedom and equality. It is based on the idea that anyone, regardless of color, can do anything and can be anything he or she wants to be. Anyone can achieve the American dream. The general idea of this principle is, "make of your life what you will". This classless concept of the American dream is what allows Americans to believe that the rewards of hard work, focus, brilliance, intelligence and perseverance are blind to class, gender and race. While this obviously does not happen in every single case, it has and still happens often enough for America to be considered mostly a classless society. This is why Barack Obama, the son of a foreign student from Kenya and a middleclass woman from Kansas could rise to become President of the United States, why Colin Powell, the son of Jamaican immigrants could rise to the levels that he did, why Condolezza Rice, a descendant of slaves could rise to the levels she did and why Bobby Jindal, the son of Indian immigrants is presently the youngest Governor in the US, why people like Oprah Winfrey and Bob Johnson could become billionaires.

I'm not saying they got to these levels because of their backgrounds, but my point is that the American system allowed them to get these levels in spite of their backgrounds.

In Britain, the situation is a bit different. Even though black people have lived in Britain for centuries, it was not until the late 1940s and 1950s that mass immigration by blacks first took place. This was mostly to fill shortages in the labor market, following the end of the World War 2.

In terms of actual integration to the point of the emergence of a powerful black middle class, it's a bit more difficult in Britain because it has always been and in many ways is still a class based society. The impact of this is that anyone, black or white, born into a social and/or economic class, would have to make miracles happen to move beyond the class they were born into. The British socio-economic structure is set up that way and has been for centuries.

Some in Britain, including politicians, have suggested that the reason why the upward mobility of black people, allowed by the American economic and political systems is a lot more difficult in Britain, is as a result of institutional racism. I disagree with this assessment, at least to an extent. The first reason why I disagree with it is because even though racism, institutional or otherwise, does exist in Britain, it is not peculiar to Britain, and I believe that Britain is still one of the most racially tolerant countries in the world.

The second reason is that I don't believe the British class system has as much to do with race as suggested, because it is a system that was in place long before black people became a factor in British society. In the past, this system only affected white Britons who did not belong to a certain socio-economic class. Now that black Britons have become a factor in British society, it affects them as well. In fact, the class system affects blacks, whites, Asians, and every other race, so I don't think it has much to do with race.

However, this class structure is still the reason why the emergence a powerful black middle class in Britain is very difficult at the moment. I used the phrase, "at the moment" because progress has been and is still being made. There are all sorts of schemes that allow for Britons of ethnic minority backgrounds to "rise above their stations". This was not the case a few decades ago, Which is why I feel confident enough to use the phrase, "at the moment" because the progress that has been made to date seemed inconceivable only two or three decades ago. Areas like the legal profession, finance, Government and even the military are now a lot more open than they used to be to Britons of any color. The result is that class and race have become less of an issue than performance and excellence.

Now, looking at both societies, a black President was always going to happen in America, before a similar situation could happen in Britain because the more powerful the black middle class in America got, the easier it was for Americans to get used to the idea of seeing a black person or black people in positions of authority.

In Britain, the lack of a powerful black middle class makes this same scenario difficult. Consequently, in Britain, the most popular black people in terms of public visibility are either sports men and women or musicians. Black people are still under-represented in politics, financial circles and other influential areas of British society.

At this point, you might ask why it is so important for the black middle class in Britain to be a lot more powerful and a lot more visible than it is now, for there to be a possibility of a black Prime Minister. The reason is very simple.

In any developed society, the middle class is the backbone. The middle class is the lifeblood of the economy and if you look at most developed countries in the world today, when the middle class does well, the country does well.

For example, in America, the middle class makes up 95% of the population. It was the emergence of a powerful black middle class in America that made it possible in what has become a meritocratic (for want of a better word) system, for African-Americans to get to the point where they could be elected and/or appointed to be Mayors (some in predominantly white towns), Governors, Senators, Congressmen and women, Senior Cabinet Secretaries, including Secretaries of State, National Security Advisers and senior military positions, including Chairman of the Joint Chiefs of Staff.

Interesting to note though, is the fact that the African-Americans that have occupied these positions were all pacesetters for Obama. As race barriers were broken, and African-Americans made inroads into these influential positions, the idea of a black President seemed less outrageous. Distant, but not outrageous.

After Obama's election victory, I got a text from a friend of mine that read, "Rosa Parks sat so that Martin Luther King could walk. Martin Luther King walked so that Barack Obama could run. Barack Obama ran and now we can fly".

The general idea of the message was that for an event as significant as electing a black American President to occur, glass ceilings need to have been broken first.

In Britain, the black middle class is only just starting to emerge, as class becomes less and less of an issue in comparison to merit. In the past, upward mobility was determined first by class, before anything else. Now, even though class still plays a significant part, merit is becoming more of a factor. This change that has occurred and is still occurring is why people like Baroness Scotland (Attorney General), Baroness Amos (Former Leader of House of Lords), Chuka Umunna (Labour Party candidate for Streatham constituency and widely regarded as the UK's Obama), Ray Lewis (Deputy Mayor of London for young people), Paul Boateng (High Commissioner to South Africa and former Chief Secretary of the Treasury), Adam Afriyie (Shadow Minister for Innovation, Universities and Skills) and Air Commodore David Case (Royal Air Force Director of Specialist Ground Training) have been able to get to the positions that they have. In the British military, black Britons now make up about 2.5% of officers from all services. This might seem like a small number, but it really isn't if you consider the fact that Britain has a population of roughly 60million people in comparison to America, which has a population of 300million and 6% representation of black officers in the US military.

I don't think anyone would argue with the fact that even two decades ago, the idea of black Britons getting to these positions seemed impossible. The more progress is made in this regard, the more visible black Britons will be in influential positions in society. The more visible black

Britons are in influential positions, the less outrageous the idea of a black British Prime Minister will be.

The second reason why I think a British Prime Minister is decades away, has to do with the political systems in both countries.

In Britain, the procedure for the ascent to the office of Prime Minister is very different from the procedure for the ascent to the office of President of The United States. While in America, anyone from any party can decide to run for President, in Britain, no one actually runs for Prime Minister. During a general election, the parties run against each other and the leader of whichever party wins the most seats in Parliament is then appointed Prime Minister by the Queen. So in actual fact, the process of selecting the party leader is the one that really determines who will be Prime Minister. This is done by party members and is largely based on the support base the candidate has within the party. And in most cases, the support a he or she is able to build is based on seniority (not in age). Although it is not an officially laid down rule, party leaders who have gone on to become Prime Minister, were Members of Parliament for over a decade first.

Look at these examples:

- Margaret Thatcher was first elected to Parliament in 1959. She was elected the Conservative Party leader in 1975 and appointed Prime Minister in 1979;

- John Major was first elected to Parliament in 1979. He was elected the Conservative Party leader in 1990 and also became Prime Minister in 1990.

- Tony Blair was first elected to Parliament in 1983. He was elected the Labor Party leader in 1994 and appointed Prime Minister in 1997.

- Gordon Brown was first elected to Parliament in 1983. He became the Labor Party leader in 2007 and was appointed Prime Minister, following the resignation of Tony Blair.

I don't believe it is at all possible for a future party leader to go on to become Prime Minister without at least a decade as an MP first. Of course an MP can decide to run for party leadership at any time he or she wants, but the fact is that no one would take such a person seriously, regardless of whatever talents he or she might possess.

This is where the American system differs and Barack Obama's candidacy is a perfect example of this difference. He had served only two years in the US Senate before announcing his intention to run for President. I don't see any scenario under which that could have happened in Britain. For all his brilliance and charisma, he would have had to "wait his turn" before he could come close to being in the running to become party leader. He delivered a powerful speech during the 2004 convention and suddenly, the national leadership of the Democratic Party began to cast him as a future Presidential candidate. Four years later, he was elected President. I don't think a powerful speech from someone running for the British Parliament would make leaders of the party consider him as a party leader in a couple of years.

You might argue at this point that this is about politics and has nothing to do with a black politician being Prime Minister. But I beg to differ. Of all the black politicians at the moment, I don't know any of them that has the kind of party base support they would need to be in serious contention for party leadership. The younger ones like Chuka Umunna are fast developing a reputation and a following, so who knows what might happen a decade or so from now. Or maybe even earlier!

So, to answer the debate question, "Could Britain have a Black Prime Minister?" My answer would be: Yes, but I don't think it will happen for another decade or more. There are those that believe it is impossible, but I would ask them to consider the fact that only a year ago, not a lot of people believed America could have a black President. They might then argue that, America is America and Britain is Britain. True, but that does not change the fact that a year ago, America or not, very few people thought it was possible. And in the world we live in today, one thing I have learnt, especially in the last year, is that, nothing is impossible.

DID YOU KNOW?

Here is some trivia for you. Ask yourself how many of the facts below you knew without fact-checking first.

1. Did you know that Abraham Lincoln was the first Republican US President?

2. Did you know that President Franklin Deleno Roosevelt was in a wheelchair during WW2?

3. Did you know that JFK stands for John Fitzgerald Kennedy and not John Frederick Kennedy, as a lot of people believe? (you'll be surprised at how many people actually think his middle name was Frederick)

4. Did you know that the official residence of the US Vice President is the US Naval Observatory in Washington and not the White House?

5. Did you know that the US Vice President is the head of the Senate, but the main duty is to act as a tie-breaker in a deadlocked vote?

6. Did you know that every President since Ronald Reagan has had an attempt made on his life? (In

the case of George Bush Sr, the attempt was made after he left office)

7. Did you know that The US Secret Service was not formed to protect the President, but to combat counterfeit currency?

8. Did you know that (as a result of 7 above) that the head of The Secret Service was the Secretary of The Treasury, until March 2003, when it was placed under the Department of Homeland Security?

9. Did you know that The US Secret Service was assigned to protect the President and Vice President in 1901 and formally assumed this as part of their duties in 1902?

10. Did you know that Bill Clinton is the last US President who will have life-time secret service protection? (all Presidents after him get protection for 10years after they leave office)

11. Did you know that the Secret Service did not start protecting Presidential candidates until after the assassination of Robert Kennedy in 1968?

12. Did you know that Barack Obama was the first US Presidential candidate to get Secret Service protection so early in an election cycle? (His protection started in May 2007, after death threats; usually, Secret Service protection of major presidential candidates starts from 120days before an election)

13. Did you know that the youngest elected US President was John Kennedy, who was 43 when he was elected? (Theodore Roosevelt, aged 42 was

the youngest to serve as President, but he took over the office after the assassination of William McKinley in 1901)

14. Did you know that two Secret Service agents have taken bullets for the President? (Agent Leslie Coffelt, was shot and killed while trying to protect President Truman from assassins in 1950; Agent Tim McCarthy was shot during the 1981 assassination attempt on Ronald Reagan. Agent McCarthy made a full recovery)

15. Did you know that President Barack Obama did not have enough clout to get a floor pass to the Democratic Convention in 2000 and had to return home to Chicago?

16. Did you know that the first woman to be nominated for the US Vice Presidency from a major political party was Geraldine Ferraro in 1984?

17. Did you know that the US Vice President, Joe Biden ran for President in 1988, when Barack Obama was 27years old?

18. Did you know that for the last 28years, there has not been a US Presidential election that did not involve either a Bush or a Clinton? (George Bush Sr was vice president from 1980 – 1988, was president from 1988 – 1992; Bill Clinton was president from 1992 – 2000; George W. Bush was president from 2000 – 2008; during the 2008 elections, Hillary Clinton contested the Democratic nomination; It'll be interesting to see if Jebb Bush will run next election cycle and Chelsea Clinton, the one after!)

19. Did you know that, "Air Force One" is a call sign and not the name of the President's plane; i.e. ANY Air Force plane the President is in, will be called Air Force One?

20. Did you know that Barack Obama is the 26th lawyer to serve as US President?

21. Did you know that every time the President flies on Air Force One, another one (Another Air Force One) flies a few miles behind?

22. Did you know that the White House has formerly been known as, "The President's Mansion, The President's Palace and The Executive Mansion? (The name, The White House was formally established in 1901 by President Theodore Roosevelt)

23. Did you know that there is no limit to the number of terms a Vice President can serve, unlike the two terms for a president?

24. Did you know that Ronald Reagan was the oldest US president? (He was 69 when he was elected and 77 at the end of his second term)?

25. Did you know that Theodore Roosevelt had a bullet lodged in his chest from an assassination attempt from 1912 till the he died in 1919? (He died of a coronary disease and not because of the bullet)

26. Did you know that the origin of "Teddy Bear" was from Theodore Roosevelt, (nicknamed Teddy), because he refused to shoot a bear that had been tied up by his staff during a hunting trip? (After this incident, there were cartoons in

newspapers showing what happened and toys of bears with the name, Teddy began to surface; that was how the name stuck)

27. Did you know that there was no official term limit for US Presidents until after the death of Franklin Roosevelt in 1945? (Roosevelt served 4 terms; before then every president served 2 terms, even though the constitution did not specify a limit. The two term limit was added as the 22nd amendment to the constitution in 1951)

28. Did you know that the President with the shortest tenure was William Harrison, who was President for only 30days before he died of pneumonia? (He served from April 1841-March 1841)

29. Did you know that if Hillary Clinton had been elected President, Bill Clinton would have been known as, "The First Gentleman?"

30. Did you know that when a senator is elected president or vice president, the state governor picks his/replacement? (as in the cases of Senators Obama and Biden)

31. Did you know that the age requirement for Presidency of the US is 35years?

32. Did you know that two US Presidents have been impeached? (Andrew Jackson in 1857 and Bill Clinton in 1998)

33. Did you know that impeachment means bringing charges against a government official, before conviction and a vote to remove or not remove from office? (There is a common misconception

that impeachment means removal from office, but it is actually only a legal statement of charges, like an indictment in criminal law. So, it is possible to be impeached without being removed from office, as in the case of Bill Clinton)

34. Did you know that the salary of the US President is $400000 per year? (This excludes expense and travel accounts)

35. Did you know that there have been two father and son Presidencies in US history? (**1.** John Adams: father, was the 2nd President of the US and served from 1797-1801 and John Quincy Adams: son, was the 6th President of the US and served from 1825-1829. **2.** George. H. W. Bush: father, was the 41st President of the US and served from 1989-1993 and George W Bush, son, is the 43rd President of the US and has served from 2001)

36. Did you know that there have been one grandfather and grandson Presidencies in US history? (William Harrison, grandfather, was the 9th US President and served from April 1841-March 1841 and Benjamin Harrison, grandson, was the 23rd US President, who served from 1889-1893)

37. Did you know that President Barack Obama only repaid his student loan four years ago, after signing his book deal?

38. Did you know that the maximum amount of money that can be contributed to a political campaign by an individual is $2300?

39. Did you know that the youngest governor in the US is Louisiana's Bobby Jindal, who is 36years old?

40. Did you know that until 1933, the President-elect did not take over as President until March, which would have been four months after the election?

TRANSCRIPT OF STATE SENATOR OBAMA'S SPEECH IN 2002 OPPOSING WAR IN IRAQ

Good afternoon. Let me begin by saying that although this has been billed as an anti-war rally, I stand before you as someone who is not opposed to war in all circumstances. The Civil War was one of the bloodiest in history, and yet it was only through the crucible of the sword, the sacrifice of multitudes, that we could begin to perfect this union, and drive the scourge of slavery from our soil. I don't oppose all wars.

My grandfather signed up for a war the day after Pearl Harbor was bombed, fought in Patton's army. He saw the dead and dying across the fields of Europe; he heard the stories of fellow troops who first entered Auschwitz and Treblinka. He fought in the name of a larger freedom, part of that arsenal of democracy that triumphed over evil, and he did not fight in vain. I don't oppose all wars. After September 11th, after witnessing the carnage and destruction, the dust and the tears, I supported this administration's pledge to hunt down and root out those who would slaughter innocents in the name of intolerance, and I would willingly take up arms myself to prevent such tragedy from happening again. I don't oppose all wars. And I know that in this crowd today, there is no shortage of patriots, or of patriotism.

What I am opposed to is a dumb war. What I am opposed to is a rash war. What I am opposed to is the cynical attempt by Richard Perle and Paul Wolfowitz and other armchair, weekend warriors in this administration to shove their own ideological agendas down our throats, irrespective of the costs in lives lost and in hardships borne.

What I am opposed to is the attempt by political hacks like Karl Rove to distract us from a rise in the uninsured, a rise in the poverty rate, a drop in the median income - to distract us from corporate scandals and a stock market that has just gone through the worst month since the Great Depression. That's what I'm opposed to. A dumb war. A rash war. A war based not on reason but on passion, not on principle but on politics. Now let me be clear - I suffer no illusions about Saddam Hussein. He is a brutal man. A ruthless man. A man who butchers his own people to secure his own power. He has repeatedly defied UN resolutions, thwarted UN inspection teams, developed chemical and biological weapons, and coveted nuclear capacity. He's a bad guy. The world, and the Iraqi people, would be better off without him.

But I also know that Saddam poses no imminent and direct threat to the United States, or to his neighbors, that the Iraqi economy is in shambles, that the Iraqi military a fraction of its former strength, and that in concert with the international community he can be contained until, in the way of all petty dictators, he falls away into the dustbin of history. I know that even a successful war against Iraq will require a US occupation of undetermined length, at undetermined cost, with undetermined consequences. I know that an invasion of Iraq without a clear rationale and without strong international support will only fan the flames of the Middle East, and encourage the worst, rather than best, impulses of the Arab world, and strengthen the recruitment arm of Al Qaeda. I am not opposed to all wars. I'm opposed to dumb wars.

So for those of us who seek a more just and secure world for our children, let us send a clear message to the President today. You want a fight, President Bush? Let's finish the fight with Bin Laden and Al Qaeda, through effective, coordinated intelligence, and a shutting down of the financial networks that support terrorism, and a homeland security program that involves more than color-coded warnings. You want a fight, President Bush? Let's fight to make sure that the UN inspectors can do their work, and that we vigorously enforce a non-proliferation treaty, and that former enemies and current allies like Russia safeguard and ultimately eliminate their stores of nuclear material, and that nations like Pakistan and India never use the terrible weapons already in their possession, and that the arms merchants in our own country stop feeding the countless wars that rage across the globe. You want a fight, President Bush?

Let's fight to make sure our so-called allies in the Middle East, the Saudis and the Egyptians, stop oppressing their own people, and suppressing dissent, and tolerating corruption and inequality, and mismanaging their economies so that their youth grow up without education, without prospects, without hope, the ready recruits of terrorist cells. You want a fight, President Bush? Let's fight to wean ourselves off Middle East oil, through an energy policy that doesn't simply serve the interests of Exxon and Mobil. Those are the battles that we need to fight. Those are the battles that we willingly join. The battles against ignorance and intolerance. Corruption and greed. Poverty and despair.

The consequences of war are dire, the sacrifices immeasurable. We may have occasion in our lifetime to once again rise up in defense of our freedom, and pay the wages of war. But we ought not -- we will not -- travel down that hellish path blindly. Nor should we allow those who would march off and pay the ultimate sacrifice, who would prove the full measure of devotion with their blood, to make such an awful sacrifice in vain

TRANSCRIPT OF STATE SENATOR BARACK OBAMA'S SPEECH AT 2004 DEMOCRATIC NATIONAL CONVENTION

On behalf of the great state of Illinois, crossroads of a nation, land of Lincoln, let me express my deep gratitude for the privilege of addressing this convention. Tonight is a particular honor for me because, let's face it, my presence on this stage is pretty unlikely. My father was a foreign student, born and raised in a small village in Kenya. He grew up herding goats, went to school in a tin-roof shack. His father, my grandfather, was a cook, a domestic servant.

But my grandfather had larger dreams for his son. Through hard work and perseverance my father got a scholarship to study in a magical place: America, which stood as a beacon of freedom and opportunity to so many who had come before. While studying here, my father met my mother. She was born in a town on the other side of the world, in Kansas. Her father worked on oil rigs and farms through most of the Depression. The day after Pearl Harbor he signed up for duty, joined Patton's army and marched across Europe. Back home, my grandmother raised their baby and went to work on a bomber assembly line. After the war, they studied on the

GI Bill, bought a house through FHA, and moved west in search of opportunity.

And they, too, had big dreams for their daughter, a common dream, born of two continents. My parents shared not only an improbable love; they shared an abiding faith in the possibilities of this nation. They would give me an African name, Barack, or "blessed," believing that in a tolerant America your name is no barrier to success. They imagined me going to the best schools in the land, even though they weren't rich, because in a generous America you don't have to be rich to achieve your potential. They are both passed away now. Yet, I know that, on this night, they look down on me with pride.

I stand here today, grateful for the diversity of my heritage, aware that my parents' dreams live on in my precious daughters. I stand here knowing that my story is part of the larger American story, that I owe a debt to all of those who came before me, and that, in no other country on earth, is my story even possible. Tonight, we gather to affirm the greatness of our nation, not because of the height of our skyscrapers, or the power of our military, or the size of our economy. Our pride is based on a very simple premise, summed up in a declaration made over two hundred years ago, "We hold these truths to he self-evident, that all men are created equal. That they are endowed by their Creator with certain inalienable rights. That among these are life, liberty and the pursuit of happiness."

That is the true genius of America, a faith in the simple dreams of its people, the insistence on small miracles. That we can tuck in our children at night and know they are fed and clothed and safe from harm. That we can say what we think, write what we think, without hearing a sudden knock on the door. That we can have an idea and start our own business without paying a bribe or hiring somebody's son. That we can participate in the political process without fear of retribution, and that our votes will he counted - or at least, most of the time.

This year, in this election, we are called to reaffirm our values and commitments, to hold them against a hard reality and see how we are measuring up, to the legacy of our forbearers, and the promise of future generations. And fellow Americans - Democrats, Republicans, Independents - I say to you tonight: we have more work to do. More to do for the workers I met in Galesburg, Illinois, who are losing their union jobs at the Maytag plant that's moving to Mexico, and now are having to compete with their own children for jobs that pay seven bucks an hour. More to do for the father I met who was losing his job and choking back tears, wondering how he would pay $4,500 a month for the drugs his son needs without the health benefits he counted on. More to do for the young woman in East St. Louis, and thousands more like her, who has the grades, has the drive, has the will, but doesn't have the money to go to college.

Don't get me wrong. The people I meet in small towns and big cities, in diners and office parks, they don't expect government to solve all their problems. They know they have to work hard to get ahead and they want to. Go into the collar counties around Chicago, and people will tell you they don't want their tax money wasted by a welfare agency or the Pentagon. Go into any inner city neighborhood, and folks will tell you that government alone can't teach kids to learn. They know that parents have to parent, that children can't achieve unless we raise their expectations and turn off the television sets and eradicate the slander that says a black youth with a book is acting white. No, people don't expect government to solve all their problems. But they sense, deep in their bones, that with just a change in priorities, we can make sure that every child in America has a decent shot at life, and that the doors of opportunity remain open to all. They know we can do better. And they want that choice.

In this election, we offer that choice. Our party has chosen a man to lead us who embodies the best this country has to offer. That man is John Kerry. John Kerry understands the ideals of community, faith, and sacrifice, because they've defined his life. From his heroic service in Vietnam to his years as prosecutor and lieutenant governor, through two decades in the United States Senate, he has devoted himself to this country. Again and again, we've seen him make tough choices when easier ones were available. His values and his record affirm what is best in us.

John Kerry believes in an America where hard work is rewarded. So instead of offering tax breaks to companies shipping jobs overseas, he'll offer them to companies creating jobs here at home. John Kerry believes in an America where all Americans can afford the same health coverage our politicians in Washington have for themselves. John Kerry believes in energy independence, so we aren't held hostage to the profits of oil companies or the sabotage of foreign oil fields. John Kerry believes in the constitutional freedoms that have made our country the envy of the world, and he will never sacrifice our basic liberties nor use faith as a wedge to divide us. And John

Kerry believes that in a dangerous world, war must be an option, but it should never he the first option.

A while back, I met a young man named Shamus at the VFW Hall in East Moline, Illinois. He was a good-looking kid, six-two or six-three, clear-eyed, with an easy smile. He told me he'd joined the Marines and was heading to Iraq the following week. As I listened to him explain why he'd enlisted, his absolute faith in our country and its leaders, his devotion to duty and service, I thought this young man was all any of us might hope for in a child. But then I asked myself: Are we serving Shamus as well as he was serving us? I thought of more than 900 service men and women, sons and daughters, husbands and wives, friends and neighbors, who will not be returning to their hometowns. I thought of families I had met who were struggling to get by without a loved one's full income, or whose loved ones had returned with a limb missing or with nerves shattered, but who still lacked long-term health benefits because they were reservists. When we send our young men and women into harm's way, we have a solemn obligation not to fudge the numbers or shade the truth about why they're going, to care for their families while they're gone, to tend to the soldiers upon their return, and to never ever go to war without enough troops to win the war, secure the peace, and earn the respect of the world.

Now let me be clear. We have real enemies in the world. These enemies must be found. They must be pursued and they must be defeated. John Kerry knows this. And just as Lieutenant Kerry did not hesitate to risk his life to protect the men who served with him in Vietnam, President Kerry will not hesitate one moment to use our military might to keep America safe and secure. John Kerry believes in America. And he knows it's not enough for just some of us to prosper. For alongside our famous individualism, there's another ingredient in the American saga.

A belief that we are connected as one people. If there's a child on the south side of Chicago who can't read, that matters to me, even if it's not my child. If there's a senior citizen somewhere who can't pay for her prescription and has to choose between medicine and the rent, that makes my life poorer, even if it's not my grandmother. If there's an Arab American family being rounded up without benefit of an attorney or due process, that threatens my civil liberties. It's that fundamental belief - I am my brother's keeper, I am my sister's keeper - that makes this country work. It's what allows us to pursue our individual dreams, yet still come together as a single American family. "E pluribus unum." Out of many, one.

Yet even as we speak, there are those who are preparing to divide us, the spin masters and negative ad peddlers who embrace the politics of anything goes. Well, I say to them tonight, there's not a liberal America and a conservative America - there's the United States of America. There's not a black America and white America and Latino America and Asian America; there's the United States of America. The pundits like to slice-and-dice our country into Red States and Blue States; Red States for Republicans, Blue States for Democrats. But I've got news for them, too. We worship an awesome God in the Blue States, and we don't like federal agents poking around our libraries in the Red States. We coach Little League in the Blue States and have gay friends in the Red States. There are patriots

249

who opposed the war in Iraq and patriots who supported it. We are one people, all of us pledging allegiance to the stars and stripes, all of us defending the United States of America.

In the end, that's what this election is about. Do we participate in a politics of cynicism or a politics of hope? John Kerry calls on us to hope. John Edwards calls on us to hope. I'm not talking about blind optimism here - the almost willful ignorance that thinks unemployment will go away if we just don't talk about it, or the health care crisis will solve itself if we just ignore it. No, I'm talking about something more substantial. It's the hope of slaves sitting around a fire singing freedom songs; the hope of immigrants setting out for distant shores; the hope of a young naval lieutenant bravely patrolling the Mekong Delta; the hope of a millworker's son who dares to defy the odds; the hope of a skinny kid with a funny name who believes that America has a place for him, too. The audacity of hope!

In the end, that is God's greatest gift to us, the bedrock of this nation; the belief in things not seen; the belief that there are better days ahead. I believe we can give our middle class relief and provide working families with a road to opportunity. I believe we can provide jobs to the jobless, homes to the homeless, and reclaim young people in cities across America from violence and despair. I believe that as we stand on the crossroads of history, we can make the right choices, and meet the challenges that face us. America!

Tonight, if you feel the same energy I do, the same urgency I do, the same passion I do, the same hopefulness I do - if we do what we must do, then I have no doubt that all across the country, from Florida to Oregon, from Washington to Maine, the people will rise up in November, and John Kerry will be sworn in as president, and John Edwards will be sworn in as vice president, and this country will reclaim its promise, and out of this long political darkness a brighter day will come. Thank you and God bless you.

TRANSCRIPT OF SENATOR BARACK OBAMA'S SPEECH ANNOUNCING CANDIDACY FOR PRESIDENT

Let me begin by saying thanks to all you who've traveled, from far and wide, to brave the cold today.

We all made this journey for a reason. It's humbling, but in my heart I know you didn't come here just for me, you came here because you believe in what this country can be. In the face of war, you believe there can be peace. In the face of despair, you believe there can be hope. In the face of a politics that's shut you out, that's told you to settle, that's divided us for too long, you believe we can be one people, reaching for what's possible, building that more perfect union.

That's the journey we're on today. But let me tell you how I came to be here. As most of you know, I am not a native of this great state. I moved to Illinois over two decades ago. I was a young man then, just a year out of college; I knew no one in Chicago, was without money or family connections. But a group of churches had offered me a job as a community organizer for $13,000 a year. And I accepted the job, sight unseen, motivated then by a single, simple, powerful idea - that I might play a small part in building a better America.

My work took me to some of Chicago's poorest neighborhoods. I joined with pastors and lay-people to deal with communities that had been ravaged by plant closings. I saw that the problems people faced weren't simply local in nature - that the decision to close a steel mill was made by distant executives; that the lack of textbooks and computers in schools could be traced to the skewed priorities of politicians a thousand miles away; and that when a child turns to violence, there's a hole in his heart no government alone can fill.

It was in these neighborhoods that I received the best education I ever had, and where I learned the true meaning of my Christian faith.

After three years of this work, I went to law school, because I wanted to understand how the law should work for those in need. I became a civil rights lawyer, and taught constitutional law, and after a time, I came to understand that our cherished rights of liberty and equality depend on the active participation of an awakened electorate. It was with these ideas in mind that I arrived in this capital city as a state Senator.

It was here, in Springfield, where I saw all that is America converge - farmers and teachers, businessmen and laborers, all of them with a story to tell, all of them seeking a seat at the table, all of them clamoring to be heard. I made lasting friendships here - friends that I see in the audience today.

It was here we learned to disagree without being disagreeable - that it's possible to compromise so long as you know those principles that can never be compromised; and that so long as we're willing to listen to each other, we can assume the best in people instead of the worst.

That's why we were able to reform a death penalty system that was broken. That's why we were able to give health insurance to children in need. That's why we made the tax system more fair and just for working families, and that's why we passed ethics reforms that the cynics said could never, ever be passed.

It was here, in Springfield, where North, South, East and West come together that I was reminded of the essential decency of the American people - where I came to believe that through this decency, we can build a more hopeful America.

And that is why, in the shadow of the Old State Capitol, where Lincoln once called on a divided house to stand together, where common hopes and common dreams still, I stand before you today to announce my candidacy for President of the United States.

I recognize there is a certain presumptuousness - a certain audacity - to this announcement. I know I haven't spent a lot of time learning the ways of Washington. But I've been there long enough to know that the ways of Washington must change.

The genius of our founders is that they designed a system of government that can be changed. And we should take heart, because we've changed this country before. In the face of tyranny, a band of patriots brought an Empire to its knees. In the face of secession, we unified a nation and set the captives free. In the face of Depression,

we put people back to work and lifted millions out of poverty. We welcomed immigrants to our shores, we opened railroads to the west, we landed a man on the moon, and we heard a King's call to let justice roll down like water, and righteousness like a mighty stream.

Each and every time, a new generation has risen up and done what's needed to be done. Today we are called once more - and it is time for our generation to answer that call.

For that is our unyielding faith - that in the face of impossible odds, people who love their country can change it.

That's what Abraham Lincoln understood. He had his doubts. He had his defeats. He had his setbacks. But through his will and his words, he moved a nation and helped free a people. It is because of the millions who rallied to his cause that we are no longer divided, North and South, slave and free. It is because men and women of every race, from every walk of life, continued to march for freedom long after Lincoln was laid to rest, that today we have the chance to face the challenges of this millennium together, as one people - as Americans.

All of us know what those challenges are today - a war with no end, a dependence on oil that threatens our future, schools where too many children aren't learning, and families struggling paycheck to paycheck despite working as hard as they can. We know the challenges. We've heard them. We've talked about them for years.

What's stopped us from meeting these challenges is not the absence of sound policies and sensible plans. What's stopped us is the failure of leadership, the smallness of our politics - the ease with which we're distracted by the petty and trivial, our chronic avoidance of tough decisions, our preference for scoring cheap political points instead of rolling up our sleeves and building a working consensus to tackle big problems.

For the last six years we've been told that our

mounting debts don't matter, we've been told that the anxiety Americans feel about rising health care costs and stagnant wages are an illusion, we've been told that climate change is a hoax, and that tough talk and an ill-conceived war can replace diplomacy, and strategy, and foresight. And when all else fails, when Katrina happens, or the death toll in Iraq mounts, we've been told that our crises are somebody else's fault. We're distracted from our real failures, and told to blame the other party, or gay people, or immigrants.

And as people have looked away in disillusionment and frustration, we know what's filled the void. The cynics, and the lobbyists, and the special interests who've turned our government into a game only they can afford to play. They write the checks and you get stuck with the bills, they get the access while you get to write a letter, they think they own this government, but we're here today to take it back. The time for that politics is over. It's time to turn the page.

We've made some progress already. I was proud to help lead the fight in Congress that led to the most sweeping ethics reform since Watergate.

But Washington has a long way to go. And it won't be easy. That's why we'll have to set priorities. We'll have to make hard choices. And although government will play a crucial role in bringing about the changes we need, more money and programs alone will not get us where we need to go. Each of us, in our own lives, will have to accept responsibility - for instilling an ethic of achievement in our children, for adapting to a more competitive economy, for strengthening our communities, and sharing some measure of sacrifice. So let us begin. Let us begin this hard work together. Let us transform this nation.

Let us be the generation that reshapes our economy to compete in the digital age. Let's set high standards for our schools and give them the resources they need to succeed. Let's recruit a new army of teachers, and give them better pay and more support in exchange for more accountability. Let's make college more affordable, and let's invest in scientific research, and let's lay down broadband lines through the heart

of inner cities and rural towns all across America.

And as our economy changes, let's be the generation that ensures our nation's workers are sharing in our prosperity. Let's protect the hard-earned benefits their companies have promised. Let's make it possible for hardworking Americans to save for retirement. And let's allow our unions and their organizers to lift up this country's middle-class again.

Let's be the generation that ends poverty in America. Every single person willing to work should be able to get job training that leads to a job, and earn a living wage that can pay the bills, and afford child care so their kids have a safe place to go when they work. Let's do this.

Let's be the generation that finally tackles our health care crisis. We can control costs by focusing on prevention, by providing better treatment to the chronically ill, and using technology to cut the bureaucracy. Let's be the generation that says right here, right now, that we will have universal health care in America by the end of the next president's first term.

Let's be the generation that finally frees America from the tyranny of oil. We can harness homegrown, alternative fuels like ethanol and spur the production of more fuel-efficient cars. We can set up a system for capping greenhouse gases. We can turn this crisis of global warming into a moment of opportunity for innovation, and job creation, and an incentive for businesses that will serve as a model for the world. Let's be the generation that makes future generations proud of what we did here.

Most of all, let's be the generation that never forgets what happened on that September day and confront the terrorists with everything we've got. Politics doesn't have to divide us on this anymore - we can work together to keep our country safe. I've worked with Republican Senator Dick Lugar to pass a law that will secure and destroy some of the world's deadliest, unguarded weapons. We can work together to track terrorists down with a stronger military, we can tighten the net around their finances, and we can improve our intelligence capabilities. But let us also understand that ultimate victory against our enemies will come only by rebuilding our alliances and exporting those ideals that bring hope and opportunity to millions around the globe.

But all of this cannot come to pass until we bring an end to this war in Iraq. Most of you know I opposed this war from the start. I thought it was a tragic mistake. Today we grieve for the families who have lost loved ones, the hearts that have been broken, and the young lives that could have been. America, it's time to start bringing our troops home. It's time to admit that no amount of American lives can resolve the political disagreement that lies at the heart of someone else's civil war. That's why I have a plan that will bring our combat troops home by March of 2008. Letting the Iraqis know that we will not be there forever is our last, best hope to pressure the Sunni and Shia to come to the table and find peace.

Finally, there is one other thing that is not too late to get right about this war - and that is the homecoming of the men and women - our veterans - who have sacrificed the most. Let us honor their valor by providing the care they need and rebuilding the military they love. Let us be the generation that begins this work.

I know there are those who don't believe we can do all these things. I understand the skepticism. After all, every four years, candidates from both parties make similar promises, and I expect this year will be no different. All of us running for president will travel around the country offering ten-point plans and making grand speeches; all of us will trumpet those qualities we believe make us uniquely qualified to lead the country. But too many times, after the election is over, and the confetti is swept away, all those promises fade from memory, and the lobbyists and the special interests move in, and people turn away, disappointed as before, left to struggle on their own.

That is why this campaign can't only be about me. It must be about us - it must be about what we can do together. This campaign must be the occasion, the vehicle, of your hopes, and your dreams. It will take your time, your energy, and your advice - to push us forward when we're doing right, and to let us know when we're not. This campaign has to be about reclaiming the meaning of citizenship, restoring our sense of common purpose, and realizing that few obstacles can withstand the power of millions of voices calling for change.

By ourselves, this change will not happen. Divided, we are bound to fail.

But the life of a tall, gangly, self-made Springfield lawyer tells us that a different future is possible.

He tells us that there is power in words.

He tells us that there is power in conviction.

That beneath all the differences of race and region, faith and station, we are one people.

He tells us that there is power in hope.

As Lincoln organized the forces arrayed against slavery, he was heard to say: "Of strange, discordant, and even hostile elements, we gathered from the four winds, and formed and fought to battle through."

That is our purpose here today.

That's why I'm in this race.

Not just to hold an office, but to gather with you to transform a nation.

I want to win that next battle - for justice and opportunity.

I want to win that next battle - for better schools, and better jobs, and health care for all.

I want us to take up the unfinished business of perfecting our union, and building a better America.

And if you will join me in this improbable quest, if you feel destiny calling, and see as I see, a future of endless possibility stretching before us; if you sense, as I sense, that the time is now to shake off our slumber, and slough off our fear, and make good on the debt we owe past and future generations, then I'm ready to take up the cause, and march with you, and work with you. Together, starting today, let us finish the work that needs to be done, and usher in a new birth of freedom on this Earth.

TRANSCRIPT OF SENATOR BARACK OBAMA'S VICTORY SPEECH ON THE NIGHT OF IOWA CAUCUSES

Thank you, Iowa.

You know, they said this day would never come.

They said our sights were set too high.

They said this country was too divided; too disillusioned to ever come together around a common purpose.

But on this January night - at this defining moment in history - you have done what the cynics said we couldn't do. You have done what the state of New Hampshire can do in five days. You have done what America can do in this New Year, 2008. In lines that stretched around schools and churches; in small towns and big cities; you came together as Democrats, Republicans and Independents to stand up and say that we are one nation; we are one people; and our time for change has come.

You said the time has come to move beyond the bitterness and pettiness and anger that's consumed Washington; to end the political strategy that's been all about division and instead make it about addition - to build a coalition for change that stretches through Red States and Blue States. Because that's how we'll win in

November, and that's how we'll finally meet the challenges that we face as a nation.

We are choosing hope over fear. We're choosing unity over division, and sending a powerful message that change is coming to America.

You said the time has come to tell the lobbyists who think their money and their influence speak louder than our voices that they don't own this government, we do; and we are here to take it back.

The time has come for a President who will be honest about the choices and the challenges we face; who will listen to you and learn from you even when we disagree; who won't just tell you what you want to hear, but what you need to know. And in New Hampshire, if you give me the same chance that Iowa did tonight, I will be that president for America.

Thank you.

I'll be a President who finally makes health care affordable and available to every single American the same way I expanded health care in Illinois - by--by bringing Democrats and Republicans together to get the job done.

I'll be a President who ends the tax breaks for companies that ship our jobs overseas and put a middle-class tax cut into the pockets of the working Americans who deserve it.

I'll be a President who harnesses the ingenuity of farmers and scientists and entrepreneurs to free this nation from the tyranny of oil once and for all.

And I'll be a President who ends this war in Iraq and finally brings our troops home; who restores our moral standing; who understands that 9/11 is not a way to scare up votes, but a challenge that should unite America and the world against the common threats of the twenty-first century; common threats of terrorism and nuclear weapons; climate change and poverty; genocide and disease.

Tonight, we are one step closer to that vision of America because of what you did here in Iowa. And so I'd especially like to thank the organizers and the precinct captains; the volunteers and the staff who made this all possible.

And while I'm at it, on "thank yous," I think it makes sense for me to thank the love of my life, the rock of the Obama family, the closer on the campaign trail; give it up for Michelle Obama.

I know you didn't do this for me. You did this-you did this because you believed so deeply in the most American of ideas - that in the face of impossible odds, people who love this country can change it.

I know this-I know this because while I may be standing here tonight, I'll never forget that my journey began on the streets of Chicago doing what so many of you have done for this campaign and all the campaigns here in Iowa - organizing, and working, and fighting to make people's lives just a little bit better.

I know how hard it is. It comes with little sleep, little pay, and a lot of sacrifice. There are days of disappointment, but sometimes, just sometimes, there are nights like this - a night-a night that, years from now, when we've made the changes we believe in; when more families can afford to see a doctor; when our children-when Malia and Sasha and your children-inherit a planet that's a little cleaner and safer; when the world sees America differently, and

America sees itself as a nation less divided and more united; you'll be able to look back with pride and say that this was the moment when it all began.

This was the moment when the improbable beat what Washington always said was inevitable.

This was the moment when we tore down barriers that have divided us for too long - when we rallied people of all parties and ages to a common cause; when we finally gave Americans who'd never participated in politics a reason to stand up and to do so.

This was the moment when we finally beat back the politics of fear, and doubt, and cynicism; the politics where we tear each other down instead of lifting this country up. This was the moment.

Years from now, you'll look back and you'll say that this was the moment - this was the place - where America remembered what it means to hope.

For many months, we've been teased, even derided for talking about hope.

But we always knew that hope is not blind optimism. It's not ignoring the enormity of the task ahead or the roadblocks that stand in our path. It's not sitting on the sidelines or shirking from a fight. Hope is that thing inside us that insists, despite all evidence to the contrary, that something better awaits us if we have the courage to reach for it, and to work for it, and to fight for it.

Hope is what I saw in the eyes of the young woman in Cedar Rapids who works the night shift after a full day of college and still can't afford health care for a sister who's ill; a young woman who still believes that this country will give her the chance to live out her dreams.

Hope is what I heard in the voice of the New

Hampshire woman who told me that she hasn't been able to breathe since her nephew left for Iraq; who still goes to bed each night praying for his safe return.

Hope is what led a band of colonists to rise up against an empire; what led the greatest of generations to free a continent and heal a nation; what led young women and young men to sit at lunch counters and brave fire hoses and march through Selma and Montgomery for freedom's cause.

Hope-hope-is what led me here today - with a father from Kenya; a mother from Kansas; and a story that could only happen in the United States of America. Hope is the bedrock of this nation; the belief that our destiny will not be written for us, but by us; by all those men and women who are not content to settle for the world as it is; who have the courage to remake the world as it should be.

That is what we started here in Iowa, and that is the message we can now carry to New Hampshire and beyond; the same message we had when we were up and when we were down; the one that can change this country brick by brick, block by block, calloused hand by calloused hand - that together, ordinary people can do extraordinary things; because we are not a collection of Red States and Blue States, we are the United States of America; and at this moment, in this election, we are ready to believe again. Thank you, Iowa.

TRANSCRIPT OF SENATOR BARACK OBAMA'S SPEECH ON RACE, "A MORE PERFECT UNION"

"We the people, in order to form a more perfect union."

Two hundred and twenty one years ago, in a hall that still stands across the street, a group of men gathered and, with these simple words, launched America's improbable experiment in democracy. Farmers and scholars; statesmen and patriots who had traveled across an ocean to escape tyranny and persecution finally made real their declaration of independence at a Philadelphia convention that lasted through the spring of 1787.

The document they produced was eventually signed but ultimately unfinished. It was stained by this nation's original sin of slavery, a question that divided the colonies and brought the convention to a stalemate until the founders chose to allow the slave trade to continue for at least twenty more years, and to leave any final resolution to future generations.

Of course, the answer to the slavery question was already embedded within our Constitution - a Constitution that had at is very core the ideal of equal citizenship under the law; a Constitution that promised its people liberty, and justice, and a union that could be and should be perfected over time.

And yet words on a parchment would not be enough to deliver slaves from bondage, or provide men and women of every color and creed their full rights and obligations as citizens of the United States. What would be needed were Americans in successive generations who were willing to do their part - through protests and struggle, on the streets and in the courts, through a civil war and civil disobedience and always at great risk - to narrow that gap between the promise of our ideals and the reality of their time.

This was one of the tasks we set forth at the beginning of this campaign - to continue the long march of those who came before us, a march for a more just, more equal, more free, more caring and more prosperous America. I chose to run for the presidency at this moment in history because I believe deeply that we cannot solve the challenges of our time unless we solve them together - unless we perfect our union by understanding that we may have different stories, but we hold common hopes; that we may not look the same and we may not have come from the same place, but we all want to move in the same direction - towards a better future for our children and our grandchildren.

This belief comes from my unyielding faith in the decency and generosity of the American people. But it also comes from my own American story.

I am the son of a black man from Kenya and a white woman from Kansas. I was raised with the help of a white grandfather who survived a Depression to serve in Patton's Army during World War II and a white grandmother who worked on a bomber assembly line at Fort Leavenworth while he was overseas. I've gone to some of the best schools in America and lived in one of the world's poorest nations. I am married to a black American who carries within her the blood of slaves and slaveowners - an inheritance we pass on to our two precious daughters. I have brothers, sisters, nieces, nephews, uncles and cousins, of every race and every hue, scattered across three continents, and for as long as I live, I will never forget that in no other country on Earth is my story even possible.

It's a story that hasn't made me the most conventional candidate. But it is a story that has seared into my genetic makeup the idea that this nation is more than the sum of its parts - that out of many, we are truly one.

Throughout the first year of this campaign, against all predictions to the contrary, we saw how hungry the American people were for this message of unity. Despite the temptation to view my candidacy through a purely racial lens, we won commanding victories in states with some of the whitest populations in the country. In South

Carolina, where the Confederate Flag still flies, we built a powerful coalition of African Americans and white Americans.

This is not to say that race has not been an issue in the campaign. At various stages in the campaign, some commentators have deemed me either "too black" or "not black enough." We saw racial tensions bubble to the surface during the week before the South Carolina primary. The press has scoured every exit poll for the latest evidence of racial polarization, not just in terms of white and black, but black and brown as well.

And yet, it has only been in the last couple of weeks

that the discussion of race in this campaign has taken a particularly divisive turn.

On one end of the spectrum, we've heard the implication that my candidacy is somehow an exercise in affirmative action; that it's based solely on the desire of wide-eyed liberals to purchase racial reconciliation on the cheap. On the other end, we've heard my former pastor, Reverend Jeremiah Wright, use incendiary language to express views that have the potential not only to widen the racial divide, but views that denigrate both the greatness and the goodness of our nation; that rightly offend white and black alike.

I have already condemned, in unequivocal terms, the statements of Reverend Wright that have caused such controversy. For some, nagging questions remain. Did I know him to be an occasionally fierce critic of American domestic and foreign policy? Of course. Did I ever hear him make remarks that could be considered controversial while I sat in church? Yes. Did I strongly disagree with many of his political views? Absolutely - just as I'm sure many of you have heard remarks from your pastors, priests, or rabbis with which you strongly disagreed.

But the remarks that have caused this recent firestorm weren't simply controversial. They weren't simply a religious leader's effort to speak out against perceived injustice. Instead, they expressed a profoundly distorted view of this country - a view that sees white racism as endemic, and that elevates what is wrong with America above all that we know is right with America; a view that sees the conflicts in the Middle East as rooted primarily in the actions of stalwart allies like Israel, instead of emanating from the perverse and hateful ideologies of radical Islam.

As such, Reverend Wright's comments were not only wrong but divisive, divisive at a time when we need unity; racially charged at a time when we need to come together to solve a set of monumental problems - two wars, a terrorist threat, a falling economy, a chronic health care crisis and potentially devastating climate change; problems that are neither black or white or Latino or Asian, but rather problems that confront us all.

Given my background, my politics, and my professed values and ideals, there will no doubt be those for whom my statements of condemnation are not enough. Why associate myself with Reverend Wright in the first place, they may ask? Why not join another church? And I confess that if all that I knew of Reverend Wright were the snippets of those sermons that have run in an endless loop on the television and You Tube, or if Trinity United Church of Christ conformed to the caricatures being peddled by some commentators, there is no doubt that I would react in much the same way

But the truth is, that isn't all that I know of the man. The man I met more than twenty years ago is a man who helped introduce me to my Christian faith, a man who spoke to me about our obligations to love one another; to care for the sick and lift up the poor. He is a man who served his country as a U.S. Marine; who has studied and lectured at some of the finest universities and seminaries in the country, and who for over thirty years led a church that serves the community by doing God's work here on Earth - by housing the homeless, ministering to the needy, providing day care services and scholarships and prison ministries, and reaching out to those suffering from HIV/AIDS.

In my first book, Dreams From My Father, I described the experience of my first

service at Trinity:

"People began to shout, to rise from their seats and clap and cry out, a forceful wind

carrying the reverend's voice up into the rafters....And in that single note - hope! - I heard something else; at the foot of that cross, inside the thousands of churches across the city, I imagined the stories of ordinary black people merging with the stories of David and Goliath, Moses and Pharaoh, the Christians in the lion's den, Ezekiel's field of dry bones. Those stories - of survival, and freedom, and hope - became our story, my story; the blood that had spilled was our blood, the tears our tears; until this black church, on this bright day, seemed once more a vessel carrying the story of a people into future generations and into a larger world. Our trials and triumphs became at once unique and universal, black and more than black; in chronicling our journey, the stories and songs gave us a means to reclaim memories that we didn't need to feel shame about...memories that all people might study and cherish - and with which we could start to rebuild."

That has been my experience at Trinity. Like other predominantly black churches across the country, Trinity embodies the black community in its entirety - the doctor and the welfare mom, the model student and the former gang-banger. Like other black churches, Trinity's services are full of raucous laughter and sometimes bawdy humor. They are full of dancing, clapping, screaming and shouting that may seem jarring to the untrained ear. The church contains in full the kindness and cruelty, the fierce intelligence and the shocking ignorance, the struggles and successes, the love and yes, the bitterness and bias that make up the black experience in America.

And this helps explain, perhaps, my relationship with Reverend Wright. As imperfect as he may be, he has been like family to me. He strengthened my faith, officiated my wedding, and baptized my children. Not once in my conversations with him have I heard him talk about any ethnic group in derogatory terms, or treat whites with whom he interacted with anything but courtesy and respect. He contains within him the contradictions - the good and the bad - of the community that he has served diligently for so many years.

I can no more disown him than I can disown the black community. I can no more disown him than I can my white grandmother - a woman who helped raise me, a woman who sacrificed again and again for me, a woman who loves me as much as she loves anything in this world, but a woman who once confessed her fear of black men who passed by her on the street, and who on more than one occasion has uttered racial or ethnic stereotypes that made me cringe.

These people are a part of me. And they are a part of America, this country that I love.

Some will see this as an attempt to justify or excuse comments that are simply inexcusable. I can assure you it is not. I suppose the politically safe thing would be to move on from this episode and just hope that it fades into the woodwork. We can dismiss Reverend Wright as a crank or a demagogue, just as some have dismissed Geraldine

Ferraro, in the aftermath of her recent statements, as harboring some deep-seated racial bias.

But race is an issue that I believe this nation cannot afford to ignore right now. We would be making the same mistake that Reverend Wright made in his offending sermons about America - to simplify and stereotype and amplify the negative to the point that it distorts reality.

The fact is that the comments that have been made and the issues that have surfaced over the last few weeks reflect the complexities of race in this country that we've never really worked through - a part of our union that we have yet to perfect. And if we walk away now, if we simply retreat into our respective corners, we will never be able to come together and solve challenges like health care, or education, or the need to find good jobs for every American.

Understanding this reality requires a reminder of how we arrived at this point. As

William Faulkner once wrote, "The past isn't dead and buried. In fact, it isn't even

past." We do not need to recite here the history of racial injustice in this country. But we do need to remind ourselves that so many of the disparities that exist in the African-American community today can be directly traced to inequalities passed on from an earlier generation that suffered under the brutal legacy of slavery and Jim Crow.

Segregated schools were, and are, inferior schools; we still haven't fixed them, fifty years after Brown v. Board of Education, and the inferior education they provided, then and now, helps explain the pervasive achievement gap between today's black and white students.

Legalized discrimination - where blacks were prevented, often through violence, from owning property, or loans were not granted to African-American business owners, or black homeowners could not access FHA mortgages, or blacks were excluded from unions, or the police force, or fire departments - meant that black families could not amass any meaningful wealth to bequeath to future generations. That history helps explain the wealth and income gap between black and white, and the concentrated pockets of poverty that persists in so many of today's urban and rural communities.

A lack of economic opportunity among black men, and the shame and frustration that came from not being able to provide for one's family, contributed to the erosion of black families - a problem that welfare policies for many years may have worsened. And the lack of basic services in so many urban black neighborhoods - parks for kids to play in, police walking the beat, regular garbage pick-up and building code enforcement - all helped create a cycle of violence, blight and neglect that continue to haunt us.

This is the reality in which Reverend Wright and other African-Americans of his generation grew up. They came of age in the late fifties and early sixties, a time when segregation was still the law of the land and opportunity was systematically constricted. What's remarkable is not how many failed in the face of discrimination, but rather how many men and women overcame the odds; how many were able to make a way out of no way for those like me who would come after them.

But for all those who scratched and clawed their way to get a piece of the American Dream, there were many who didn't make it - those who were ultimately defeated, in one way or another, by discrimination. That legacy of defeat was passed on to future generations - those young men and increasingly young women who we see standing on street corners or languishing in our prisons, without hope or prospects for the future. Even for those blacks who did make it, questions of race, and racism, continue to define their worldview in fundamental ways. For the men and women of Reverend Wright's generation, the memories of humiliation and doubt and fear have not gone away; nor has the anger and the bitterness of those years. That anger may not get expressed in public, in front of white co-workers or white friends. But it does find voice in the barbershop or around the kitchen table. At times, that anger is exploited by politicians, to gin up votes along racial lines, or to make up for a politician's own failings.

And occasionally it finds voice in the church on Sunday morning, in the pulpit and in the pews. The fact that so many people are surprised to hear that anger in some of Reverend Wright's sermons simply reminds us of the old truism that the most segregated hour in American life occurs on Sunday morning. That anger is not always productive; indeed, all too often it distracts attention from solving real problems; it keeps us from squarely facing our own complicity in our condition, and prevents the African-American community from forging the alliances it needs to bring about real change. But the anger is real; it is powerful; and to simply wish it away, to condemn it without understanding its roots, only serves to widen the chasm of misunderstanding that exists between the races.

In fact, a similar anger exists within segments of the white community. Most working-

and middle-class white Americans don't feel that they have been particularly privileged by their race. Their experience is the immigrant experience - as far as they're concerned, no one's handed them anything, they've built it from scratch. They've worked hard all their lives, many times only to see their jobs shipped overseas or their pension dumped after a lifetime of labor. They are anxious about their futures, and feel their dreams slipping away; in an era of stagnant wages and global competition, opportunity comes to be seen as a zero sum game, in which your dreams come at my expense. So when they are told to bus their children to a school across town; when they hear that an African American is getting an advantage in landing a good job or a spot in a good college because of an injustice that they themselves never committed; when they're told that their fears about crime in urban neighborhoods are somehow prejudiced, resentment builds over time.

Like the anger within the black community, these resentments aren't always expressed in polite company. But they have helped shape the political landscape for at least a generation. Anger over welfare and affirmative action helped forge the Reagan Coalition. Politicians routinely exploited fears of crime for their own electoral ends. Talk show hosts and conservative commentators built entire careers unmasking bogus claims of racism while dismissing legitimate discussions of racial injustice and inequality as mere political correctness or reverse racism.

Just as black anger often proved counterproductive,

so have these white resentments distracted attention from the real culprits of the middle class squeeze - a corporate culture rife with inside dealing, questionable accounting practices, and short-term greed; a Washington dominated by lobbyists and special interests; economic policies that favor the few over the many. And yet, to wish away the resentments of white Americans, to label them as misguided or even racist, without recognizing they are grounded in legitimate concerns - this too widens the racial divide, and blocks the path to understanding.

This is where we are right now. It's a racial stalemate we've been stuck in for years. Contrary to the claims of some of my critics, black and white, I have never been so naïve as to believe that we can get beyond our racial divisions in a single election cycle, or with a single candidacy - particularly a candidacy as imperfect as my own.

But I have asserted a firm conviction - a conviction rooted in my faith in God and my faith in the American people - that working together we can move beyond some of our old racial wounds, and that in fact we have no choice if we are to continue on the path of a more perfect union.

For the African-American community, that path means embracing the burdens of our past without becoming victims of our past. It means continuing to insist on a full measure of justice in every aspect of American life. But it also means binding our particular grievances - for better health care, and better schools, and better jobs - to the larger aspirations of all Americans -- the white woman struggling to break the glass ceiling, the white man whose been laid off, the immigrant trying to feed his family. And it means taking full responsibility for own lives - by demanding more from our fathers, and spending more time with our children, and reading to them, and teaching them that while they may face challenges and discrimination in their own lives, they must never succumb to despair or cynicism; they must always believe that they can write their own destiny.

Ironically, this quintessentially American - and yes, conservative - notion of self-help found frequent expression in Reverend Wright's sermons. But what my former pastor too often failed to understand is that embarking on a program of self-help also requires a belief that society can change.

The profound mistake of Reverend Wright's sermons is not that he spoke about racism in our society. It's that he spoke as if our society was static; as if no progress has been made; as if this country - a country that has made it possible for one of his own members to run for the highest office in the land and build a coalition of white

and black; Latino and Asian, rich and poor, young and old -- is still irrevocably bound

to a tragic past. But what we know -- what we have seen - is that America can change. That is true genius of this nation. What we have already achieved gives us hope - the audacity to hope - for what we can and must achieve tomorrow.

In the white community, the path to a more perfect union means acknowledging that what ails the African-American community does not just exist in the minds of black people; that the legacy of discrimination - and current incidents of discrimination, while less overt than in the past - are real and must be addressed. Not just with words, but with deeds - by investing in our schools and our communities; by enforcing our civil rights laws and ensuring fairness in our criminal justice system; by providing this generation with ladders of opportunity that were unavailable for previous generations. It requires all Americans to realize that your dreams do not have to come at the expense of my dreams; that investing in the health, welfare, and education of black and brown and white children will ultimately help all of America prosper.

In the end, then, what is called for is nothing more, and nothing less, than what all the world's great religions demand - that we do unto others as we would have them do unto us. Let us be our brother's keeper, Scripture tells us. Let us be our sister's keeper. Let us find that common stake we all have in one another, and let our politics reflect that spirit as well.

For we have a choice in this country. We can accept a politics that breeds division, and conflict, and cynicism. We can tackle race only as spectacle - as we did in the OJ trial - or in the wake of tragedy, as we did in the aftermath of Katrina - or as fodder for the nightly news. We can play Reverend Wright's sermons on every channel, every day and talk about them from now until the election, and make the only question in this campaign whether or not the American people think that I somehow believe or sympathize with his most offensive words. We can pounce on some gaffe by a Hillary supporter as evidence that she's playing the race card, or we can speculate on whether white men will all flock to John McCain in the general election regardless of his policies.

We can do that.

But if we do, I can tell you that in the next election, we'll be talking about some other distraction. And then another one. And then another one. And nothing will change.

That is one option. Or, at this moment, in this election, we can come together and say, "Not this time." This time we want to talk about the crumbling schools that are stealing the future of black children and white children and Asian children and Hispanic children and Native American children. This time we want to reject the cynicism that tells us that these kids can't learn; that those kids who don't look like us are somebody else's problem. The children of America are not those kids, they are our kids, and we will not let them fall behind in a 21st century economy. Not this time.

This time we want to talk about how the lines in the Emergency Room are filled with whites and blacks and Hispanics who do not have health care; who don't have the power on their own to overcome the special interests in Washington, but who can take them on if we do it together.

This time we want to talk about the shuttered mills that once provided a decent life for men and women of every race, and the homes for sale that once belonged to Americans from every religion, every region, every walk of life. This time we want to talk about the fact that the real problem is not that someone who doesn't look like you might take your job; it's that the corporation you work for will ship it overseas for nothing more than a profit.

This time we want to talk about the men and women of every color and creed who serve together, and fight together, and bleed together under the same proud flag. We want to talk about how to bring them home from a war that never should've been authorized and never should've been waged, and we want to talk about how we'll show our patriotism by caring for them, and their families, and giving them the benefits they have earned.

I would not be running for President if I didn't believe with all my heart that this is what the vast majority of Americans want for this country. This union may never be perfect, but generation after generation has shown that it can always be perfected. And today, whenever I find myself feeling doubtful or cynical about this possibility, what gives me the most hope is the next generation - the young people whose attitudes and beliefs and openness to change have already made history in this election.

There is one story in particularly that I'd like to leave you with today - a story I told when I had the great honor of speaking on Dr. King's birthday at his home church, Ebenezer Baptist, in Atlanta.

There is a young, twenty-three year old white woman named Ashley Baia who organized for our campaign in Florence, South Carolina. She had been working to organize a mostly African-American community since the beginning of this campaign, and one day she was at a roundtable discussion where everyone went around telling their story and why they were there.

And Ashley said that when she was nine years old, her mother got cancer. And because she had to miss days of work, she was let go and lost her health care. They had to file for bankruptcy, and that's when Ashley decided that she had to do something to help her mom.

She knew that food was one of their most expensive

costs, and so Ashley convinced her mother that what she really liked and really wanted to eat more than anything else was mustard and relish sandwiches. Because that was the cheapest way to eat.

She did this for a year until her mom got better, and she told everyone at the roundtable that the reason she joined our campaign was so that she could help the millions of other children in the country who want and need to help their parents too.

Now Ashley might have made a different choice. Perhaps somebody told her along the way that the source of her mother's problems were blacks who were on welfare and too lazy to work, or Hispanics who were coming into the country illegally. But she didn't. She sought out allies in her fight against injustice.

Anyway, Ashley finishes her story and then goes around the room and asks everyone else why they're supporting the campaign. They all have different stories and reasons. Many bring up a specific issue. And finally they come to this elderly black man who's been sitting there quietly the entire time. And Ashley asks him why he's there. And he does not bring up a specific issue. He does not say health care or the economy. He does not say education or the war. He does not say that he was there because of Barack Obama. He simply says to everyone in the room, "I am here because of Ashley."

"I'm here because of Ashley." By itself, that single moment of recognition between that young white girl and that old black man is not enough. It is not enough to give health care to the sick, or jobs to the jobless, or education to our children.

But it is where we start. It is where our union grows

stronger. And as so many generations have come to realize over the course of the two-hundred and twenty one years since a band of patriots signed that document in Philadelphia, that is where the perfection begins

TRANSCRIPT OF SENATOR BARACK OBAMA'S DECLARATION OF VICTORY SPEECH AT THE CONCLUSION OF DEMOCRATIC PRIMARIES

Tonight, after fifty-four hard-fought contests, our primary season has finally come to an end.

Sixteen months have passed since we first stood together on the steps of the Old State Capitol in Springfield, Illinois. Thousands of miles have been traveled. Millions of voices have been heard. And because of what you said – because you decided that change must come to Washington; because you believed that this year must be different than all the rest; because you chose to listen not to your doubts or your fears but to your greatest hopes and highest aspirations, tonight we mark the end of one historic journey with the beginning of another – a journey that will bring a new and better day to America. Tonight, I can stand before you and say that I will be the Democratic nominee for President of the United States.

I want to thank every American who stood with us over the course of this campaign – through the good days and the bad; from the snows of Cedar Rapids to the sunshine of Sioux Falls. And tonight I also want to thank the men and woman who took this journey with me as fellow candidates for President.

At this defining moment for our nation, we should be proud that our party put forth one of the most talented, qualified field of individuals ever to run for this office. I have not just competed with them as rivals, I have learned from them as friends, as public servants, and as patriots who love America and are willing to work tirelessly to make this country better. They are leaders of this party, and leaders that America will turn to for years to come.

That is particularly true for the candidate who has traveled further on this journey than anyone else. Senator Hillary Clinton has made history in this campaign not just because she's a woman who has done what no woman has done before, but because she's a leader who inspires millions of Americans with her strength, her courage, and her commitment to the causes that brought us here tonight.

We've certainly had our differences over the last sixteen months. But as someone who's shared a stage with her many times, I can tell you that what gets Hillary Clinton up in the morning – even in the face of tough odds – is exactly what sent her and Bill Clinton to sign up for their first campaign in Texas all those years ago; what sent her to work at the Children's Defense Fund and made her fight for health care as First Lady; what led her to the United States Senate and fueled her barrier-breaking campaign for the presidency – an unyielding desire to improve the lives of ordinary Americans, no matter how difficult the fight may be. And you can rest assured that when we finally win the battle for universal health care in this country, she will be central to that victory. When we transform our energy policy and lift our children out of poverty, it will be because she worked to help make it happen. Our party and our country are better off because of her, and I am a better candidate for having had the honor to compete with Hillary Rodham Clinton.

There are those who say that this primary has somehow left us weaker and more divided. Well I say that because of this primary, there are millions of Americans who have cast their ballot for the very first time. There are Independents and Republicans who understand that this election isn't just about the party in charge of Washington, it's about the need to change Washington. There are young people, and African-Americans, and Latinos, and women of all ages who have voted in numbers that have broken records and inspired a nation.

All of you chose to support a candidate you believe in deeply. But at the end of the day, we aren't the reason you came out and waited in lines that stretched block after block to make your voice heard. You didn't do that because of me or Senator Clinton or anyone else. You did it because you know in your hearts that at this moment – a moment that will define a generation – we cannot afford to keep doing what we've

been doing. We owe our children a better future. We owe our country a better future. And for all those who dream of that future tonight, I say – let us begin the work together. Let us unite in common effort to chart a new course for America.

In just a few short months, the Republican Party will arrive in St. Paul with a very different agenda. They will come here to nominate John McCain, a man who has served this country heroically. I honor that service, and I respect his many accomplishments, even if he chooses to deny mine. My differences with him are not personal; they are with the policies he has proposed in this campaign.

Because while John McCain can legitimately tout moments of independence from his party in the past, such independence has not been the hallmark of his presidential campaign.

It's not change when John McCain decided to stand with George Bush ninety-five percent of the time, as he did in the Senate last year.

It's not change when he offers four more years of Bush economic policies that have failed to create well-paying jobs, or insure our workers, or help Americans afford the skyrocketing cost of college – policies that have lowered the real incomes of the average American family, widened the gap between Wall Street and Main Street, and left our children with a mountain of debt.

And it's not change when he promises to continue a policy in Iraq that asks everything of our brave men and women in uniform and nothing of Iraqi politicians – a policy where all we look for are reasons to stay in Iraq, while we spend billions of dollars a month on a war that isn't making the American people any safer.

So I'll say this – there are many words to describe John McCain's attempt to pass off his embrace of George Bush's policies as bipartisan and new. But change is not one of them.

Change is a foreign policy that doesn't begin and end with a war that should've never been authorized and never been waged. I won't stand here and pretend that there are many good options left in Iraq, but what's not an option is leaving our troops in that country for the next hundred years – especially at a time when our military is overstretched, our nation is isolated, and nearly every other threat to America is being ignored.

We must be as careful getting out of Iraq as we were careless getting in - but start leaving we must. It's time for Iraqis to take responsibility for their future. It's time to rebuild our military and give our veterans the care they need and the benefits they deserve when they come home. It's time to refocus our efforts on al Qaeda's leadership and Afghanistan, and rally the world against the common threats of the 21st century – terrorism and nuclear weapons; climate change and poverty; genocide and disease. That's what change is.

Change is realizing that meeting today's threats requires not just our firepower, but the power of our diplomacy – tough, direct diplomacy where the President of the United States isn't afraid to let any petty dictator know where America stands and what we stand for. We must once again have the courage and conviction to lead the free world. That is the legacy of Roosevelt, and Truman, and Kennedy. That's what the American people want. That's what change is.

Change is building an economy that rewards not just wealth, but the work and workers who created it. It's understanding that the struggles facing working families can't be solved by spending billions of dollars on more tax breaks for big corporations and wealthy CEOs, but by giving a the middle-class a tax break, and investing in our crumbling infrastructure, and transforming how we use energy, and improving our schools, and renewing our commitment to science and innovation. It's understanding that fiscal responsibility and shared prosperity can go hand-in-hand, as they did when Bill Clinton was President.

John McCain has spent a lot of time talking about trips to Iraq in the last few weeks, but maybe if he spent some time taking trips to the cities and towns that have been

hardest hit by this economy – cities in Michigan, and Ohio, and right here in Minnesota – he'd understand the kind of change that people are looking for.

Maybe if he went to Iowa and met the student who works the night shift after a full

day of class and still can't pay the medical bills for a sister who's ill, he'd understand that she can't afford four more years of a health care plan that only takes care of the healthy and wealthy. She needs us to pass health care plan that guarantees insurance to every American who wants it and brings down premiums for every family who needs it. That's the change we need.

Maybe if he went to Pennsylvania and met the man who lost his job but can't even afford the gas to drive around and look for a new one, he'd understand that we can't afford four more years of our addiction to oil from dictators. That man needs us to pass an energy policy that works with automakers to raise fuel standards, and makes corporations pay for their pollution, and oil companies invest their record profits in a clean energy future – an energy policy that will create millions of new jobs that pay well and can't be outsourced. That's the change we need.

And maybe if he spent some time in the schools of South Carolina or St. Paul or where he spoke tonight in New Orleans, he'd understand that we can't afford to leave the money behind for No Child Left Behind; that we owe it to our children to invest in early childhood education; to recruit an army of new teachers and give them better pay and more support; to finally decide that in this global economy, the chance to get a college education should not be a privilege for the wealthy few, but the birthright of every American. That's the change we need in America. That's why I'm running for President.

The other side will come here in September and offer a very different set of policies and positions, and that is a debate I look forward to. It is a debate the American people deserve. But what you don't deserve is another election that's governed by fear, and innuendo, and division. What you won't hear from this campaign or this party is the kind of politics that uses religion as a wedge, and patriotism as a bludgeon – that sees our opponents not as competitors to challenge, but enemies to demonize. Because we may call ourselves Democrats and Republicans, but we are Americans first. We are always Americans first.

Despite what the good Senator from Arizona said tonight, I have seen people of differing views and opinions find common cause many times during my two decades in public life, and I have brought many together myself. I've walked arm-in-arm with community leaders on the South Side of Chicago and watched tensions fade as black, white, and Latino fought together for good jobs and good schools. I've sat across the table from law enforcement and civil rights advocates to reform a criminal justice system that sent thirteen innocent people to death row. And I've worked with friends in the other party to provide more children with health insurance and more working families with a tax break; to curb the spread of nuclear weapons and ensure that the American people know where their tax dollars are being spent; and to reduce the influence of lobbyists who have all too often set the agenda in Washington.

In our country, I have found that this cooperation happens not because we agree on everything, but because behind all the labels and false divisions and categories that define us; beyond all the petty bickering and point-scoring in Washington, Americans are a decent, generous, compassionate people, united by common challenges and common hopes. And every so often, there are moments which call on that fundamental goodness to make this country great again.

So it was for that band of patriots who declared in a Philadelphia hall the formation of a more perfect union; and for all those who gave on the fields of Gettysburg and Antietam their last full measure of devotion to save that same union.

So it was for the Greatest Generation that conquered fear itself, and liberated a continent from tyranny, and made this country home to untold opportunity and prosperity.

So it was for the workers who stood out on the picket lines; the women who shattered glass ceilings; the children who braved a Selma bridge for freedom's cause.

So it has been for every generation that faced down the greatest challenges and the most improbable odds to leave their children a world that's better, and kinder, and more just.

And so it must be for us.

America, this is our moment. This is our time. Our time to turn the page on the policies of the past. Our time to bring new energy and new ideas to the challenges we face. Our time to offer a new direction for the country we love.

The journey will be difficult. The road will be long. I face this challenge with profound humility, and knowledge of my own limitations. But I also face it with limitless faith in the capacity of the American people. Because if we are willing to work for it, and fight for it, and believe in it, then I am absolutely certain that generations from now, we will be able to look back and tell our children that this was the moment when we began to provide care for the sick and good jobs to the jobless; this was the moment when the rise of the oceans began to slow and our planet began to heal; this was the moment when we ended a war and secured our nation and restored our image as the last, best hope on Earth. This was the moment – this was the time – when we came together to remake this great nation so that it may always reflect our very best selves, and our highest ideals. Thank you, God Bless you, and may God Bless the United States of America.

TRANSCRIPT OF SENATOR BARACK OBAMA'S ACCEPTANCE SPEECH AT 2008 DEMOCRATIC NATIONAL CONVENTION

To Chairman Dean and my great friend Dick Durbin; and to all my fellow citizens of this great nation;

With profound gratitude and great humility, I accept your nomination for the presidency of the United States.

Let me express my thanks to the historic slate of candidates who accompanied me on this journey, and especially the one who traveled the farthest - a champion for working Americans and an inspiration to my daughters and to yours -- Hillary Rodham Clinton. To President Clinton, who last night made the case for change as only he can make it; to Ted Kennedy, who embodies the spirit of service; and to the next Vice President of the United States, Joe Biden, I thank you. I am grateful to finish this journey with one of the finest statesmen of our time, a man at ease with everyone from world leaders to the conductors on the Amtrak train he still takes home every night.

To the love of my life, our next First Lady, Michelle Obama, and to Sasha and Malia - I love you so much, and I'm so proud of all of you.

Four years ago, I stood before you and told you my story - of the brief union between a young man from Kenya and a young woman from Kansas who weren't well-off or well-known, but shared a belief that in America, their son could achieve whatever he put his mind to.

It is that promise that has always set this country apart - that through hard work and sacrifice, each of us can pursue our individual dreams but still come together as one American family, to ensure that the next generation can pursue their dreams as well.

That's why I stand here tonight. Because for two hundred and thirty two years, at each moment when that promise was in jeopardy, ordinary men and women - students and soldiers, farmers and teachers, nurses and janitors -- found the courage to keep it alive.

We meet at one of those defining moments - a moment when our nation is at war, our economy is in turmoil, and the American promise has been threatened once more.

Tonight, more Americans are out of work and more are working harder for less. More of you have lost your homes and even more are watching your home values plummet. More of you have cars you can't afford to drive, credit card bills you can't afford to pay, and tuition that's beyond your reach.

These challenges are not all of government's making. But the failure to respond is a direct result of a broken politics in Washington and the failed policies of George W. Bush.

America, we are better than these last eight years. We are a better country than this.

This country is more decent than one where a woman

in Ohio, on the brink of retirement, finds herself one illness away from disaster after a lifetime of hard work.

This country is more generous than one where a man in Indiana has to pack up the equipment he's worked on for twenty years and watch it shipped off to China, and then chokes up as he explains how he felt like a failure when he went home to tell his family the news.

We are more compassionate than a government that lets veterans sleep on our streets and families slide into poverty; that sits on its hands while a major American city drowns before our eyes.

Tonight, I say to the American people, to Democrats and Republicans and Independents across this great land - enough! This moment - this election - is our chance to keep, in the 21st century, the American promise alive. Because next week, in Minnesota, the same party that brought you two terms of George Bush and Dick Cheney will ask this country for a third. And we are here because we love this

country too much to let the next four years look like the last eight. On November 4th, we must stand up and say: "Eight is enough."

Now let there be no doubt. The Republican nominee, John McCain, has worn the uniform of our country with bravery and distinction, and for that we owe him our

gratitude and respect. And next week, we'll also hear about those occasions when he's broken with his party as evidence that he can deliver the change that we need.

But the record's clear: John McCain has voted with George Bush ninety percent of the time. Senator McCain likes to talk about judgment, but really, what does it say about your judgment when you think George Bush has been right more than ninety percent of the time? I don't know about you, but I'm not ready to take a ten percent chance on change.

The truth is, on issue after issue that would make a difference in your lives - on health care and education and the economy - Senator McCain has been anything but independent. He said that our economy has made "great progress" under this President. He said that the fundamentals of the economy are strong. And when one of his chief advisors - the man who wrote his economic plan - was talking about the anxiety Americans are feeling, he said that we were just suffering from a "mental recession," and that we've become, and I quote, "a nation of whiners." A nation of whiners? Tell that to the proud auto workers at a Michigan plant who, after they found out it was closing, kept showing up every day and working as hard as ever, because they knew there were people who counted on the brakes that they made. Tell that to the military families who shoulder their burdens silently as they watch their loved ones leave for their third or fourth or fifth tour of duty. These are not whiners. They work hard and give back and keep going without complaint. These are the Americans that I know.

Now, I don't believe that Senator McCain doesn't care what's going on in the lives of Americans. I just think he doesn't know. Why else would he define middle-class as someone making under five million dollars a year? How else could he propose hundreds of billions in tax breaks for big corporations and oil companies but not one penny of tax relief to more than one hundred million Americans? How else could he offer a health care plan that would actually tax people's benefits, or an education plan that

Omololu Elegbe

would do nothing to help families pay for college, or a plan that would privatize Social Security and gamble your retirement?

It's not because John McCain doesn't care. It's because John McCain doesn't get it.

For over two decades, he's subscribed to that old, discredited Republican philosophy - give more and more to those with the most and hope that prosperity trickles down to everyone else. In Washington, they call this the Ownership Society, but what it really means is - you're on your own. Out of work? Tough luck. No health care? The market will fix it. Born into poverty? Pull yourself up by your own bootstraps - even if you don't have boots. You're on your own.

Well it's time for them to own their failure. It's time for us to change America.

You see, we Democrats have a very different measure of what constitutes progress in this country.

We measure progress by how many people can find a job that pays the mortgage; whether you can put a little extra money away at the end of each month so you can someday watch your child receive her college diploma. We measure progress in the 23 million new jobs that were created when Bill Clinton was President - when the average American family saw its income go up $7,500 instead of down $2,000 like it has under George Bush.

We measure the strength of our economy not by the number of billionaires we have or the profits of the Fortune 500, but by whether someone with a good idea can take a risk and start a new business, or whether the waitress who lives on tips can take a day off to look after a sick kid without losing her job - an economy that honors the dignity of work.

The fundamentals we use to measure economic strength are whether we are living up to that fundamental promise that has made this country great - a promise that is the only reason I am standing here tonight.

Because in the faces of those young veterans who come back from Iraq and Afghanistan, I see my grandfather, who signed up after Pearl Harbor, marched in Patton's Army, and was rewarded by a grateful nation with the chance to go to college on the GI Bill.

In the face of that young student who sleeps just three hours before working the night shift, I think about my mom, who raised my sister and me on her own while she worked and earned her degree; who once turned to food stamps but was still able to send us to the best schools in the country with the help of student loans and scholarships.

When I listen to another worker tell me that his factory has shut down, I remember all those men and women on the South Side of Chicago who I stood by and fought for two decades ago after the local steel plant closed.

And when I hear a woman talk about the difficulties of starting her own business, I think about my grandmother, who worked her way up from the secretarial pool to middle-management, despite years of being passed over for promotions because she was a woman. She's the one who taught me about hard work. She's the one who put off buying a new car or a new dress for herself so that I could have a better life. She poured everything she had into me. And although she can no longer travel, I know that she's watching tonight, and that tonight is her night as well.

I don't know what kind of lives John McCain thinks that celebrities lead, but this has been mine. These are my heroes. Theirs are the stories that shaped me. And it is on their behalf that I intend to win this election and keep our promise alive as President of the United States.

What is that promise?

It's a promise that says each of us has the freedom to make of our own lives what we will, but that we also have the obligation to treat each other with dignity and respect.

It's a promise that says the market should reward drive and innovation and generate growth, but that businesses should live up to their responsibilities to create American jobs, look out for American workers, and play by the rules of the road.

Ours is a promise that says government cannot solve all our problems, but what it should do is that which we cannot do for ourselves - protect us from harm and provide every child a decent education; keep our water clean and our toys safe; invest in new schools and new roads and new science and technology.

Our government should work for us, not against us. It should help us, not hurt us. It should ensure opportunity not just for those with the most money and influence, but for every American who's willing to work.

That's the promise of America - the idea that we are responsible for ourselves, but that we also rise or fall as one nation; the fundamental belief that I am my brother's keeper; I am my sister's keeper.

That's the promise we need to keep. That's the change

we need right now. So let me spell out exactly what that change would mean if I am President.

Change means a tax code that doesn't reward the lobbyists who wrote it, but the American workers and small businesses who deserve it.

Unlike John McCain, I will stop giving tax breaks to corporations that ship jobs overseas, and I will start giving them to companies that create good jobs right here in America.

I will eliminate capital gains taxes for the small businesses and the start-ups that will create the high-wage, high-tech jobs of tomorrow.

I will cut taxes - cut taxes - for 95% of all working families. Because in an economy like this, the last thing we should do is raise taxes on the middle-class.

And for the sake of our economy, our security, and the future of our planet, I will set a clear goal as President: in ten years, we will finally end our dependence on oil from the Middle East.

Washington's been talking about our oil addiction for the last thirty years, and John McCain has been there for twenty-six of them. In that time, he's said no to higher fuel-efficiency standards for cars, no to investments in renewable energy, no to renewable fuels. And today, we import triple the amount of oil as the day that Senator McCain took office.

Now is the time to end this addiction, and to understand that drilling is a stop-gap measure, not a long-term solution. Not even close.

As President, I will tap our natural gas reserves, invest in clean coal technology, and find ways to safely harness nuclear power. I'll help our auto companies re-tool, so that the fuel-efficient cars of the future are built right here in America. I'll make it easier for the American people to afford these new cars. And I'll invest 150 billion dollars over the next decade in affordable, renewable sources of energy - wind power and solar power and the next generation of biofuels; an investment that will lead to new industries and five million new jobs that pay well and can't ever be outsourced.

America, now is not the time for small plans.

Now is the time to finally meet our moral obligation to provide every child a world-class education, because it will take nothing less to compete in the global economy. Michelle and I are only here tonight because we were given a chance at an education. And I will not settle for an America where some kids don't have that chance. I'll invest in early childhood education. I'll recruit an army of new teachers, and pay them higher salaries and give them more support. And in exchange, I'll ask for higher standards and more accountability. And we will keep our promise to every young American - if you commit to serving your community or your country, we will make sure you can afford a college education.

Now is the time to finally keep the promise of affordable, accessible health care for every single American. If you have health care, my plan will lower your premiums. If you don't, you'll be able to get the same kind of coverage that members of Congress give themselves. And as someone who watched my mother argue with insurance companies while she lay in bed dying of cancer, I will make certain those companies stop discriminating against those who are sick and need care the most.

Now is the time to help families with paid sick days and better family leave, because nobody in America should have to choose between keeping their jobs and caring for a sick child or ailing parent.

Now is the time to change our bankruptcy laws, so that your pensions are protected ahead of CEO bonuses; and the time to protect Social Security for future generations.

And now is the time to keep the promise of equal pay for an equal day's work, because I want my daughters to have exactly the same opportunities as your sons.

Now, many of these plans will cost money, which is why I've laid out how I'll pay for every dime - by closing corporate loopholes and tax havens that don't help America grow. But I will also go through the federal budget, line by line, eliminating programs that no longer work and making the ones we do need work better and cost less - because we cannot meet twenty-first century challenges with a twentieth century bureaucracy.

And Democrats, we must also admit that fulfilling America's promise will require more than just money. It will require a renewed sense of responsibility from each of us to recover what John F. Kennedy called our "intellectual and moral strength." Yes, government must lead on energy independence, but each of us must do our part to make our homes and businesses more efficient. Yes, we must provide more ladders to success for young men who fall into lives of crime and despair. But we must also admit that programs alone can't replace parents; that government can't turn off the television and make a child do her homework; that fathers must take more responsibility for providing the love and guidance their children need.

Individual responsibility and mutual responsibility - that's the essence of America's promise.

And just as we keep our keep our promise to the next generation here at home, so must we keep America's promise abroad. If John McCain wants to have a debate about who has the temperament, and judgment, to serve as the next Commander-in-Chief, that's a debate I'm ready to have.

For while Senator McCain was turning his sights to Iraq just days after 9/11, I stood up and opposed this war, knowing that it would distract us from the real threats we face. When John McCain said we could just "muddle through" in Afghanistan, I argued for more resources and more troops to finish the fight against the terrorists who actually attacked us on 9/11, and made clear that we must take out Osama bin Laden and his lieutenants if we have them in our sights. John McCain likes to say that he'll follow bin Laden to the Gates of Hell - but he won't even go to the cave where he lives.

And today, as my call for a time frame to remove our troops from Iraq has been echoed by the Iraqi government and even the Bush Administration, even after we learned that Iraq has a $79 billion surplus while we're wallowing in deficits, John McCain stands alone in his stubborn refusal to end a misguided war.

That's not the judgment we need. That won't keep America safe. We need a President who can face the threats of the future, not keep grasping at the ideas of the past.

You don't defeat a terrorist network that operates in

eighty countries by occupying Iraq. You don't protect Israel and deter Iran just by talking tough in Washington. You can't truly stand up for Georgia when you've strained our oldest alliances. If John McCain wants to follow George Bush with more tough talk and bad strategy, that is his choice - but it is not the change we need.

We are the party of Roosevelt. We are the party of Kennedy. So don't tell me that Democrats won't defend this country. Don't tell me that Democrats won't keep us safe. The Bush-McCain foreign policy has squandered the legacy that generations of Americans -- Democrats and Republicans - have built, and we are here to restore that legacy.

As Commander-in-Chief, I will never hesitate to defend this nation, but I will only send our troops into harm's way with a clear mission and a sacred commitment to give them the equipment they need in battle and the care and benefits they deserve when they come home.

I will end this war in Iraq responsibly, and finish the fight against al Qaeda and the Taliban in Afghanistan. I will rebuild our military to meet future conflicts. But I will also renew the tough, direct diplomacy that can prevent Iran from obtaining nuclear weapons and curb Russian aggression. I will build new partnerships to defeat the threats of the 21st century: terrorism and nuclear proliferation; poverty and genocide; climate change and disease. And I will restore our moral standing, so that America is once again that last, best hope for all who are called to the cause of freedom, who long for lives of peace, and who yearn for a better future.

These are the policies I will pursue. And in the

weeks ahead, I look forward to debating them with John McCain.

But what I will not do is suggest that the Senator takes his positions for political purposes. Because one of the things that we have to change in our politics is the idea that people cannot disagree without challenging each other's character and patriotism.

The times are too serious, the stakes are too high for this same partisan playbook. So let us agree that patriotism has no party. I love this country, and so do you, and so does John McCain. The men and women who serve in our battlefields may be Democrats and Republicans and Independents, but they have fought together and bled together and some died together under the same proud flag. They have not served a Red America or a Blue America - they have served the United States of America.

So I've got news for you, John McCain. We all put our country first.

America, our work will not be easy. The challenges we face require tough choices, and Democrats as well as Republicans will need to cast off the worn-out ideas and politics of the past. For part of what has been lost these past eight years can't just be measured by lost wages or bigger trade deficits. What has also been lost is our sense of common purpose - our sense of higher purpose. And that's what we have to restore.

We may not agree on abortion, but surely we can agree on reducing the number of unwanted pregnancies in this country. The reality of gun ownership may be different for hunters in rural Ohio than for those plagued by gang-violence in Cleveland, but don't tell me we can't uphold the Second Amendment while keeping AK-47s out of the hands of criminals. I know there are differences on same-sex marriage, but surely we can agree that our gay and lesbian brothers and sisters deserve to visit the person they love in the hospital and to live lives free of discrimination. Passions fly on immigration, but I don't know anyone who benefits when a mother is separated from her infant child or an employer undercuts American wages by hiring illegal workers. This too is part of America's promise - the promise of a democracy where we can find the strength and grace to bridge divides and unite in common effort.

I know there are those who dismiss such beliefs as happy talk. They claim that our insistence on something larger, something firmer and more honest in our public life is just a Trojan Horse for higher taxes and the abandonment of traditional values. And that's to be expected. Because if you don't have any fresh ideas, then you use stale tactics to scare the voters. If you don't have a record to run on, then you paint your opponent as someone people should run from.

You make a big election about small things.

And you know what - it's worked before. Because it feeds into the cynicism we all have about government. When Washington doesn't work, all its promises seem empty. If your hopes have been dashed again and again, then it's best to stop hoping, and settle for what you already know.

I get it. I realize that I am not the likeliest candidate for this office. I don't fit the typical pedigree, and I haven't spent my career in the halls of Washington.

But I stand before you tonight because all across

America something is stirring. What the nay-sayers don't understand is that this election has never been about me. It's been about you.

For eighteen long months, you have stood up, one by one, and said enough to the politics of the past. You understand that in this election, the greatest risk we can take is to try the same old politics with the same old players and expect a different result. You have shown what history teaches us - that at defining moments like this one, the change we need doesn't come from Washington. Change comes to Washington. Change happens because the American people demand it - because they rise up and insist on new ideas and new leadership, a new politics for a new time.

America, this is one of those moments.

I believe that as hard as it will be, the change we need is coming. Because I've seen it. Because I've lived it. I've seen it in Illinois, when we provided health care to more children and moved more families from welfare to work. I've seen it in Washington, when we worked across party lines to open up government and hold lobbyists more accountable, to give better care for our veterans and keep nuclear weapons out of terrorist hands.

And I've seen it in this campaign. In the young people who voted for the first time, and in those who got involved again after a very long time. In the Republicans who never thought they'd pick up a Democratic ballot, but did. I've seen it in the workers who would rather cut their hours back a day than see their friends lose their jobs, in the soldiers who re-enlist after losing a limb, in the good neighbors who take a stranger in when a hurricane strikes and the floodwaters rise.

This country of ours has more wealth than any nation, but that's not what makes us rich. We have the most powerful military on Earth, but that's not what makes us strong. Our universities and our culture are the envy of the world, but that's not what keeps the world coming to our shores.

Instead, it is that American spirit - that American promise - that pushes us forward

even when the path is uncertain; that binds us together in spite of our differences; that makes us fix our eye not on what is seen, but what is unseen, that better place around the bend.

That promise is our greatest inheritance. It's a promise I make to my daughters when I tuck them in at night, and a promise that you make to yours - a promise that has led immigrants to cross oceans and pioneers to travel west; a promise that led workers to picket lines, and women to reach for the ballot.

And it is that promise that forty five years ago today, brought Americans from every corner of this land to stand together on a Mall in Washington, before Lincoln's Memorial, and hear a young preacher from Georgia speak of his dream.

The men and women who gathered there could've heard many things. They could've heard words of anger and discord. They could've been told to succumb to the fear and frustration of so many dreams deferred.

But what the people heard instead - people of every creed and color, from every walk of life - is that in America, our destiny is inextricably linked. That together, our dreams can be one. "We cannot walk alone," the preacher cried. "And as we walk, we must make the pledge that we shall always march ahead. We cannot turn back."

America, we cannot turn back. Not with so much work to be done. Not with so many children to educate, and so many veterans to care for. Not with an economy to fix and cities to rebuild and farms to save. Not with so many families to protect and so many lives to mend. America, we cannot turn back. We cannot walk alone. At this moment, in this election, we must pledge once more to march into the future. Let us keep that promise - that American promise - and in the words of Scripture hold firmly, without wavering, to the hope that we confess.

Thank you, God Bless you, and God Bless the United States of America.

TRANSCRIPT OF PRESIDENT-ELECT BARACK OBAMA'S VICTORY SPEECH ON ELECTION, NOVEMBER 4, 2008

If there is anyone out there who still doubts that America is a place where all things are possible; who still wonders if the dream of our founders is alive in our time; who still questions the power of our democracy, tonight is your answer.

It's the answer told by lines that stretched around schools and churches in numbers this nation has never seen; by people who waited three hours and four hours, many for the very first time in their lives, because they believed that this time must be different; that their voice could be that difference.

It's the answer spoken by young and old, rich and poor, Democrat and Republican, black, white, Latino, Asian, Native American, gay, straight, disabled and not disabled — Americans who sent a message to the world that we have never been a collection of red states and blue states; we are, and always will be, the United States of America.

It's the answer that led those who have been told for so long by so many to be cynical, and fearful, and doubtful of what we can achieve to put their hands on the arc of history and bend it once more toward the hope of a better day.

It's been a long time coming, but tonight, because of what we did on this day, in this election, at this defining moment, change has come to America.

I just received a very gracious call from Sen. McCain. He fought long and hard in this campaign, and he's fought even longer and harder for the country he loves. He has endured sacrifices for America that most of us cannot begin to imagine, and we are better off for the service rendered by this brave and selfless leader. I congratulate him and Gov. Palin for all they have achieved, and I look forward to working with them to renew this nation's promise in the months ahead.

I want to thank my partner in this journey, a man who campaigned from his heart and spoke for the men and women he grew up with on the streets of Scranton and rode with on that train home to Delaware, the vice-president-elect of the United States, Joe Biden.

I would not be standing here tonight without the unyielding support of my best friend for the last 16 years, the rock of our family and the love of my life, our nation's next first lady, Michelle Obama. Sasha and Malia, I love you both so much, and you have earned the new puppy that's coming with us to the White House. And while she's no longer with us, I know my grandmother is watching, along with the family that made me who I am. I miss them tonight, and know that my debt to them is beyond measure.

To my campaign manager, David Plouffe; my chief strategist, David Axelrod; and the best campaign team ever assembled in the history of politics — you made this happen, and I am forever grateful for what you've sacrificed to get it done.

But above all, I will never forget who this victory truly belongs to — it belongs to you.

I was never the likeliest candidate for this office. We didn't start with much money or many endorsements. Our campaign was not hatched in the halls of Washington — it began in the backyards of Des Moines and the living rooms of Concord and the front porches of Charleston.

It was built by working men and women who dug into what little savings they had to give $5 and $10 and $20 to this cause. It grew strength from the young people who rejected the myth of their generation's apathy; who left their homes and their families for jobs that offered little pay and less sleep; from the not-so-young people who braved the bitter cold and scorching heat to knock on the doors of perfect strangers; from the millions of Americans who volunteered and organized, and proved that more than two centuries later, a government of the people, by the people and for the people has not perished from this earth. This is your victory.

I know you didn't do this just to win an election, and I know you didn't do it for me.

You did it because you understand the enormity of the task that lies ahead. For even as we celebrate tonight, we know the challenges that tomorrow will bring are the greatest of our lifetime — two wars, a planet in peril, the worst financial crisis in a century. Even as we stand here tonight, we know there are brave Americans waking up in the deserts of Iraq and the mountains of Afghanistan to risk their lives for us. There are mothers and fathers who will lie awake after their children fall asleep and wonder how they'll make the mortgage, or pay their doctor's bills, or save enough for college. There is new energy to harness and new jobs to be created; new schools to build and threats to meet and alliances to repair.

The road ahead will be long. Our climb will be steep. We may not get there in one year, or even one term, but America — I have never been more hopeful than I am tonight that we will get there. I promise you: We as a people will get there.

There will be setbacks and false starts. There are many who won't agree with every decision or policy I make as president, and we know that government can't solve every problem. But I will always be honest with you about the challenges we face. I will listen to you, especially when we disagree. And, above all, I will ask you join in the work of remaking this nation the only way it's been done in America for 221 years — block by block, brick by brick, callused hand by callused hand.

What began 21 months ago in the depths of winter must not end on this autumn night. This victory alone is not the change we seek — it is only the chance for us to make that change. And that cannot happen if we go back to the way things were. It cannot happen without you.

So let us summon a new spirit of patriotism; of service and responsibility where each of us resolves to pitch in and work harder and look after not only ourselves, but each other. Let us remember that if this financial crisis taught us anything, it's that we cannot have a thriving Wall Street while Main Street suffers. In this country, we rise or fall as one nation — as one people.

Let us resist the temptation to fall back on the same partisanship and pettiness and immaturity that has poisoned our politics for so long. Let us remember that it was a man from this state who first carried the banner of the Republican Party to the White House — a party founded on the values of self-reliance, individual liberty and national unity. Those are values we all share, and while the Democratic Party has won a great victory tonight, we do so with a measure of humility and determination to heal the divides that have held back our progress.

As Lincoln said to a nation far more divided than ours, "We are not enemies, but friends... Though passion may have strained, it must not break our bonds of affection." And, to those Americans whose support I have yet to earn, I may not have won your vote, but I hear your voices, I need your help, and I will be your president, too.

And to all those watching tonight from beyond our shores, from parliaments and palaces to those who are huddled around radios in the forgotten corners of our world — our stories are singular, but our destiny is shared, and a new dawn of American leadership is at hand. To those who would tear this world down: We will defeat you. To those who seek peace and security: We support you. And to all those who have wondered if America's beacon still burns as bright: Tonight, we proved once more that the true strength of our nation comes not from the might of our arms or the scale of our wealth, but from the enduring power of our ideals: democracy, liberty, opportunity and unyielding hope.

For that is the true genius of America — that America can change. Our union can be perfected. And what we have already achieved gives us hope for what we can and must achieve tomorrow.

This election had many firsts and many stories that

will be told for generations. But one that's on my mind tonight is about a woman who cast her ballot in Atlanta. She's a lot like the millions of others who stood in line to make their voice heard in this

election, except for one thing: Ann Nixon Cooper is 106 years old.

She was born just a generation past slavery; a time when there were no cars on the road or planes in the sky; when someone like her couldn't vote for two reasons —

because she was a woman and because of the color of her skin. And tonight, I think about all that she's seen throughout her century in America — the heartache and the hope; the struggle and the progress; the times we were told that we can't and the people who pressed on with that American creed: Yes, we can.

At a time when women's voices were silenced and their hopes dismissed, she lived to see them stand up and speak out and reach for the ballot. Yes, we can.

When there was despair in the Dust Bowl and depression across the land, she saw a nation conquer fear itself with a New Deal, new jobs and a new sense of common purpose. Yes, we can.

When the bombs fell on our harbor and tyranny threatened the world, she was there to witness a generation rise to greatness and a democracy was saved. Yes, we can.

She was there for the buses in Montgomery, the hoses in Birmingham, a bridge in Selma and a preacher from Atlanta who told a people that "We Shall Overcome." Yes, we can.

A man touched down on the moon, a wall came down in Berlin, a world was connected by our own science and imagination. And this year, in this election, she touched her finger to a screen and cast her vote, because after 106 years in America, through the best of times and the darkest of hours, she knows how America can change. Yes, we can.

America, we have come so far. We have seen so much. But there is so much more to do. So tonight, let us ask ourselves: If our children should live to see the next century; if my daughters should be so lucky to live as long as Ann Nixon Cooper, what change will they see? What progress will we have made?

This is our chance to answer that call. This is our moment. This is our time — to put our people back to work and open doors of opportunity for our kids; to restore prosperity and promote the cause of peace; to reclaim the American Dream and reaffirm that fundamental truth that out of many, we are one; that while we breathe, we hope, and where we are met with cynicism, and doubt, and those who tell us that we can't, we will respond with that timeless creed that sums up the spirit of a people: Yes, we can.

Thank you, God bless you, and may God bless the United States of America.